JUSTICE
FOR BONNIE

Karen Foster and
I.J. Schecter

D0062534

BERKLEY

New York

BERKLEY
An imprint of Penguin Random House LLC
penguinrandomhouse.com

ISBN: 9780593100622

Berkley premium edition / September 2014
Berkley trade paperback edition / December 2019

Printed in the United States of America
1   3   5   7   9   10   8   6   4   2

Cover photo: *Karen Foster* © Jim Lavrakas / Anchorage Daily News / MCT via Getty Images
Book design by Elke Sigal

Most Berkley books are available at special quantity discounts for
bulk purchases for sales promotions, premiums, fund-raising, or educational use.
Special books, or book excerpts, can also be created to fit specific needs.
For details, write: SpecialMarkets@penguinrandomhouse.com.

To Bonnie, my guardian angel,
who gives me strength and protects me daily,
and to my father, who stood by my side until his death.

To all survivors and victims
who have suffered incredible loss and pain.
My heart goes out to you all.

Love and hugs,
—Karen Foster

To the miracles of my life, Julian, Oliver, and Charlotte.
You three make the world make sense.

And to any parent who has lost a child
and somehow found the strength and courage to go on.
You are heroes all.

—I.J. Schecter

ACKNOWLEDGMENTS

FROM I.J. SCHECTER

I am indebted to Karen Foster and to Bonnie's siblings and extended family, for being so candid about the tragedy they have endured together, and for answering every one of my questions, even the toughest ones. Karen and her family gave me access to a world of unending pain and unfathomable resilience to make sure Bonnie's story could be told properly and her memory honored in the right way. It is a great privilege to help tell this story, and I hope it allows Karen and her family some measure of catharsis while encouraging those in positions of power to ensure that our laws are designed to protect citizens and support families of victims.

My deepest gratitude also goes to Shannon Jamieson Vazquez, our keen-eyed editor at The Berkley Publishing Group, who was responsible for bringing Bonnie's story to print in the first place, and who possesses both of the attributes one hopes for in an editor: a ruthless eye for detail, and a deep sensitivity to the material itself.

FROM KAREN FOSTER

I first would like to thank all the people who have supported me and my family through this unspeakable tragedy; those who jumped into action to get things done, get laws changed and those who simply took time to give us a hug, drop us a note, showing us that they cared.

Thank you to all the other victims who have helped me, shared their stories, and worked with me to help change our laws.

Thank you to all the lawmakers who took time to listen to my story and the stories of many other families, then made changes in our laws so fewer people would have to suffer as we did. Thanks to the governors who have supported and signed "Collection of DNA on Felony Arrest" bills into law. Thank you to the lawmakers who ensure our law enforcement and crime labs are sufficiently funded to do their jobs.

Thank you to all those who work in the crime labs across the United States and Canada. It is with your help and dedication that more criminals will be successfully prosecuted. You are the backbone—and the new heroes—of our justice system.

Thank you to those who read this book and share it with lawmakers in states without collection of DNA on arrest laws. We need to ensure all fifty states and Canada collect DNA on arrest. It will save lives and so much pain.

Thank you to Paul Miovas and Jenna Gruenstein and Timothy Hunyor for being the most understanding and kind prosecution team a family could ask for. Without your skillful prosecution this story could have turned into a bigger tragedy and injustice.

Thank you to Mel and Arlene Schecter, for bringing my story to their son I.J., and for encouraging both of us to write this book. I.J. was the perfect person to help me through such a daunting project, and turned seventeen years of hell into an amazing book. He took all my stories, rantings, news reports, and the trial scripts and made it all come together. He is truly an amazing and talented writer.

ACKNOWLEDGMENTS ix

Thank you to Shannon Jamieson Vazquez, our editor, for all her talent, patience, and understanding.

Thank you to all my children, Jason, Adam, Samantha; my stepchildren, Jesse, Alex, and Sarah; and all my grandchildren. Without you, I could not have survived this tragedy. You have truly enriched my life, and I know Bonnie is so very proud of you all.

Lastly, Bonnie, you will never be forgotten. We love you dearly.

1

I wake up from the dream uneasy.

My boyfriend, Jim, is holding my shoulders and assuring me it was only a dream. *There is no woman; no one went over the edge of our sailboat.* I'm disoriented because I seldom remember my dreams, but this one was vivid. I saw a woman wearing a shorty—a wet suit with short sleeves and cut-off legs—fall over into the water off the side of our boat. I didn't know who she was.

We're right here, Jim's telling me. *Karen, it's me; there's no one else here; it was just a dream.* I must have dozed off, I realize—no matter how much I've sailed, the sea air still gets to me.

Slowly, I cross over the hazy line into consciousness again, and Jim's voice brings me all the way back out of the nightmare. I relax, and soon our gentle progress up the Gulf Coast of Florida lulls me back into sleep. I'm glad that I'm still tired enough from our travels to slip right back over that line, and am happy to drift away again.

Two days earlier, on Monday, September 26, 1994, Jim and I had boarded a red-eye flight from Anchorage, Alaska, to Tampa,

Florida, Jim's original stomping grounds, then chartered a thirty-seven-foot Island Packet sailboat out of St. Petersburg and started our way up Florida's western lip. The announcement two months earlier that Jim's younger brother Ken was getting married on the opposite corner of the continent had given us the perfect excuse for this trip. Jim and I had been seeing each other for less than two years but living together half that time, attempting to merge two families into one: his three kids, ranging in age from eight to thirteen, and my two youngest kids, aged twelve and thirteen, in a modest hillside home in Anchorage. Jason, my twenty-year-old son, lived in his own apartment with his girlfriend, Traci; Bonnie, my eighteen-year-old daughter, had moved out to live with my ex-husband, Gary, where she could have a room of her own. The decision crushed me, but I understood it. She was a young woman who wanted her space, something in short supply in my house. Adam, my thirteen-year-old son, and Samantha, my twelve-year-old daughter, did week-on, week-off between Gary's place and mine.

My relationship with Jim is far from perfect, but it works well enough. We've gone away together a couple of times before, both times to Mexico, where he owns some property. While we're gone, my kids stay with Gary, and his kids stay at his ex's place.

We have a few days to enjoy St. Marks before the wedding on Saturday. On Sunday, we will sail back down the coast and then fly home to our regular lives in Anchorage, where Jim works as a firefighter and paramedic, me as a Realtor and reserve police officer, each of us navigating the strange chapter of our midforties, finding happiness in each other and trying to steer our kids along decent paths.

After two days of enjoying the calm of the boat and the freedom of the water, we neared our destination: the port town of St. Marks, population three hundred, home to the locally famous Posey's Oyster Bar, "Home of the Topless Oyster." It's ironic, then, that it was on the front edge of an oyster bed where we inadvertently grounded ourselves while navigating up the channel into St. Marks. It was the middle of the night, and there wasn't a soul around to help. Jim told me our only choice was to wait for the tide to come up. I had no better solution. With each wave, we heard the scratching of our hull against the oyster bed. We weren't in any danger, since the water was shallow enough to stand in, should it come to that—not to mention warm, unlike the waters in Alaska—but the feeling of helplessness, and the sound of the boat being damaged, dampened the light spirit we'd shared all day. Eventually, with nothing else to do, I fell asleep.

"The stars are moving."

Jim's voice startled me awake. I wasn't sure if I'd been asleep for hours or minutes.

"Huh?"

"The stars are moving. The tide's come in!"

He was right—we were floating. Jim turned the motor on and slowly backed us into the channel. He grew up diving for bottles in the St. Marks River and zipping up and down it in power boats, but we both realized we still shouldn't have done this after dark.

By the time we arrived at the St. Marks Marina, it was almost morning. As Jim and I settled into our berths, he told me that the spot where we were grounded was smack in the middle of Alligator Bay. I didn't know whether he was joking, but we smiled at each other, and, soothed by the rocking of the boat against the dock, fell asleep.

On Wednesday morning, September 28, Ken and his bride-to-be, Valeri, drive the twenty miles from Tallahassee to St. Marks to meet us and spend the day. We lunch, walk, and shop. Jim's father—also named Jim—and his stepmother, Mary, join us for dinner. It is my first time meeting them. As the stranger in the group, I feel a bit on the outside, but Valeri is a sweetheart, Jim Sr. and Mary are lovely, and there is lots of joking and kindness. I eat grouper for the first time. Everything is pleasant, fun, and serene.

After dinner, the six of us part ways. Jim and I drive to a historic local lighthouse, said to be the first in the New World, which sits at the mouth of the St. Marks River six miles from town. Though it's late by the time we get back to the boat and the sun has long since set, the thick Florida humidity still hangs heavy, and the small fans on the boat provide little relief. By the time we settle into bed, Jim in the V-berth, me in the quarter berth in the back of the boat, we're both irritable. A silly argument about nothing takes root, but we both see that each of us is reacting to the heat and the hour. We apologize, kiss, and go to sleep.

It's three in the morning when I feel the boat lurch. I'm startled by the sound of footsteps—the third time in two days that I've been jolted out of sleep. I jump out of the narrow quarter berth and alert Jim, who scrambles to his feet.

Suddenly, there's a knock on the companionway, the door separating the upper deck from the cabin below. I ask who's there.

"It's Ken."

I slide the trio of panels up and out of their grooves. Ken is looking down at Jim and me. I wonder what he's doing there, what could be important enough that he'd drive back to the marina at such a late hour.

The answer is obvious on his face. Ken is normally the kind of person who smiles by default. During our day together, he'd been even happier than usual, a man thrilled to have found his other half.

Now, his face has changed as completely as the difference between the sunset I'd loved the night before and the darkness that had followed it. His eyes are misting, and he has the kind of expression no one ever wants to see on someone else's face. It is the kind of expression that says, "I'm sorry for what I'm about to tell you."

2

Every parent knows that you live in fear from the moment your child is born. At first, you just pray they'll keep breathing every night and wake up again in the morning. Later, you worry that they might fall in with the wrong crowd, do something dumb to fit in, get in the car with a stranger. Sometimes you let your mind go to the darkest places, maybe only as a way of being able to shove the bad thoughts aside and remind yourself it won't happen. You live in a safe town. You've taught them to make good decisions. They have sensible friends. You falsely convince yourself of their immunity every way you can. The bad thoughts invade your head, you let them in temporarily, and then you violently push them out, a little less at peace than you were before.

You do it a hundred times, a thousand. Every time you hear a terrible news story, or tragedy touches an acquaintance. All the while, you watch your children grow, thankful to God or whatever you believe in, endlessly grateful at the miracle they represent. When they experience pain, you hate it, but you say the same thing every time it happens: if this is the worst, it isn't so bad. They fall off a slide and get a scrape, then cry and hug you till it's better. They miss the winning shot or let in the winning goal—you hurt like hell for them in the moment, but you know they'll get over it and be stronger in the end. A girlfriend or boyfriend dumps them, and you see heartbreak in their eyes for the first time. It tears you apart, but you know they have to go through it, and you say to yourself, again, if it's the worst thing they'll ever experience, it's not so bad. You count yourself lucky. You can sleep again that night.

"What is it?" I ask Ken.

"It's Bonnie," he responds, his voice cracking. "She's . . . she was in a hiking accident."

Everyone reacts differently to bad news—or, more specifically, to the moment before you're about to get hit with it. Some people get mad. Others get sad or afraid. What I feel is offended and angry, because I can't figure out why Ken would drive such a long way in the middle of the night just to tell me such a terrible lie. He's obviously gone off the deep end. Or someone is playing a cruel joke on me, through him, and he's been gullible enough to fall for it. It's obviously a mistake.

The fact that he just keeps staring at me and saying "I'm sorry" is getting under my skin even more.

"Who told you that?" I demand.

Ken holds out a yellow Post-it with something scrawled on it, but I don't take it from him. No matter what your reaction is to bad news, we all do one thing similar: we keep it at arm's length for as long as we can. We keep it outside the realm of reality by refusing any evidence. I could keep Ken's words at bay if they were just words. People lie all the time, for plenty of reasons. But this Post-it is something with the potential to break down my refusal to believe. I don't want to look at it.

"I'm so sorry," he says again, the bastard. "An Alaska State Trooper called me." He's still holding out the evil yellow Post-it, like something poisonous that he wants to get out of his hands. "He told me to get the message to you. This is his number."

I don't want to take it, but my hand reaches out. Once the Post-it is in my hands, I don't want to look at it, either—but I look. A meaningless name and an unknown phone number.

Each of these moments happens in slow-motion. My senses are amped up, and at the same time, everything collapses inward. I feel both chilled and overheated, like a sudden wave of the flu. I feel exposed and at the same time claustrophobic. From a strange place outside of my body, I see myself shaking and my legs going at the knees.

"No, not my Bonnie. How do they know?" I hear myself say. I don't know why I'm even implying I may actually believe Ken's lie.

"I don't know," he says. "They just told me to have you call them." I want to beat some sense into him.

Jim and I dress while Ken and Valeri wait in the cockpit above. I have no idea what I'm putting on. I'm still trying to figure out who's behind this awful joke and why.

We climb off the boat. I'm still holding the sickening Post-it. With only a radio on the boat, we find a pay phone outside a small store near the dockmaster's office. I try to dial the number, but I can't hold the phone because my hand is shaking too much. Jim dials instead and reaches a switchboard operator. He gives her the number on the Post-it and the name of the trooper, then hands me the phone, rubbing my back.

"I'm sorry; I don't recognize that name," she says. I repeat the request, more insistently, and her tone stiffens. She asks me for my patience, reminds me it's eleven P.M. in Anchorage, and suggests I call back in the morning.

"I've just been told my daughter died in a hiking accident," I tell her. There is a pause.

"One moment, please," she says. I wait on the other end of the line, as if this situation was no different from a regular conversation on a regular day. When you're suddenly faced with information that throws your entire world out of whack, it's the most mundane acts, like a phone call, that seem the most bizarre. The news that my daughter is no longer alive doesn't match up with the need to be put on hold. None of it fits.

Finally, a different voice comes on the line. "Hello, this is Sergeant Mike Marrs of the Alaska State Troopers. Is this Karen Campbell, Bonnie Craig's mom?" Although we divorced two years ago, I still use Gary's last name, while Bonnie has my first husband's name.

"Yes."

"I'm so sorry to have to tell you this, Mrs. Campbell. Bonnie's body was found out at McHugh Creek. She fell off a cliff, Mrs. Campbell. She's dead. I'm very sorry."

If everyone acts differently in the way they brace for bad news, the same is true of how we react when it's no longer possible to deny. In my case, as I speak to a trooper telling me that my eighteen-year-old daughter is dead, I snap into detective mode.

Outside of my day job selling real estate, I've spent the previous two and a half years as an unpaid volunteer undercover reserve officer with the Anchorage Police Department. I've gone through the police academy and earned the right to pick assignments. I've worked drug raids and undercover buys. I regularly choose the toughest shifts in the worst areas. I've been an adrenaline junkie since I was cut out of my mother's womb, and it's never gone away.

My parents sent the police to look for me five or six times when I was a kid because I was out wandering, looking for something to give me a rush. I spent time as a news reporter, getting a thrill out of being in front of the camera, and I still wanted that thrill.

The Anchorage Police Department and the Alaska State Troopers share mutual contempt; each agrees that the other doesn't know its ass from its elbow. My instinct is already to ask for the case to be handed over to the APD. I know the homicide guys there, and they're good. I could get things done.

I've helped collar some bad people. Not the kind who give up grudges easily. My mind threatens to go to a very bad place, but I refuse it because there's no point in allowing myself to consider that possibility at the moment. I'm in the first mental stage of doing what I've become so used to doing: trying to solve a puzzle.

"Who was she with?" I ask.

"No one, Mrs. Campbell. She was out there alone."

Sergeant Marrs's voice is flat and serious. I wonder, how many other calls like this has he made before? He must have talked down a dozen mothers like me, a hundred. He has his script and his instructions to stay composed and not let the shocked person on the other end let him get worked up, which would only be counterproductive. I've never done one of these calls myself, nor a live visit to deliver the news. Either would be a nightmare.

"How did she get there?" I can feel my voice coming back into my body. I'm used to this kind of exchange. "She doesn't drive, so how?" I'm happy to start poking holes in the story. I wonder how long it will take to show that they have the wrong person, that it isn't Bonnie at all. McHugh Creek is ten miles from her bus route, for God's sake.

"We don't know, ma'am."

"What time did you find her?" I wish I had a notepad.

"About two-thirty this afternoon," says Sergeant Marrs.

"No," I say, trying not to scream at this fool. "She would have been in class. She'd never miss. How did you identify her?"

"She didn't have a wallet or any ID on her," he says. "Her name was on her class ring, and we pulled up her state ID. We identified her from that picture."

A class ring could easily get switched. He sounds harebrained.

"Has Gary or anyone identified her?" Gary may not be Bonnie's biological father, but he's the dad who raised her.

"No—we were going to wait for you."

Another hole in the story. No one who really knows Bonnie has even seen the body of this poor girl, whoever she is. What an incredible mix-up. I consider calling Bonnie's boyfriend, Cameron, who will no doubt know where she is. Even though he left Anchorage a few months earlier to study architecture at the University of California, Berkeley, the two of them still talk or e-mail multiple times per day.

Sergeant Marrs is asking me to calm down. I don't know why he's saying this, since I feel very focused. But the part of me that's still on the outside looking in can hear me cry and scream.

"Could she have been raped?" I don't know why I ask this question. I'm mad at myself for saying these words, and I want to take them back.

"No, Mrs. Campbell. All her clothes were on. Nothing was ripped or torn. All her buttons were done up, as was her zipper."

"That doesn't mean someone wasn't raped!" Sergeant Marrs's refusal to be logical is making it hard for me to concentrate. "I work with the Anchorage Police Department. I was just involved in a big drug bust before I left."

"Ma'am? I'm sorry?"

"I work with the police department. We just did a big bust. Maybe they thought it was me? Bonnie looks just like me."

"No, Mrs. Campbell. She died from a fall off a cliff. Up at McHugh Creek, as I said. It was over thirty feet, ma'am. I'm very sorry."

I want to climb through the phone and throttle him until he stops saying Bonnie is dead. It sounds asinine. I want to talk to someone who knows what they're doing. "If it's Bonnie, it's not a hiking accident. It's got to be murder!"

"No, ma'am. It was a hiking accident. If it were an act of retribution, they would have used guns. Or there would have been duct tape, something binding her. We know how those kinds of acts are carried out and what they look like. This wasn't murder, or rape, Mrs. Campbell. I'm afraid it was just a tragic accident. She fell from a great height."

The detective inside me is still pressing forward. If they don't think it was murder, they won't have investigated it as a crime scene. They'll have investigated it as an accident, which means next to no investigation at all.

"Did the troopers at the scene collect evidence?"

"There was no evidence to collect, ma'am. As I said, we ID'd her from her class ring. There's nothing else to look for, I'm afraid."

First Ken drives over in the middle of the night to give me this awful story about Bonnie being dead. Then I'm forced to talk to an inept switchboard operator who could only complain about how late it was in Alaska. Now this trooper doesn't seem to know which end is up, telling me that the person they'd found was wearing Bonnie's class ring and that she'd mysteriously fallen off a thirty-foot cliff at McHugh Creek. A stumble and thirty-foot plunge, just like that—no explanation? The poor girl, whoever she is. It's like a conspiracy of incompetence.

"I'm in Florida," I say. "I'll be on the next plane back."

———————

I hear myself on the phone with my ex-husband Gary, telling him that none of it is making any sense. I hear him agreeing with me that whatever happened couldn't have been an accident.

I'd been mad at Gary already, and that anger now multiplies. Late last week, I had called his place, where Adam and Samantha would be staying while Jim and I were gone, only to find out from Bonnie that Gary had taken a sudden business trip to New Orleans and wouldn't be back for a week. I was furious. He and I had a clear agreement never to be out of state at the same time. Gary had known about my vacation with Jim for Ken's wedding weeks in advance, yet his trip now meant he'd still be away when we left for Florida.

Bonnie, confident and proud in her ability to handle babysitting her younger brother and sister by herself for a few days, had defended Gary, not wanting me to get into a fight with him over it. "It's all right, Mom," she'd said. "Don't worry. Come on, I'm eighteen." I'd felt my temperature rising as I'd agreed she was perfectly capable, but that that wasn't the point. The point was that it wasn't appropriate for her to be asked to look after her brother and sister when their father was supposed to be there. When he'd *agreed* to be there.

"Everything's fine, Mom," Bonnie had said. "Don't worry. I love you. Just enjoy your vacation. I'll be fine." Now people are telling me these are the last words I will ever hear her say.

As I think these thoughts, I slip out of my comfort zone as a detective and back to being just a mother, and it's nearly intolerable. Part of me is threatening to fly away, but I try to stay anchored to Gary's voice so I can take in everything he's telling me. The divorce hasn't made our relationship any easier. He's more annoyed with every child-support check he has to write, and I'm annoyed that it bothers him, since it's a drop in the bucket compared to what he makes. We see each other at the hockey arena for Adam's games, and he barely acknowledges my presence. By association, he doesn't like Jim, and the feeling is mutual. But we know we have to put our differences aside now. What's more important is the exchange of information.

Gary tells me that a pair of Alaska State Troopers had knocked on his door around ten that evening. He and the kids had already been wondering why Bonnie wasn't home. Seeing the troopers' serious faces, Gary feared the worst. Samantha had heard Bonnie leave early in the morning for her 7:00 A.M. English class. But she hadn't come home and hadn't called. As Gary tells me the story, I take cold comfort in hearing that he and the kids were together.

I hear myself tell Gary that I need to call my parents. I see my hand place the phone back in its cradle and then pick it up again to dial the number for St. Catharines, Ontario, a little town of parks, gardens, and trails along the Niagara River, a stone's throw from the world's longest peaceful border. I feel no peace inside me. I feel a knife sinking into my soul.

The words coming out are vague as I tell my parents that people are trying to convince me their granddaughter is dead. I think I can hear the cries of denial coming from my parents on the other end. "I'll call you when I get to Anchorage," I hear myself say. I hang up the phone again. I feel like I just want to keep making phone calls. I need information.

We are back at the boat and I am watching myself stuff clothes into a duffel bag. Jim is trying to console me, but he is not packing a bag of his own. I feel confused at the thought that he is planning to stick me on a plane back to Alaska alone. I see myself ask him. He has arranged to get me on the next flight out, he says. It is not an answer.

We all pile into Ken's truck on the way to the Tallahassee Airport. It is the early hours of the morning. Jim is beside me, holding my hand. There are intentionally few streetlamps in this part of Florida, so it is very dark. I see that I am still holding the Post-in in my free hand. I am still irritated at Ken. I am still aggravated with the useless dispatcher. I am irate with Jim. I am furious at the trooper for trying to tell me Bonnie slipped off the edge of a cliff, fell thirty feet, and will never breathe again.

At the airport, a few red-eye customers mill about, and a handful of weary-looking staff manage the desks. Jim is speaking with a ticket agent. I am at a pay phone, making another call. I hear the voice of my friend Cara, saying, "Please leave a message, and I'll get back to you as soon as I can." I've called her out of desperation. Cara is a local news reporter. She is connected. She'll know what's happening.

My body starts to shake again, and then my knees go. I'm in a heap on the floor, screaming into the receiver. "Cara, please pick up!" I am shouting in the middle of the nearly empty airport. "Cara, the Alaska State Troopers are telling me Bonnie is dead! They're telling me they found her out at McHugh Creek. Oh, my God, Cara, please pick up. Please check it out. Find out if it's really Bonnie, please, I need your help. Please!"

I hear myself tell Cara a version of the same message I'd given the trooper. "I'm in Florida. I'll be back later today." Then I am pulling myself up and making another call—to another friend, Michelle. She will know what's going on.

Again the phone rings and rings; then I hear Michelle saying, "Hi, I can't come to the phone right now . . ." and I buckle a second time. As I gaze at the ticket counter, I see Jim look my way. He watches me there on the floor, under the pay phone, the handle dangling from its cord above my face. I see him turn back toward the agent and ask for a second ticket.

———————

I am in a dark airplane in the early-morning hours with only the soft drone of the engines invading my thoughts. Beside me, Jim's head rests against his shoulder, a small blanket bunched against the side of his head. He has tried to stay awake for my sake, but the fatigue has overcome him. Maybe a dozen other people occupy the plane, most asleep.

I see myself sobbing, shaking my head, rubbing my hands together. I feel paralyzed by remoteness from the truth. Mostly I rock slowly in my seat, up and down, wondering what in heaven's name is going on and when I will wake up from what must be a nightmare.

Part of me insists that when we arrive at the airport, Bonnie will be there, ashamed that she's caused us to return for a silly mistake. She'll tell us how it happened, it will all sound logical, and despite the inconvenience of coming home, we'll have a laugh about it, because it will have been a result of something out of her control. She'll still feel guilty about it, because that's the kind of kid she is. I'll tell her again and again that she did nothing wrong; it's just the cost of a plane ticket, inconsequential as long as she's okay. Mix-ups happen, nothing to get upset about. She'll give me one of her great hugs and it will be done.

My mind goes back over certain moments again and again, unable to let go of the possibility that my police work may have drawn the wrong kind of vengeance from the wrong kind of people. I see myself a few years earlier, a wet-behind-the-ears reporter for KIMO 13 News, an ABC affiliate, covering the police and courts, compelled by that world, listening to the police scanner out of fascination even when there was no story to follow. In the newsroom, they teased me about my obsession with the scanner and my desire to be first on the scene for the next big story. One of my colleagues asked me if I turned the scanner off during sex.

I think back to a couple of years earlier, to my first pivotal conversation with Captain Tom Walker of the Anchorage Police Department, who told me the department was in need of female officers and that I'd make a great candidate. I recall telling Gary that same evening that I wanted to do it. I'd already taken the criminal justice and EMT courses; I knew my stuff and could hit the ground running. He agreed I should go for it; but, in retrospect, I wondered if it was because he was confident I wouldn't make it.

When I joined the police academy, Gary realized I *could* handle it, and as I neared graduation, he told me he didn't want a gun in the house and wasn't comfortable looking across the bed at a trained killer. He said he'd rather see me come home in a body bag than find out I'd killed someone. I asked if he'd really rather see the mother of his children dead than learn that she'd offed some scumbag, and he said yes—that he couldn't live with the idea of my having killed another human being. Our marriage, already shaky by that point, couldn't survive the situation.

The day of my graduation from the academy, in September 1992, Gary told the kids we were getting a divorce. Jason was eighteen, Bonnie sixteen, Adam eleven, Samantha ten. "Mom, you gotta do what's important to you," Adam told me, his preteen wisdom and selflessness warming me.

I joined the Patrol Unit for that first exciting shift, twelve hours' worth, driving through the worst neighborhoods in town. Given the choice of shifts, I chose Friday and Saturday nights, when the real action happened. I was chomping at the bit to get out there. With few women in the department, I was often called to the hospital to see women who'd been assaulted. I got called out on Special Details, Search and Rescues. Soon, after working the streets enough and learning the ropes out on patrol, I was asked to join the Metro Unit to carry out undercover drug buys. I felt important. I felt productive. I felt like I was making a difference.

Rarely did I feel in danger—even when the inevitable curveballs made improvisation a necessity. I remembered one buy when I was wired and hiding my 40-millimeter Glock on the small of my back under my plainclothes outfit. After picking up the informant, I saw the undercover car behind lose track of us. I continued on to do the deal and played dumb, but I knew that if something went down, I'd be on my own. Then I picked up the dealer and handled the transaction at a bowling alley on the south end of town. (The point wasn't to bust him; it was to gather evidence with the goal of bringing down the entire ring.) I loved the rush, never really felt nervous. The adrenaline obscured the nerves.

The same thing happened during a bust outside a hotel where I'd arranged a buy from a known dealer. We had a sharpshooter stationed on the parking-garage roof, and two other undercover officers—the bellman and the guy unloading luggage from a car, posing as a guest. I was supposed to sit in the passenger seat, get the drugs, then remove the key from the ignition, signaling the others to move. But what we hadn't talked about was what to do if there were other people in the vehicle—like the dealer's kids, which was exactly who he showed up with in the backseat. I wasn't sure whether to abandon the deal, but I decided to get the drugs, then pull my gun and announce myself as police. The others jumped to it, backing me up, and the dealer was taken away. No one was hurt. The arrest was successful.

But I also remember the one night when a fellow officer, Officer Dan Seeley, responded to a simple domestic-disturbance call. Seeley's wife, who worked in dispatch, heard the call. At the house, an estranged husband, crazed and armed, shot and killed Officer Seeley in the line of duty, then chased his own family to a nearby house, shot and killed his two young kids, shot his wife, then put a bullet in his own head. I'd gone to the ER after Officer Seeley was pronounced dead and stood honor guard alongside his body. I had trained under him, shared meals with him. My heart broke for his wife and family.

But bad guys don't exist in isolation. Bad guys know other bad guys, and they have long memories. I stare out the airplane window into the black early-morning sky. Soon I hear the pilot's voice announcing that we are starting our descent. Tallahassee to Chicago, Chicago to Anchorage. We have passed through the entire continental United States and slanted through the Canadian Yukon. I pray I will see my beautiful daughter and be able to wrap my arms around her. Please, God. Please.

The flight attendants have been made aware of our situation. With awkward sympathetic looks, they shepherd me and Jim off of the plane ahead of the other passengers. We nod blankly at the pilot and cabin staff as we disembark and walk along the jetway into the quiet cavern of the terminal.

Despite my prayers, Bonnie is not there to hug me and tell me it was all a big mistake. She is not there for me to assure and for-give. Instead, Bert McQueen, the police chaplain, greets us, along with Sergeant Marrs, who is much larger in person than I imagined from our phone conversation.

Jim and I both know Bert well. He hugs me and asks us to come sit down and talk in one of the terminal's makeshift confer-ence rooms.

After we sit down in the hard plastic chairs, Bert says, "Karen, Jim, I'm so sorry. It's a terrible tragedy for Bonnie to go in this way, in a hiking accident."

"It's not an accident," I snap. "If it's really Bonnie, it's got to be murder."

Bert looks back at me with a different expression. "Karen, I want you to know how terrible we all feel. The thoughts of the entire community are with you. Everyone is here to offer their support."

He is trying to comfort me, but not to correct me. He believes what the troopers have told him about Bonnie accidentally slipping off a cliff, in a place where she never went and could hardly have reached by herself.

"Mrs. Campbell," says Sergeant Marrs, "I hate to discuss prac-tical matters with you, but there are some things that need to be done. First, a picture of Bonnie is required. As you know, it's stan-dard procedure. And, of course, you'll have to come down to the funeral home and . . ."

He can hardly bring himself to say it: *ID her.* I stand up and walk out of the room, Jim trailing. I think I can hear Bert saying "Karen . . ." My head is swimming.

Bert and Sergeant Marrs catch up to us, and numbly we walk with them out of the terminal and into the cruiser. I'm in a fog during the drive to Gary's house, staring out the window. Bert and Sergeant Marrs may or may not be saying things to me.

We reach the house, and I rush to the front door. My kids, Jason, Adam, and Samantha, are all there. They throw themselves into my arms and erupt into sobs. Gary is behind them. We repeat the same things over and over. It doesn't make sense. It cannot have happened. Not Bonnie. No. No. No. We are sharing the first wave of pain that will continue to loop back through us forever.

Samantha fills in more details for me from the previous night, when the troopers came to deliver the news. Hearing the knock, she and Adam had taken a secret spot at the top of the stairs to watch the conversation between them and Gary on the front porch. Then they'd seen their dad drop to his knees and scream, "Not Bonnie!" People's worlds explode at different moments. For me, it was the moment on the boat when Ken held out the Post-it; for my kids, it was watching their father's heart get torn out of him.

They'd never seen their dad cry before. Then they'd watched him break apart. Crumpled on the floor, he'd sobbed and screamed, repeating Bonnie's name. The trooper had stood unemotionally, asking questions, repeating how sorry he was to be the bearer of this news. Samantha tells me that she and Adam stayed watching from the top of the stairs and prayed that Bonnie was still alive. They were hoping it was just a bad accident, she said, and that the trooper had gotten it wrong. When the troopers asked how to get in touch with me, Adam and Samantha had given him Jim's ex-wife's number, and she had in turn given them Ken's.

––––––––––––

Eventually, Jim and I accompany Bert and Sergeant Marrs to the funeral home. I know that the only way to prove that the girl who died at McHugh Creek isn't Bonnie will be to look into her face. It will be awful, but it is the only way. I am silent in the cruiser, again looking out the window, wondering what's going on. A day ago, I was on a sailboat in Florida, relaxed and untroubled.

Approaching the door of the funeral home, I feel a wave of nausea. Another thing I've never had to do in my volunteer police work is participate in this dreadful exercise, though I've imagined it often enough. The people from the home talk to me. I don't listen. They are saying something meant to prepare me and calm me down. Not a word registers. I see them turn, and I follow them into a room where a white sheet covers a body on a metal gurney.

You try to keep it at bay. You deny it at first. You get mad; you disbelieve. As the evidence starts to become real, the feeling builds. A Post-it, a conversation, a class ring. Everyone around you is trying to convince you of something that can't be true, because if it's true, you won't be able to handle it. You don't let it in; you refuse it with everything you have. Then the sheet is pulled down, and it is your daughter's face you see there, perfectly still, unmoving, unbreathing, and refusal is no longer possible.

3

What people say is true. You have only two choices: go on or don't. It isn't a conscious decision, at least not at first. It's a reaction, based on, I suppose, a variety of factors. As I look down at my daughter's face, the knowledge that she is dead hits me fully. I can no longer refute it, no matter how badly I want to. A part of me departs instantly, never to come back. It is the part that was my beautiful baby girl.

It is not false mysticism to say that when one of your children dies, part of you dies along with her. Your child is a component of you. She is part of your spirit and your energy. When you hear a parent describing a time when his or her child almost ran into traffic and saying "I nearly died," it isn't a lie. Any parent knows that at those moments, you feel a tangible part of your soul drain away. "I nearly had a heart attack," people say. "It took a year off my life," they joke. None of the statements are figurative. Each near miss is a small death inside.

The part of you that is connected to your child dies the moment she dies, or at least the moment you can no longer pretend she's alive. That part, sadly, is not up to you. There will always be a hole in your heart, which nothing can close.

But the rest is up to you.

I make the decision without knowing I'm making it. Trying to solve the puzzle is easier than accepting that Bonnie is gone. Why Bonnie? Why me? What did I do to deserve this? The questions come, and I can't avoid them, and there is no answer. The funeral director is telling me I can come back tomorrow with my family to spend time with Bonnie—that she isn't ready yet, whatever that means. Jim and I are escorted to the cruiser and taken to the police station to talk further with the troopers. We sit at a desk.

Before they have a chance to speak, I say, "It has to be murder." I start asking questions. I tell them Bonnie would have been carrying her book bag and keys. She had pepper spray on her key chain. I ask if there was any evidence of its having being used. They assure me that if it had been used, there would have been residue evident at the scene. It would not have washed off even in the glacier-fed water of McHugh Creek. That's true. Pepper spray is oily—you need detergent to wash it off. They insist there was no evidence of the pepper spray being deployed in any way.

I question how Bonnie was discovered, surprised to realize it's taken me so long to ask. A young woman was hiking along the creek taking pictures, they tell me, when she saw a body floating in the water. She raced back to her car, drove back toward Anchorage, and pulled into a weigh station, where she told the attendant she needed to call the police.

That's all I learn at the troopers' headquarters. The rest of the conversation is a blur. As Jim and I leave the police station, I feel like I'm moving through a vacuum. But within minutes of returning home, I am assaulted by an unending stream of phone calls from, it seems, every media outlet in Anchorage. People elsewhere in the country tend to see Alaska as an outpost, but Anchorage is a city with a population similar to Pittsburgh, Cleveland, or St. Louis. Big enough to have major media but small enough that word spreads fast.

Though out of the media now, I'm still tight with a lot of news reporters in the city. Many of the people who are calling for interviews know me, which they feel gives them extra license to ask. But no one has to twist my arm—I *want* to talk, and I want people to listen. I say yes to everyone who requests my time, and in the hours and days that follow I hear myself repeating the words "It's murder" again and again. I'm only partly aware of who I'm talking to or what station or newspaper they represent. I know instinctively that the media is one way, maybe the best way, of helping find out who did this. I will talk as long as they will let me.

I remember, from my own days as a reporter, one mother I spoke to after her eighteen-year-old son was shot by an airport security officer. The officer had chased the boy over a long distance, finally hunting him down as he ran from his car only half a mile from his house. Within hours of his being declared dead at the scene, the boy's mother told me through her tears that her son had never done anything worse than steal a Stop sign. I remember wanting to help let the world know that he hadn't been a threat—he'd just been trying to get home safely to his mother, fleeing from an enraged officer. I remember wanting his mother to have the chance to defend him and tell her side. He was a good kid, and now he was dead. It wouldn't do anything to help her heal, but it might help others understand that he didn't have to die.

I was comfortable inside the trooper station, asking questions, beginning to pull apart the mystery. I cannot absorb the idea that Bonnie is dead, so that was a temporarily acceptable alternative. But my strange, sudden celebrity is jarring me out of that comfortable mode. It is so far from real that I can't even begin to connect it to what I knew before. The reporters want to know what I think, what my theories are, whether I accept what the State Troopers are telling me. I *don't* accept what the troopers are telling me, and I make this known because it is what I feel.

I cry more than I sleep. Taking care of my other kids suddenly seems an impossible task. My pain is threatening to overwhelm me, so what can I do for them? I try to stay focused on the investigation, but the tidal wave of emotion inside me is, like a real wave, unrelenting. I can't turn off the switch, and I can't ask the wave to pause while I get myself together.

We hug. We hold each other and squeeze each other and cry. Jason goes home to Traci. I send Adam and Samantha to their dad's house, out from under the glare of the media. I have said yes to anyone willing to give me exposure and thereby, hopefully, try to unearth information the troopers seem uninterested in trying to find. The kids aren't used to the media attention, and it's not fair to them. For now, I just need them to be safe and away from the craziness.

One after another, the reporters file into my home, set up their lights, attach mics to my lapel, and begin their apologetic interviews. They ask why I think it's murder. They ask what I think happened. I tell them I don't know what happened, and I'm not making guesses, but I know it wasn't an accident. The interviews are broadcast and printed. By the next day, Bonnie's death is a citywide storm, and, before long, word of the case has spread across the state.

Eventually I do sleep, exhausted from pain and tears and the shrieking disbelief in my head. When there is nothing left for that day, my eyes close and my brain takes mercy on me by shutting off, at least temporarily.

I wonder if, when I wake up again, I might forget where I am, or what's happened. For just a fleeting moment, I wonder if I will be able to pretend.

The moment doesn't come. I wake up and the pain is waiting there, always.

We go to the funeral home—Jim, Gary, Jason, Adam, Samantha, and I. I am scared for my kids, and my only thought is to protect them from seeing something that they will never get over. I accept that they need to speak to detectives about Bonnie, but I will not force them to look at anything they don't need or want to. Extra emotional scars are not going to help.

But the kids say they want to see their sister, and I trust them, so I'm allowing it. We all enter the same room I went into the day before. More of the sheet has been pulled down today, exposing Bonnie's forearms and hands. I'm the first to approach her body. I take one of her hands in mine, put it against my forehead and start to sob. I don't want to do this in front of the kids, but I've never hidden anything from them before, and anyway, I am torn open. There is no way to hold it inside.

As I cry and hold my dead daughter's hand, I notice something odd about her fingers. The knuckles are bigger than they should be. I slide the sheet farther down, toward her waist. Her arms are bruised in several places.

"Get the troopers back in here," I say.

"What is it?" Jim says.

I look up at him. "These are defensive wounds."

"Excuse me, Mrs. Campbell?" It is the funeral director, poking his head through the door. "I'm very sorry, but whenever you're ready, we're going to need to talk about arrangements. Please take as much time as you need."

"Just a minute," I tell the director. "You need to call the troopers and get them back here." I call the troopers' office myself and tell them they need to return immediately to take pictures. I inform them about Bonnie's hands and arms, wondering how they missed her bruises and broken knuckles in the first place. Gary, Jim, and the kids see the condition of Bonnie's body and are equally startled. Even my twelve- and thirteen-year-old children notice obvious signs of things not being right, but I'm supposed to accept that the troopers just happened to miss how Bonnie's arms are bruised up and down? Their reaction is weirdly nonchalant. I know all too well that at any time, in any town of moderate size, there is more than one disaster to investigate, and more than one family dealing with heartbreak. But I also know evidence when I see it, and the casual attitude they seem to have toward this crime is baffling.

I call my supervisor at APD and the sergeant in Homicide. I tell them what I've seen and plead with them to take over the case. They both tell me the same thing: they wish they could, but it's a matter of jurisdiction. Their hearts are breaking for me, but their hands are tied.

We pick out a coffin. It is the most surreal thing I have done in my life, as though we are choosing window blinds or a washing machine. The director has his list of questions we have to answer and decisions we need to make. There is no way to describe the strangeness of this conversation.

We agree that we want to preserve Bonnie's body as much as possible. We know she must be buried, and we know there has to be a funeral. But we will put her in a cement vault, so that exhumation is possible later, for evidence. If it really had been an accident,

I would have had her body cremated. But the thought of losing any potential evidence is overwhelming. I won't do it. It could be the difference between finding out who did this to my daughter and never knowing. I answer every question that the director asks from the viewpoint of solving the case. I can only assume that other moms in my position use other tricks on themselves to get through this horrible task of choosing which kind of box your child is going to spend eternity in.

Out of the blue, Gary tells us about a conversation he had with Bonnie once, in which she told him she'd like to be buried in Prince Edward Island, at a cemetery in Summerside, his hometown, where most of his family still live. He tells me that Bonnie told him she wanted to be buried there because it was so peaceful and beautiful.

I can't believe he's talking about the funeral at all. I can't believe he's talking about burying our daughter, much less telling me that she was talking about *where* to be buried. I ask him why he and Bonnie were talking about such things at all. It just came up, he says. They talked about all kinds of things together. He says he wants to send her body there, and he adds that he's certain she would have liked the funeral services to be held at the Rabbit Creek Community Church, not far from his home in Anchorage.

Send her body there. I'm stunned at the way he's talking about Bonnie, alive and smiling two days ago. I have been to Summerside and am trying to figure out why Gary is so sure that's where Bonnie would like to be taken. I ask him again how they started talking spontaneously about where she'd like to be buried. He tells me again that they were close; it just came up. I think my kids would want their sister to be buried in Anchorage, where they can visit her, not almost five thousand miles away.

I ignore the comment for now, in part because the TV stations and newspaper reporters are stepping up their efforts, and when we walk out of the funeral home, there they are again, like a pack moving together via a collective tracking device. They have gathered more information now, who knows from what sources, and their questions are more pointed. But they hardly need to ask questions, because I am still more than willing to talk. I stand in front of their microphones, cameras, and notepads and ask them the same questions I want answers to. How did she get to McHugh Creek? Why are the troopers so sure it was an accident? Where are her keys? Where is her backpack?

I hear myself say the same thing over and over: "It was murder." The media is getting exactly what they want from me, and I am happy to give it. I'll tell anyone who will listen. I will do whatever I need to do to catch my daughter's killer.

4

You hear it said all the time: there's no bigger tragedy than a parent outliving their child. Often, the next comment you hear involves God, or faith. *Thank goodness they have their faith to get them through. At least she has the Lord on her side.*

Organized religion doesn't really figure much in our lives. While pondering the funeral specifics, I think about St. George's Anglican Church in Chateauguay, Quebec, the place of worship I knew as a child. I picture my Christian household and the way my father would encourage me to attend services with him every Sunday. It was mainly because he enjoyed watching me sing in the choir that he pressed me so much to go.

At least I'm pretty sure that was the reason. Although technically my dad was born Anglican, I never thought God played as big a role in his life as family did, though sometimes it seemed the two did compete for attention. I think he must have known I went mostly for him, and I'm fairly sure he was okay with that. I always felt that church was a place for him to relax and think, and to smile as his daughter sang hymns. His work was his real temple; I believe it was when he was designing those circuit boards for the new touch-tone telephones that he felt most alive, most like a person of importance.

My father, Kaj Larsen, grew up on a farm in a small country town in Canada and went to university at night to get an electrical engineering degree. He was the quintessential company man. I remember sitting by his side at the age of ten and listening to him explain the technology that was allowing the old rotary phones to change to ones with buttons. He'd get excited telling me about the star and pound buttons. He'd show me the inner workings of the phone with a magnifying glass so I could appreciate the intricate beauty of the thing. One day, he'd tell me, people will be able to turn off their lights and water their lawns from their phones. I'd smile at his flights of fancy and hug him.

For nearly four decades he worked on phones, taking pleasure in helping develop the miraculous new technology. When his commitment proved irrelevant and Northern Electric filed for bankruptcy, he lost a third of his pension and plenty of benefits, but I don't think he ever blamed them or regretted his dedication. You can't control things that are out of your control, he would say. All you can do is work hard, try to be a good person, and hope for the best.

I picture my mother, Bernice, growing up Catholic outside of Montreal with twelve brothers and sisters, believing in God but averse to attending church. It was only at the urging of my father that she would join us on Christmas and Easter. I was pretty certain that, after heading straight into part-time work as a secretary while having me and my two older brothers within a three-year span, she used whatever spare time she could get to have some moments to herself rather than to pray.

When my brothers, Andrew and Kaj, got older and stopped going to church, my father didn't make much of it. But when I wanted to stop, he was disappointed, telling me what a letdown it would be not to see me there on Sunday morning in the choir. I kept going, but my sense of obligation fought against a growing sense of resentment. It wasn't long before other things took priority. At my high school graduation dance, I started dating a classmate named Gordon Craig. By the following week, we were going steady, and soon after, at the age of seventeen, I became pregnant with Jason, and conversations with my father regarding church took a backseat.

Gordon and I got married in July of 1973. We moved to Calgary, then had Bonnie in 1976. The following year, my brother Kaj, our father's namesake, died after a long coma following a car accident. My parents had stayed by Kaj's hospital bedside in Montreal every day from August until the end of October 1977. They read to him, talked to him, hugged and kissed him, asked for signals from him, all the while wondering if he was somewhere in there, hearing them but unable to respond. On Halloween night, my sister-in-law Marilyn decided that Kaj would want Michael, their two-year-old son, to be able to enjoy Halloween, so she put off that day's hospital visit. It was the first day since the accident that Kaj didn't receive a visitor. The same night, after holding on for two months, he—or his body—finally decided to let go.

I remember talking to the minister at his funeral. We would never know if Kaj made the decision somewhere inside to relinquish the fight or whether the connections in his brain finally just stopped working. I can still hear the minister explaining to me that God loves all his children, and that Kaj will be going to heaven, since hell is really only here on Earth.

Kaj's death made me realize that Gordon and I were just two horses pulling a cart together, and nothing more. There were no fights and few disagreements. He was a great father, helpful around the house. But in the face of my brother's death, Gordon showed as little emotion as he'd shown about everything else for nearly five years, and I couldn't live with it. We walked into a local attorney's office, got a friendly divorce for three hundred dollars and change, and Gordon promptly disappeared from our lives. Though our houses were less than a mile apart and I allowed him unlimited visitation, he chose to see the kids only on their birthdays and Christmas. He told me he wanted to stay out of their way and let them, and me, start a new life. "Don't you want to see your kids?" I asked him. "Of course," he said, "but it's better if I step aside." So he stepped aside.

———————

The day after we visit the funeral home, Sergeant Marrs calls and again asks if I'll come down to the station. Good, I think—they must have found something more. As long as I am getting information, I think I may be able to survive, because information may lead to answers, and answers will lead to justice. Without the feeling that something is being done, it is hard to imagine being able to go from day to day.

"Hello, Mrs. Campbell," says Sergeant Marrs as I walk in. "Please sit down. How are you feeling?"

"It's Karen. Do you have new information?" I ask.

"Not at this time, unfortunately. Listen—Karen—we'd like to ask you to back off with the media. It isn't a good idea for you to be calling Bonnie's death murder when we have no evidence to support that statement."

"No evidence? What about broken knuckles and bruised arms? That's not evidence?"

"Look at it this way. The more the media knows and talks about, the less likely it is that someone will give us what we need to solve the case. We didn't want the reporters to get wind of the fact that Bonnie's backpack and keys were missing, because once they get a bit of a story, obviously they're going to try to get the rest of it, and that may hinder our efforts."

"What efforts?" I say. "I'm not seeing the efforts you're talking about."

"We'd like to ask you to act as though you agree it was a hiking accident for now. We aren't saying you're wrong. But we're hoping that someone will come forward with the right kind of information to help us move forward in the investigation."

"So you are investigating it as a murder?"

"We're investigating all possibilities."

"Then you agree it wasn't an accident."

"It's an investigation, Karen. We're in the midst of creating posters asking for information about Bonnie's death. The only thing the media tends to do is hamper an investigation, not help it. Would you like a glass of water or a cup of coffee? You seem upset."

"Telling me your strategy at this point is a little late. Did you not think the reporters would ask me questions? Did you think they would accept that it was an accident? Why would they accept it any more than me?"

"We're concerned about you trying to take the investigation into your own hands."

"I'm trying to get information. I don't see you guys trying. I've been an undercover reserve officer for—"

"I understand how you feel. I want to assure you that we are doing a lot, and that, having done countless investigations like this in the past, we know the right way to conduct them. There's always information. Someone knows something. It's just a matter of how to go about getting it."

"Right. So how are you planning to get it? What are you planning to investigate?"

"I'd like to ask you to trust us for now. I know how hard this is for you."

"You do? Has one of your children ever been murdered?"

"Karen, I'm very sorry for what's happened. We all are. We want to find the person responsible. I'm asking you to let us do our jobs."

"That's what I'm asking, too. For you to do your jobs. So far doing your job has involved telling me my daughter's death was an accidental thirty-foot fall off a cliff and then having me point out to you that her knuckles were broken and her arms were bruised. I'd love to know what other parts of your job you're doing."

Sergeant Marrs doesn't allow himself to be baited. "There's one more thing. We need you, Gary, Adam, and Samantha to come down to the station tomorrow so we can get prints and hair samples from all of you. It's part of the elimination process."

I know procedure, so it doesn't surprise me to hear him ask for prints and DNA samples from Gary. But I don't understand asking it of me or the kids. "Why do you need samples from me and the kids? We aren't suspects."

"No, you aren't. But if we ask Gary by himself, we're concerned he might lawyer up. As you know, we're going to bring in anyone who might have crossed Bonnie's path that day and collect DNA samples from them. But the process needs to include her family members, too."

"Doesn't it seem cruel to you to put a twelve- and thirteen-year-old through that?"

"We thought you could explain it to them somehow. It would certainly be easier for us to obtain a sample from Gary this way."

"Are you saying you think Gary may have done this?"

"We have no opinion or belief whatsoever regarding Gary. We're simply following protocol—as you're aware. Would you excuse me for a minute?"

Sergeant Marrs gets up from the desk before I answer, but it doesn't matter, because in my mind all I can hear is Gary telling me he wants to ship Bonnie's body to Summerside. I ask myself why he would want Bonnie's body out of the country. No answer comes. I ask myself how well you really get to know someone, even after more than twelve years of marriage.

I think of the evening Gary and I met, just a few weeks after Gordon and I got our friendly divorce. I was in one of the Calgary Sheraton's conference rooms, quietly taking my seat among the fifty or so others looking forward to an introductory session by a group that offers a speed-reading program, something called Evelyn Wood. The woman at the front of the room began selling the twelve-week course and explaining how it would increase our reading speed in ways we could scarcely imagine.

My divorce from Gordon wouldn't be final until the mandatory three-month waiting period was up. I had half-joked to Gordon when we got married that I was taking out a five-year renewable on him. Now, after five years, I chose not to renew. Still in my early twenties, I was navigating new emotional territory. Evenings like this were a good tonic. They stimulated my brain, and they allowed me to meet people. One of the people I met was Gary Campbell.

I noticed him lingering in the registration line. I had no actual interest in signing up for the course because the cost was ridiculous, but I asked for his number with the ruse that I would like to call him when he's done the course so I could ask him whether he thought it was worth the time and money.

Three months later, I dialed the number I hadn't thrown out.

Gary had no idea who I was. I reminded him about our interaction at the introductory class, and he remembered, or pretended to, and offered to share all of the course material with me so I could save the money. I was charmed.

We met at a restaurant and talked for hours, then walked along the quiet streets and talked more. The leaves were red, yellow, and orange, and the air was crisp. A week later, he cooked me dinner at his place. He told me he was an engineer for Esso, Canada's version of Exxon.

We got married in our backyard in the summer of 1980, Gary in a suit, me in a cream gown and a lace cowboy hat. My parents and my surviving brother, Andrew, were there; Gary's parents were not, but his brother Alex came. Jason and Bonnie, all of five and three, looked adorable, him carrying the ring, her the basket of flowers. Our son, Adam, arrived the following March; our daughter, Samantha, the spring after.

BP recruited Gary and made him an offer he couldn't refuse. For the next decade, the company moved us around, from Calgary to Walnut Creek, California, to Anchorage, Alaska, to Midland, Texas (where we adopted an American Eskimo dog, whom the kids named Avalanche), then from Midland to Houston, and, finally, just as the leaves started to fall in late 1989, from Houston back to Anchorage. Gary left first, with all four of the kids and the dog, while I stayed behind for an extra month to finish the journalism degree I'd started at the University of Houston. I don't like not finishing what I start.

Gary and the kids arrived in Anchorage in time for Halloween, and a week before Christmas, my degree finished, I got in the Chevy van and headed for St. Catharines to meet Gary, the kids, and my parents for the holidays. We shipped the van to Anchorage and flew back together.

As the nineties dawned, Gary and I began to realize that things had changed. Following Gary around the continent had worn me down. I'd become unsure who I was, other than a doting wife who'd uprooted her children for a new city almost every year for a decade. The conversation became unavoidable. When it's over, you know it's over. By the fall of 1992, it was over.

"Karen?"

Sergeant Marrs has returned to the desk with a cup of coffee.

"Here you go, if you'd like. I was wondering if you've had a chance to think about what we discussed. About bringing the kids in with Gary to provide prints and hair samples."

"Yes," I say. "We'll do it. Whatever might help."

"We really appreciate it. I know it isn't an easy thing to ask of the kids. I promise we'll make it as quick and painless as possible."

Painless. It's an odd word to choose. He will try to make it painless for a thirteen-year-old boy and his twelve-year-old sister to come to a police station and give fingerprints so that samples tied to them may be eliminated if found during the investigation? Nothing will be painless again. At least Jason, who doesn't live at the house and therefore doesn't need his prints eliminated, can be spared this part.

I tell Gary and the kids that we need to provide prints and samples. The kids are a bit bewildered, and Gary is slightly hesitant, but no one argues. We all just want to get through this nightmare.

We arrive at the station. Sergeant Marrs greets me with a nod and asks us to come one by one into the back room, the kids first. I again ask Adam and Samantha if they're okay to do this, and they say it's fine. I believe them. When you're still trying to process the fact that your older sister has been murdered, being asked to press your thumb onto an inkpad and donate a strand of hair is nothing.

Gary goes next; me last. A moment before I leave, Sergeant Marrs asks to have a word. He guides me into a hallway.

"Karen," he says, "Gary's clean. I asked the kids about the day of Bonnie's death, and they independently said they saw him scraping ice off the car before getting in and leaving for work. Around seven. Their reports are consistent."

I say nothing.

"We've also received verification from multiple individuals at his workplace that he was there during the day. We can rule him out."

"Thank you," I say.

Later, from home, I call Gary. "I'm not letting her body go to PEI," I say.

"Karen?"

"There's no way you're taking her body to Summerside."

"It's what she wanted."

"Right, during your conversations with her about when she's going to die and where she wants to be buried. What if they need more evidence? What if they need to exhume the body? I am not sending her to Canada."

"Why did you steal a picture of her off my mantel?" he asks me.

"What?"

"I had a picture of Bonnie there, and now it's gone. What did you do with it?"

"It was the picture we gave the troopers. Stop acting paranoid. I'm coming to get her stuff," I tell him.

"You can't."

"What do you mean I can't?"

"You want me to give the police my fingerprints and DNA, fine. But that doesn't mean you're allowed to come into my house and take her stuff away." The kids had told me that Gary had put a lock on Bonnie's bedroom door.

"She's my daughter," I say.

"She's our daughter, Karen."

I call Sergeant Marrs.

"I'm sorry, Karen," he says, "but you know I can't help you with that. That's for the courts. You'll have to get an injunction. If you can do that, I can then meet you at the house to make sure you're safe while you retrieve her possessions. But I'm afraid that's where my authority ends."

I drive down to the courthouse, fighting tears. I speak to a judge, explaining to her that my ex-husband is holding my dead daughter's things hostage. I see the judge hand me a piece of paper. I call Sergeant Marrs back.

"Give me two hours," he says.

That afternoon, Jim and I take his van to Gary's house. Sergeant Marrs is parked in his cruiser at the front curb. He gets out and nods at us both.

"Just you," he says to me.

"Jim can't go in?"

"No. And I don't have the authority to help you, either. My job here is to ensure a peaceful situation and guarantee your safety, Karen. I need both hands free at all times. Can't be carrying boxes."

I take a breath and ring the doorbell. Gary opens it to find me and Sergeant Marrs, and, standing beside the van at the curb, Jim.

"I'm here to get Bonnie's things," I say, handing Gary the court order. He grabs it with one hand while looking straight at me, then, after a moment, looks down at it. He glances at Sergeant Marrs, shoves the paper back toward me, and steps to the side.

Gary leads us toward Bonnie's room. He still hasn't said a word. He unlocks the door and steps out of the way, still not taking his eyes off me. I know he won't do anything foolish with Sergeant Marrs here, but it unsettles me anyway.

With each item of Bonnie's that I place into a box, a fresh bolt of pain slices through me. I make myself as numb as I can, though tears are streaming down my cheeks. One by one, I carry boxes and laundry baskets out of the house and hand them to Jim.

As I pack Bonnie's things, I start to wonder whether I might find clues or answers in any of them. Now all I want to do is get home and start going through all of it. Get back into detective mode. Stop being the mother for a day. An hour. A minute. Eventually, I do go through them, and I send the troopers items I think might be useful, like Bonnie's bank statements or the automobile classifieds she'd been looking through. But none of it provides a clue to what's happened. It is now just a box of my late daughter's things.

———————

The next two days are a blur, as we make preparations for the funeral. Some people call, offering their help and support, while others avoid me in public. I quickly come to learn that one of the most difficult parts of losing a child, or at least the part that is hardest for me to get used to, is my new image as the mother of the girl who was murdered. People cross the street to avoid me because it's far easier than the effort of trying to come up with something intelligent or useful to say. It's tough for them to know how much a simple hug or word of condolence would help; or maybe they know it, but it's hard as hell to really step up and do anything that they think the suffering person will find helpful. People avoid pain. Now I am pain. I cease to be anything else.

The calendar changes from September to October. I'm sitting in the kitchen staring at the coffee pot in a daze when Jim walks in and says something about returning to Florida.

"Hm?"

"I have to fly back down, Karen. To take the sailboat back to the charter company in St. Pete's."

"Are you serious?"

"Yes. No one else can do it. It's in my name."

"Tell me you're joking," I say. "Find someone else to do it."

"I can't. All of our stuff is still on it."

"So pay the company to ship it to us."

"I'll be back for the funeral."

"How do you know that?"

"I promise."

"I cannot believe you're going to leave me."

"I'll be back in time. Don't worry."

"Jim. Call someone and arrange to have the stuff sent back. You don't need to go." I can't suggest he ask Ken, since Ken is getting married literally hours from now. Jim was supposed to be the best man.

"Karen, I have to. Come on; be reasonable. It's all our stuff. I'll be back."

Jim leaves the kitchen. I go back to staring at the coffee pot.

A few hours later, the funeral director calls, asking me to come by. We need to take care of payment, he says. I've been a self-employed Realtor for the past ten months, and in six of those months, I've made nothing. The bill from the funeral home is fifteen thousand dollars. I know no bank is going to loan me a dime, and I know I can count on nothing from Gary, who refuses to help since I won't agree to send Bonnie to Prince Edward Island. Jim, who is always hard up for cash, is no help, either.

I sit across from the funeral director and explain my circumstances, asking him to send me a bill.

"This is, um, a sticky situation," he says. "We can't release the body without the bill being paid. I know that must be difficult to accept. I'm sorry—it's just policy."

The newest surge of disbelief washes over me. Bonnie's body is being held hostage by a funeral parlor unless I can come up with thousands of dollars I don't have. Every time I think this strange nightmare can't get more surreal, it does. I begin to pull out my credit cards.

"You'll have to split it across different cards. Here—this one, and, I guess, this one. I think there might be enough room between them to cover it."

"Thank you," the funeral director says, quietly sweeping both cards into his hands. "Would you excuse me? I'll just take a minute to process these, and then we can discuss what happens next."

Tears are rolling down my face. My poor baby girl.

———————————

I've never been inside Rabbit Creek Community Church, a stone's throw from Gary's house, though he tells me that Bonnie attended services there from time to time and enjoyed them. "Loved them" were the words he used. I don't know whether I believe that, but since I don't have an affiliation with any church in particular at the moment, I've deferred to Gary. Rabbit Creek it is.

I move through the day of the funeral in a fog. Waking up saddens me. Putting on the dark clothes numbs me. Entering the church makes my blood boil. I don't know the minister here, and it feels like he's using Bonnie's murder to drum up business. A big funeral is great free advertising for new parishioners, after all, and Bonnie's funeral is big. Rabbit Creek Community Church is overflowing with attendees, so many that some have to stand and listen from the foyer. Bonnie's friends, my friends, dozens of the officers, sergeants, and detectives I've worked with at APD, including the chief, the chaplain, and a number of reserve officers. Gary's colleagues from BP. Parents of Bonnie's friends. Neighbors.

Sergeant Marrs has also informed me, and me alone, that there are also five undercover Alaska State Troopers here scanning the crowd in case Bonnie's killer decides to show up. Sometimes the perverse mix of guilt, curiosity, and connection makes such people do such things. You never know.

During the moments I come back into my body and feel present, I take comfort in the show of support, but most of the time I alternate between a faraway haze and simmering anger. I spend a lot of time staring at the flowers. For years I'd felt that flowers at a funeral were a waste of money. At my brother's funeral, that opinion changed. I realized they were the one superficially uplifting element in a relentlessly sad and painful event. Rabbit Creek Community Church is bursting with arrangements of every type. In every direction I look there are yellows, whites, pinks, and greens—colors of softness, tenderness.

People walk in silence toward the altar, quietly unfold pieces of paper, and speak about Bonnie. They are a blur to me, shadows drifting across my eyes, vague impressions of people, words, and tears. I hear snippets of things, the things I already know about my daughter.

She was such a responsible person. Someone you could always count on.

She was so nurturing to her younger siblings. Always liked to help them make good decisions.

She would get up in the morning and decide to have a good day, every day.

Her friends called her Tigger because she was so bouncy and fun to be around.

She coached kids in swimming.

After her friend Katie died as a result of a drunk-driving accident, she started SADD, Students Against Drunk Driving.

She was the first girl to be on the Service High School wrestling team.

Gordon Craig, my first husband, Bonnie's birth father, is there. He has flown in from Calgary. Gary Campbell, my second husband, Bonnie's true father, is there, as is his brother, Alex, who also flew in from Calgary. Jim Foster, my current partner, is there, too, having returned from Florida an hour before the service. They are all there to say good-bye.

I come slightly out of my haze when I see Cameron Miyasaki, Bonnie's boyfriend, enter. He has flown back from California for the funeral. I'd often caught Bonnie recording herself singing and talking on cassette tapes to send to him at Berkeley. Now, though his sweet, kind face is the same, he is a shell, barely able to compose himself. His shoulders are slumped, and his chin droops.

I do not make the effort to walk to the front of the room and address everyone. Some things you know are impossible. I'd requested that the song "Peace, Perfect Peace," by Bishop E. H. Bickersteth, be played near the end of the service. I am aware enough to register the fact that the wrong version comes over the speakers. I hear myself cry out, "That's the wrong one!" People don't know what I am saying. They assume it is confused, anguished ranting. My mother hushes me and offers empty words of consolation. Beside her, my father is a stone. My brother, Andrew, who also flew in from St. Catharines, sits on the other side of me, his hand on my shoulder. Each bit of strength from someone helps.

I want to be present for Jason, Adam, and Samantha. My surviving children. It makes me fume to have to think of them that way. It is hard enough to put one foot in front of the other and breathe in and out continuously, but I know they need me. I fear that there are hours, maybe days, when I forget that I need to be there for them. I feel myself sinking into the obsessive quest to find Bonnie's murderer and feel powerless to stop it.

I walk out of the narthex of the Rabbit Creek Community Church with Jason, Adam, and Samantha at my side, our arms interlaced. Afterward, I go back in and ask the kids to help me carry out as many of the potted plants or baskets as they can manage. We collect one rose from each arrangement to keep forever. One wreath in particular is really lovely. It seems just the kind Bonnie would like. I don't know who it's from, but I take it with me.

The next morning I wake up, look at the especially lovely wreath, and spend the next several hours duplicating it with silk flowers. I hang it on the front door. Then I sit down in the kitchen, stare at the phone, and wait.

5

I t is one week after my daughter has been murdered. I will say that to myself a thousand more times—*My daughter has been murdered*—and never get any better at processing the words. I've managed a fitful sleep, the best I can hope for. I arise at 4:45 A.M., put on some clothes, quietly make myself a pot of coffee, and drive to Gary's house on Vern Drive.

I've decided to replicate Bonnie's exact route to the bus stop, the one she would have taken on the day of her death. At exactly 5:00 A.M., I start out on foot from Gary's house, just as she did. I have told both Jim and the troopers about my plan to retrace Bonnie's steps in the hope of finding a clue or catching some insight. Jim knows nothing he can say will stop me. The troopers seem indifferent to whatever I do.

I walk the couple of minutes north to Legacy Drive, then, after a brief jog east, turn back north again onto Lake Otis Parkway, which covers nearly the north-south length of Anchorage. Lake Otis Parkway is well lit and, for the first part of my walk, runs through neighborhoods on both sides. It's hard to imagine Bonnie in any danger walking along this road.

At the same time, I am not happy to realize that my daughter never shared with me how far she had to walk to reach the bus, because she never wanted to contradict the idea that living with her dad made it easier for her to get to school and work. That's what she'd told me, so that's what I'd believed.

After fifteen minutes, I am still nowhere near her bus stop. As I continue along Lake Otis Parkway, a chilling memory from more than a decade earlier surfaces. I was at home in Calgary when, around noon, I got a call from Bonnie and Jason's school telling me they had only just arrived. Shocked, I asked where my seven-year-old son and five-year-old daughter had been since eight-thirty that morning, when they'd left home to catch the bus. The receptionist told me that some man had dropped them off. I was instantly terrified and sickened. I'd told both Bonnie and Jason, again and again, never, under any circumstances, to accept a stranger's invitation into a car. I raced to the school in a panic, imagining sexual abuse and worse. Jason and Bonnie were together in the school office, looking normal. I hugged and kissed them then, fighting tears, asked what had happened and who they'd been with. I looked them both in the eyes and told them it was important that they tell Mommy the truth. Jason explained that they'd been late and had missed their bus. Not wanting to get in trouble, they'd decided to walk to school instead. Jason had memorized the route, which ran along a two-lane expressway.

As they walked, a man who worked for one of the oil-field service companies stopped alongside and told them they really shouldn't be walking along a freeway like this, and that their mother would probably be worried if she knew. He offered to take them to school in his car. Jason told the man that they weren't allowed to get into a car with a stranger. The man handed Jason his business card, said he had children, too, and that they could trust him to drive them to school to make sure they'd get there safely.

The man drove them to school and told them to have a good day and not to walk on the freeway again, which was dangerous. Jason, concerned that he and Bonnie would get in trouble for accepting the man's offer, threw the business card in the garbage can in front of the school.

I thanked my son and daughter for telling me the truth—a mother can sense whether her child is lying—and told them I was proud of them. Once I was sure they were okay, and I assured them they weren't in trouble, I left the office and went straight to the garbage can at the front of the school. The business card was there, just as Jason said. Now I knew for certain that they'd been telling the truth. Why would a predator leave his business card? I called the number on it and introduced myself to the man who answered. He complimented my children, telling me that Jason and Bonnie had been walking hand in hand, their free hands swinging their lunch pails. Jason had been very protective of his little sister, the man noted.

Later that day, when the kids arrived home from school, I sat them down to say they would never get in trouble for missing the bus, and that if it happened again, they should turn back for home. When the other mothers in the community learned about the incident, they told their children the same thing. *Just come home. You can always come home, where it's safe.*

My memory of that incident is broken by the familiar sound of a moose coming from the large undeveloped block of land to the east. As I turn, the moose is already in motion toward me. Like any Alaskan, I'm well aware that moose, though docile in nature, will protect their territory just like any other animal, and though they may look awkward, they can be deadly if they give chase.

I run immediately north, and find the only protection I can: a lamppost, maybe a foot wide. The moose walks toward the lamppost and we begin a strange dance, me circling around it and him slowly following with his huge body.

Finally, a red pickup truck stops to offer assistance, and the moose nonchalantly saunters back into the brush. I thank the man for stopping, but the moose seems to have lost interest, so I tell the driver I'm fine to continue on.

I'm proceeding up Lake Otis when my unusually aggressive companion again emerges from the foliage. I use the same tactic as before, running to the nearest lamppost and resuming the odd dance, keeping the twelve-inch barrier between me and the huge animal.

This time it is an Alaska State Trooper car that stops at the side of the road. Again the moose retreats as I walk to the car. The trooper doesn't recognize me, but when I tell him the same thing I'd told the driver of the pickup—that I'm Bonnie Craig's mother and am walking her route to try to gather clues—he offers to let me off farther down Lake Otis, past the wooded area and clear of the moose's terrain. I hop in, and the trooper drives me half a mile down the road, where there are houses all around; the moose is no longer a concern. I continue walking north until I reach Bonnie's bus stop.

I have walked for forty-five minutes. I am furious with Gary for allowing Bonnie to walk this far every morning to catch the bus to school, not to mention for keeping me in the dark about it. The route along Lake Otis is the only one. Did Bonnie encounter the same moose? Maybe she saw it more than once. Maybe on that morning it acted more aggressive than usual, and her killer had happened by in a car, offering a ride. I'd have accepted a ride from the man in the pickup myself had it been just a week earlier, when my daughter was still alive.

Beyond this observation, though, I learn nothing more from my replication of the route. All I gain is the sequence of images I've assembled in my own head: of Bonnie walking; then being snatched away; then being beaten and, likely, raped; then finally being tossed off the cliffside at McHugh Creek to her death. As I walk back, I see the words *HELP ME* spray-painted on the plywood frame of a partially constructed apartment complex. I ask myself if the troopers have seen this or looked into it.

Now, just after six o'clock in the morning, Lake Otis Parkway and its surrounding streets are abuzz with people. How could someone have taken her without anyone else noticing?

Later, I get in my car and drive to, and stop at, various parking lots—at the university, at McHugh Creek, at other trailheads on the way out of the city. With the leaves falling and blowing, I keep up hope that her backpack will be found. I get out of the car and scour the ditches. I get down in a walking crouch and move slowly along, a foot at a time, an inch, praying for a trace of evidence, not knowing what I'm looking for but hoping to find it anyway.

I think about the moose and realize I never yelled at it or used any commonsense defenses, like the pepper spray I keep attached to my key ring at all times. I know Bonnie had pepper spray on her key ring, too. I'd given it to her for protection and insisted that she always carry it. In my training with the police department, I'd seen its effect on would-be attackers. I'd felt it myself—to be approved to carry it on your belt, you had to get sprayed with it in the face and then still be able to call dispatch via the handheld radio—also on your belt—and give your location, while protecting your weapon from being taken by a suspect and somehow extricating yourself from the situation. I had managed to pass the test, but it made clear to me the defense that the spray offered. At times I had more faith in it than my gun.

But I hadn't thought to use mine on the moose. Instead I'd done that slow dance around the lamppost with the beast, twice. I've always thought of myself as someone who keeps her head in an emergency. Bonnie was the same. It's hard for me to imagine it would be easy for anyone, even a man, to force Bonnie into a car easily. She was a wrestler. She was tough, scrappy.

But she was still a young girl, and a man bent on abduction has a different kind of strength. What hell my daughter must have endured.

When I walk in the door, Jim is there. "Listen," he says, placing his hands on my shoulders, "I need to go to Mexico in a few weeks to take care of some paperwork."

Mexico. It is the last thing I need to hear. After traveling with his ex-wife to a fishing village called San Blas, nestled between Mazatlán and Puerto Vallarta, Jim had been coaxed into buying property with some bungalows on the water because it was minutes from the ocean, and he was convinced that the initial investment would pay handsome dividends over time. True to his dreamer's nature, he pictured a house on the beach; a restaurant frequented by happy, sun-kissed travelers and locals; and a constant flow of revenue. One IRS lien and one bankruptcy later, the property generates little to no income, and Jim can't buy a damn thing. The only thing he can claim is the duplex in Anchorage his ex-wife lives in.

"Come with me. We won't be gone long."

"Not a chance," I say. "How can I do that?"

"Look, there's nothing you can do here right now. The troopers are doing everything they can, and they'll call us when they have information. Getting out of town for a few days might be just the thing."

If I go, I'm leaving my kids alone. What might happen to them while I'm gone? I don't know if I'll ever be able to go away again.

"Just think about it, okay?" he says. "Not for me. For you. I have to leave on Thursday, in the morning. It would just be for a few days."

By the Wednesday night before Jim is scheduled to leave for Mexico, I'm still filled with fear at the idea of leaving my kids. But part of me has started to think Jim might be right, that taking a few days to escape wouldn't be the worst idea in the world. In the predawn hours of Thursday, I hastily and messily pack a suitcase, still panic-stricken but deciding it will be better to be in Mexico with Jim than alone in the house in Anchorage—the kids are at Gary's—doing nothing but facing my thoughts. It already seems like an eternity since the murder, and still I've received no information from the troopers.

With the pit in my stomach growing, we board the plane. Jim is quiet on the flight, pleased that he has persuaded me to come, feeling he has done his duty for now by physically, if not emotionally, removing me from the darkness.

Arriving in San Blas, I am restless. I tell Jim I need to do something. It is impossible for him to understand the turmoil inside me and the difficulty of sitting still. When we get to his property, I gather whatever cleaning products I can find. The rest I buy at the local hardware store, along with painting supplies. I spend the next two days scrubbing, cleaning, and painting any door or surface I can find.

Jim cautiously approaches me as I apply a second coat of white to the front wall. "Hey," he says. "Listen, I know you want to be doing stuff instead of just sitting around. But the beach is right there, and we haven't taken advantage. Let's go relax a bit. It will be good for you."

It's the same thing he said about coming on the trip, which has been anything but good for me. It isn't his fault. I could be on Jupiter right now and I'd feel the same. It isn't the world outside I will have to learn how to manage for the rest of my life; it is the world inside. But I consent to go to the beach.

"Great," Jim says again. "It will be good for you."

Jim relaxes in a beach chair with a cerveza and a magazine. I walk along the sand, then wade a distance out into the water. As I run my fingertips along the surface of the water, I find myself thinking about the little wooden box Bonnie made me as a kid. It was lined with fabric to make a hinge. On the top, it read, "Mom, I needed you . . ." and then, under the lid, "every step of the way." Inside was a heart with "# 1 Mom" written on it. But I wasn't there for her. Tears stream down my cheeks. Oh, God, I wasn't there for her. That she wrote it in past tense makes it all the more haunting.

Back at the house, I seek the mercy of sleep, but I'm unable to close my eyes. When Jim is around, I stifle the sounds of my crying or find refuge elsewhere, outside the house, where I let the tears come until they are spent for another day, another hour. My jaw tightens until my head throbs. I try hard to snap out of it, but I know the next wave is never far behind.

Soon after we land back in Anchorage, I pick up multiple messages at home from people asking when I'll be home from vacation. The kids tell me that Gary has been informing people Jim and I decided to take a short vacation in Mexico. I'm stunned to think that he'd want to paint me in that kind of light. I guess he has his reasons.

I have coped with things before. I have gone through multiple marriages and divorces. I have lost one of my brothers. I have coped, and I have dealt.

But it is now mid-November, six weeks after my daughter has been murdered—*My daughter has been murdered*—and I am struggling. My hands shake when I try to pour myself a cup of coffee. Getting dressed seems like a giant task. Keeping a focused thought in my head is near impossible. I cry for my daughter more than I thought it was possible to cry. I sob at night until I am exhausted enough to sleep. When I think the tears have been depleted, more come.

The detective inside me expected answers in the immediate days after Bonnie's murder and still questions why none have arrived. I wait for the phone to ring. It never does. I wait for word that the troopers have someone in custody or at least a list of suspects. They don't. Or if they do, they aren't telling me. Being left in the dark is, in a sense, worse than the initial news of Bonnie's murder. I crash, mentally and physically, worrying my family instead of making sure my other kids are healthy and coping.

I begin to inundate Sergeant Marrs and the other troopers with calls, demanding to know what they are doing or finding, offering suggestions on where they should look or what they can do. It is clear they don't want my help. The more I call, the more annoyed with me they become. I am not asking them to tell me the case has been solved. I am asking them to tell me what they are doing to try to solve it.

The less they reveal, the more I come to believe in their incompetence. On the occasions I do get through, I am given vague, generic information.

"We're talking to the appropriate people and pursuing the appropriate leads, Mrs. Campbell. I can't really be more specific than that at the moment. We have to be very careful about information getting into the wrong hands."

"The wrong hands?"

"In an investigation like this, information has to be kept very secure, because if something gets leaked, there is the very real possibility that the one person who knows something critical may become nervous and not come forward."

"But my hands are not the wrong hands. I'm Bonnie's mother."

"Absolutely. But there is a specific protocol for an investigation of this type, and it must be followed. Experience tells us that."

"Sergeant Marrs, this is awfully frustrating. I don't know why you and the others won't share anything with me. I have no idea what you are or aren't doing. You can imagine how it feels." I'm trying to be diplomatic. I was taught to start with diplomacy in any situation and only shift gears if that doesn't work.

"I understand, Mrs. Campbell. I assure you that we're talking to lots of folks and doing everything we can to move the investigation forward. In these kinds of situations, we'd always like things to move faster, but they rarely do. For the person in your position, it naturally feels like progress is even slower. We want the same thing as you, which is to find the person who did this and to put them away. We are working on every lead we have."

"Thank you—but those are very general statements. What am I supposed to do with them? Why can't I be told who you're speaking with or where you're looking? I have no idea what you've found out, if anything. It's my daughter, but you won't let me get involved."

"It's important that you let us do our jobs."

His tone changes when he says this. He is willing to offer me endless ambiguous statements about the investigation in general, but as soon as I offer my assistance, his hackles go up. Underneath the words he is saying, I can hear the actual statement: *We're the detectives. You aren't. Do your job, and let us do ours.*

In their minds, my job is to sit aside and do nothing. I've never done that before, and I'm not about to start doing it now. The more I talk in circles with Sergeant Marrs, the more resentful I become at being put off like this. They want me to act like a victim. I have no interest in being a victim, because I am not the victim. My murdered daughter is the victim. I am the one surviving, and I could act like a survivor if they would let me. But they don't believe a regular citizen, police-trained or not, can do anything but sit by while they do their jobs. If they even *are* doing their jobs. I have no way of knowing.

"Mike," I say in a later, similar conversation, "while I guess I can appreciate what you're trying to tell me, the fact is I'm Bonnie's mother. It's also the case that I've spent years training as an undercover police officer, I've participated in drug busts, I know how investigations work, and, protocol or not, I could be of use in the investigation if—"

"Mrs. Campbell?"

"Karen."

"Karen. I'm sorry to interrupt. I really can't disclose to you anything more than I've already said at this point. I want to assure you that we will share with you any significant development in the case before it's told to anyone else. We can't provide you daily updates because unfortunately things do work slower than that, and if we spend the majority of our time keeping you in the loop on every small development, it will compromise our ability to move the case forward and eventually solve it. I hope you can trust what I'm saying. I sympathize with the helpless position I'm sure you feel you're in."

"Several people have told me they've left messages for you or the other troopers with potential information about Bonnie or the case that might help, and no one has called them back."

"I will definitely look into that. I apologize. It's fine if they're offering information, but you understand that if people are asking questions, we can't give any answers."

I have received frequent calls from people telling me they have contacted the troopers on the case to provide whatever tidbits of information they can or mention potentially suspicious individuals but that the troopers never respond. I wonder two things. First, why the troopers aren't following up on every lead they can. And second, why they aren't informing me about the information they're getting.

"What about hiring a private investigator? I'll pay for it."

"That would be a conflict of interest," Sergeant Marrs responds. "We can't share information as long as the investigation is open."

"What if it's a retired state trooper?"

"I'm afraid it still wouldn't be of any help, Karen. I assure you we've deployed every resource and are carrying out the proper steps."

"I'd like to believe that, but I have no evidence."

"Again, we want to make sure we're using our time in the best way possible, and that is by conducting the investigation and then reporting relevant information to you as it's discovered. There will be days, or sometimes weeks, when we unfortunately have nothing to report. I understand how frustrating that must be, but when you don't hear from us, it isn't because we're hiding anything from you. It's because we don't have anything to tell."

I'm not satisfied. Sergeant Marrs is compassionate and, I believe, sincere, but I still can't understand why I seem to be the last person who finds out anything about the case in which my own daughter is the victim.

"Karen, if I could mention one thing. There's a support group. It's called Victims for Justice. I've been involved with them a number of times in these kinds of situations and have seen them help people who face circumstances similar to yours. They do a number of things, including helping people file for victim's compensation. I'm not prying into your personal affairs, but I know firsthand how a situation like this can affect everything, from the dynamics at home to finances. They can help you figure out ways the state might be able to help you defray certain costs. I encourage you to give them a call. May I give you the number?"

———————

I stare at the piece of paper on which I've just scrawled the number. Ever since seeing Ken hold out the yellow Post-it on the boat, phone numbers on scraps of paper are now sources of pain.

I don't think I need the help Sergeant Marrs and the other troopers think I do. I don't need their help dealing with my private hell—what I need is for them to let down their silly arrogance and allow me to participate in the case. What I want is to find the person who killed my daughter. I can handle pain. Sitting in a circle sharing with others is not going to help me do that.

I realize I am crying again.

I dial the number.

A woman named Janice answers. She knows who I am and does most of the talking. I am small-voiced and somehow ashamed to be calling.

"Why don't you come down for a chat?" Janice says. "I'd really like to meet you. We have a lot in common."

The Victims for Justice office is a room in an old run-down building in downtown Anchorage. I walk up a flight of wooden stairs, follow the arrow printed on the small sign with the hand-done organizational logo, and approach a small dank room with poor lighting.

"Pretty easy to tell we're a nonprofit, isn't it?"

I turn to see a small, thin woman with short dark hair, maybe ten years older than me, smiling an easy smile. "You must be Karen. I'm Janice Lienhart. I'm glad you came. Will you sit down?"

We sit at a long dining room table.

"This table was donated, like everything else," Janice says. "We're struggling to get funding, but I'm not really one to give up."

Janice tells me her story—how nine years earlier, in 1985, a fourteen-year-old girl named Winona Fletcher and her nineteen-year-old boyfriend, Cordel Boyd, broke into Janice's parents' home while on a burglary spree and shot both of them, as well as her aunt, execution-style. It was a random thrill-kill: Winona and Cordel had merely wanted to find out what it would be like to kill someone. Janice's parents were sixty-nine and seventy years old; her aunt seventy-six.

When Janice and her sister Sharon had tried to get information regarding the case, they'd discovered that victims had no standing in the criminal justice process. Because she was a minor at age fourteen, Winona Fletcher had gone through a mini trial called a waiver hearing to determine if she should be charged as an adult. The hearing was closed to the public, including Janice and Sharon's family.

"We were just so angry," Janice says in a soft den-mother voice. "Imagine finding that out. The families themselves, the ones who should be taken care of, actually have no status. They're literally left to deal with things on their own. It was up to us to try to have Winona tried as an adult. Everything was being done behind closed doors, and we as a family were not given a stitch of information for the longest time, so we had no idea what was going on. She was a juvenile, so it was all kept very secret. Had she been tried as a juvenile, she would have done some rehab in a treatment facility and then walked free at twenty. We had to become the advocates for ourselves. It was insane."

"What happened to Winona?" I ask.

"Finally, she was tried as an adult and put away. Two counts of first-degree murder and one second-degree. Two hundred and ninety-seven years. Later, it was reduced to a hundred and thirty-five. She'll be eligible for parole at age sixty. Cordel was guilty of first-degree on all three murders. What my sister and I went through was a nightmare. We didn't want others to have to endure the same. So we started Victims for Justice. It started very grass-roots. We're still small, but we've made some inroads. And we can help you in certain ways. When you're in this position, it can be very tricky to negotiate the system. We've lobbied the legislature pretty hard, and we've managed to make some changes—though we want to make more."

Janice and I talk awhile longer. She tells me about how her family came to Alaska from Wyoming in the 1940s, how her father was a construction superintendent who built housing for military families. We talk about her sister Sharon and their special bond, cemented by this unspeakable tragedy. She offers to help me file for something called victim's compensation to help get financial support from the state. Those forms make doing your taxes seem like a walk in the park, Janice tells me, so it helps to have someone in your corner who knows their way around the details. Since she seems to know how to get things done, I tell her that I have asked the troopers to see Bonnie's autopsy report multiple times only to be told over and over that I can't. She says she might be able to help, but doesn't mention anything further about it.

When I get home, I do more research, and I learn that Janice has vastly understated what Victims for Justice has achieved. Thanks to her organization, victims' rights in Alaska are now en-shrined in a voter-approved constitutional amendment. They have not made small inroads; they have changed laws. I read about the

JUSTICE FOR BONNIE   63

things she has done. She is tenacious. She has been through hell and has dedicated her life to helping others survive the same. In all the reading I do, I notice that she is never visible in photographs. It seems she's intentionally kept herself out of the limelight.

I call her back.

"You were being modest," I say.

"I don't think about what we've done," she says. "I think about how much there still is to do."

I like this woman.

"Karen?" she says.

"Yes?"

"Would you consider attending a group-support session? And before you answer, let me say something. When my parents and aunt were killed, the first thing people suggested was for me to do counseling, and I said no. I felt it was a waste of time, because I didn't want to sit around crying with a bunch of strangers when I could be out fighting for justice instead. But I was wrong. Just take down the date and time. Okay?"

"Sure," I say noncommittally. I think about it frequently for the next week, mostly deciding it isn't for me, just as Janice said she felt when people made the same suggestion. But when the following Wednesday arrives, I find myself at the door of the Victims for Justice office, feeling nervous and embarrassed. I'm about to turn around and head back to the car when the door opens and Janice appears.

"Glad you came," she says, taking my hand and guiding me inside. I meet Janice's sister Sharon, whose big presence and gregarious energy directly contrast Janice's soft-spoken strength. The two sisters introduce me to the dozen or so other people present, all of whom greet me with sympathetic hugs and knowing expressions. Their eyes tell me that we are all on different parts of the same journey.

We sit on simple folding chairs arranged in a circle, and people begin to speak. The purpose of group-support sessions isn't guidance or problem solving; it's simply to be heard. We go around the room and lay out our respective tragedies. There is no judgment and no competition. Each story is unbearable. Yet we continue to tell, and we continue to listen.

Janice and Sharon say as little as possible, simply going around the room to make sure everyone has a chance to speak. Each of us seems to feel the pain of the others. Our jaws drop as we hear not only the stories of loss and family heartbreak but also of the continued revictimization—by the law, the media, employers, and prosecutors. Boxes of tissues sit on a table in the middle of the circle. We reach for them frequently. I have felt acutely aware of having been pushed aside by those I would have expected to help, but in my self-focus, I never realized that there were other people experiencing the same things.

At the end of the session, I exchange hugs with everyone, Janice and Sharon last, then walk to my car. I feel bonded to a room of people whom I didn't know a few hours ago. They, like me, have stopped trying to figure out whether the pain will ever subside. They, like me, are just trying to survive the day. We survive by knowing that others are facing the same struggle. That we are not alone.

I am not alone.

I walk in the door at home emotionally sapped but at the same time uplifted. I know I will return to the group again, to feel what I've just felt—buoyed up, just slightly, above the water line.

The phone rings.

"Hello. Is this Karen?"

"Yes," I say. I don't recognize the voice.

"Karen, my name is Sandy Cassidy. I know you don't know me, and I never met your daughter, but I wanted to let you know that I, and many in the community, feel so saddened and sickened to hear about her death. I've been following it in the newspaper and on TV. I wanted to let you know that I'd like to help in some way, if I could."

I'm flabbergasted. In the past few months, I've mostly encountered avoidance from others, apart from my dearest friends. Even many of those people whom I'd considered close acquaintances have been conspicuous in their absence. Knowing how to act around someone who has lost a child is nearly impossible. I get it.

"That's very kind of you," I say to Sandy. "I really appreciate it. I feel like I've been spinning my wheels."

"I think it would help you to get out there in the newspaper and on the news so that no one forgets about Bonnie. My husband Maurice and I would like to help you keep it in the public eye. We can form a group. Maybe get a reward fund going. I'm sure there's a way we can help find out who did this."

I have never heard of Sandy Cassidy, and I can't imagine why she is so invested in Bonnie. But I'm grateful for her words nonetheless. For the first week or two after Bonnie was killed, I talked to the media as much as I could, desperate to rally support and get people talking about the fact that it couldn't have been an accident. But I've been a reporter, and I know as well as anyone that a story, no matter how big, stops being a story fast.

After those first couple of weeks, I went quiet, both because I knew the story would inevitably slide to the back page and also because, at that point, part of me was saying it was no longer fair to continue bombarding people with it. They had their own problems to deal with. For more than two months, I've hardly said a word publicly about the case.

I can only think of one thing to say to Sandy: "Do you have children?"

"Yes," she says. "Maurice and I have a daughter. She attends the university. He's taking some classes there, too. Karen, may I come up and see you so we could talk about this? I have some specific ideas I'd like to share."

"Sure."

"When would be a good time for you?"

"How about now?"

Sandy shows up at my door an hour later. She is a little taller than me and a little heavier, with a caring face.

"Hi," she says, reaching out to hug me. "It's nice to meet you. I'm so sorry for what you're going through."

"Thank you," I say. "Come on in."

Sandy and I sit in my living room. "I hope you don't think I'm being presumptuous," she says. "I don't mean to tell you what to do. It's just, I'm sure you're feeling a bit frustrated and impatient, and I think some of my ideas would help you get the word out and keep it out. No matter what the story is, it's front and center one day, but then other stories come along and push it aside, and before long everyone's forgotten about it. But there are ways of keeping it out there so people don't forget."

"My BA is in journalism and public communication," I tell Sandy. "I've done some local TV reporting. I know a lot of the media around here. But I haven't really thought about ways to keep the media involved. I did all those interviews right afterward, but then it kind of faded away."

"That's what tends to happen. It's only page one for so long. But if you keep it on people's minds . . . sooner or later you get a hit. Something. If you mount a campaign, if there's enough coverage, eventually someone may feel guilty enough to come forward.

Not necessarily the person who did it, but someone who knows something. There are a dozen reasons why people don't come forward. If they're allowed to just forget about it, it makes it much easier. But if you keep it in the spotlight, it makes it a lot harder to keep a secret."

"That makes sense," I say. "I guess I've been kind of wallowing in self-pity. I've been doing a lot of looking around, but on my own. The troopers haven't exactly been cooperative."

"I understand. Between you and me, there's more than one reason to keep the case in the media. One reason is to try to encourage people who know something to come forward. But second, once the media latches on to a story, they'll be like bloodhounds on the troopers. They'll be calling them every day for updates and statements. They may be able to hide from you, but they can't hide from the entire Anchorage media."

Part of me wonders why this stranger wants to help me. But right now, I don't care. "I'm very grateful for this," I tell Sandy.

"Not at all," she says. "We really want to do it. I can't imagine what it would be like to be in your position. Maurice and I consider this the least we can do. Shall we get down to business?"

Any doubts I have about Sandy's intentions disappear within the first few minutes of her being in my home. She tells me of her work with Habitat for Humanity and other charitable causes. I believe what my gut is telling me. Sandy is simply one of those people who believe they have a civic duty to help others in need.

She lays out various ideas and asks what I think about them. Getting signs, bumper stickers, and posters printed and placing them around town. Giving more interviews—lots of them. Getting articles into the paper. Going on local TV shows. Doing bus ads. Scheduling memorials and vigils, to get the community involved.

"I think it's normal for people who have suffered the way you have to find it difficult to deal with the press," Sandy says, "or maybe they feel disheartened when, like I said, initially there's all this coverage, giving them hope, and then suddenly it all seems to go away. You kind of feel victimized by the media, where at first you thought they were going to be helpful. The truth is the media are only there to do their jobs, which is to report on current stories. So it's our job to make sure it remains current."

I know this, of course. I've been one of those media hounds who people sneer at. I know the rules of the game. But there's no script for this, and no rehearsal for the position I'm in now. Sandy and I talk for a long time. I thank her several more times. I find I have little else to say, which is unusual for me. As she leaves, we exchange hugs.

Sandy calls the next morning to tell me she has initiated a group called Friends and Family of Bonnie Craig. I put her in touch with Janice, who helps set it up as a nonprofit and gets one of her contacts from Victims for Justice to do the tax forms. Sandy tells me she has also started to post messages and design flyers to solicit support from the community. Finally, she and Maurice have made the first donation toward a reward fund that will be used to solicit information.

"Karen?" she says.

I'm on the other end, looking at the phone. "Sorry. I'm here."

"Did you hear everything I said?"

"Yes. Yes, I heard."

"Are you on board with it? Is it okay?"

"Yes, of course. Thank you, Sandy. Thank you."

With Sandy's encouragement, I pull myself out of my fog and start doing everything I can to ensure Bonnie's case doesn't fade from the public eye. I provide content for articles in the *Anchorage Daily News*. I give more TV interviews. Before I can blink, the reward fund grows to five thousand dollars, making me cry with gratitude. A few weeks after my first conversation with Sandy, I am walking outside when I see my daughter's face pass me on the side of a bus, next to the words *Who Killed Bonnie?*

With each bit of coverage, more leads come in. I know from my undercover work that most of these leads will amount to nothing, but it is a positive sign not only that people have information to give but also that they are willing to give it. From friends and neighbors, I learn that Bonnie's case, and the mystery of her death, has again become a common topic of conversation. Where previously people avoided me, now they seek me out. Frequently, strangers ask me if I'm Bonnie Craig's mom. When I say I am, they give me hugs. Soon it seems everyone is discussing the case again. Or, at the very least, they are aware of it. It's been nearly three months, and people are preparing for family holiday celebrations. But they haven't forgotten—not yet.

Some of the leads come directly to me. With every piece of information I receive, I telephone Sergeant Marrs and relay what I've learned. He nearly always says the same thing: "Thank you. We'll look into it." If someone mentions a possible suspect to me, I tell Sergeant Marrs about it. "Thank you," he says. "We'll look into it." I follow up weekly. "Thanks for calling," he says. "We're looking into it." On one occasion, I forward information provided to me about a potential suspect and ask Sergeant Marrs if the individual has a criminal record. "We can't tell you that," he says. I can go online and find out more than the state troopers investigating the case are telling me.

In my mind I fantasize that, with the holidays approaching, and the heightened collective awareness by those in the community, the person responsible for my daughter's murder will get drunk or high and end up accidentally talking. Revealing something. Maybe even be swayed by the Christmas spirit and feel compelled to do the right thing. Maybe this monster will see families celebrating or mothers and fathers embracing their children and be so gnawed by guilt and shame that he—probably he—will feel obliged to admit what he's done. It will be just like in the movies. He will see the ads and the flyers. He'll know the walls are closing in on him. He'll realize that, in the end, he can't outrun the law. He'll throw his hands up and cry, "I did it!"

But this doesn't happen. I hear nothing from the troopers, and soon the discussions about Bonnie's case again start to fade as conversations turn instead to the excitement of the holidays and family vacations and presents under the tree. The snow and cold come to Anchorage. Soon it is New Year's. I hear the celebrations outside and parties going on in the neighborhood. Looking through my bedroom window, I hear festive voices and see people smiling and throwing their arms around each other. Midnight comes. The calendar turns from 1994 to 1995. I sit on my bed and cry.

6

On the second day of 1995, I call Sergeant Mike Marrs, wish him Happy New Year, and ask if Bonnie was raped.

"Karen, we can't confirm or deny that," he tells me. My rage at his response threatens to erupt. Though I'm sure the troopers feel I'm a nuisance, I've been keeping my feelings in check, at least in my conversations with Sergeant Marrs and the others.

"Why not?" I ask.

"I assure you we'll reveal that information as soon as it becomes clear."

"Reveal that information? I'm not the public. This isn't a press conference. I'm Bonnie's mother."

"Yes, of course. I understand that, and I know you're hungry for information. We all are. But anything we could tell you in that respect would be mere speculation."

"How can that be? It's been over three months."

"Things take time, Karen."

I know what he wants to say: *Bonnie's case isn't our only one.* I know that. I've been on his side. But I'm not asking who did it. I'm asking whether someone forced himself on my daughter.

"Karen, are you still there?"

"Yes, I'm here."

"I received a call from your friend a couple of weeks ago. Ms. Lienhart."

I have been attending regular support meetings at the Victims for Justice office, and Janice Lienhart has willingly taken up the mantle of Bonnie's case, pushing for various rights on my behalf—including the right to see the autopsy report. I haven't been told a word of what it contains.

"I know you're very interested in seeing the autopsy report on Bonnie, and I assure you I'm doing everything I can to make that happen."

I'd asked Sergeant Marrs about it in the immediate weeks after Bonnie's death. The topic was brushed under the carpet. It was just another question I'd felt they hoped I would stop asking if they ignored me enough. But I will not be a silent party to a hidden investigation while my daughter's killer roams free.

A week later, the phone rings again.

"Karen?"

It's Sergeant Marrs. By now, I recognize his voice as easily as I do one of my children's.

"Hi, Mike."

"How are you?"

"Fine." I'm not interested in small talk.

"Karen, you're at liberty to see the report."

"The autopsy report?"

"Yes."

"What happened?"

"I'm not sure, but I've been authorized to invite you to come down and meet with the medical examiner to have a look at it. I'm sorry it's taken so long."

It's about time is all I can think of saying. Instead, I call Janice.

"Thank you," I say when she answers.

"Don't thank me," Janice says. "You can't go alone. I'm heading out of town. Who can you get to come with you?"

"Oh no!" I exclaim. "Cara Lee! But, they may not be happy about that! She's a reporter!"

"Perfect! Call her right away."

I know it's a gruesome task, but Cara has seen a lot as a reporter. She will know the questions to ask and remember what the medical examiner says.

A half-hour later I am at the Trooper's Post sitting on a chair near the front desk. Cara arrives a few minutes behind me.

Sergeant Marrs steps out from behind a door. He greets me, then looks disapprovingly at Cara. He recognizes her as a reporter. I quickly let him know. "Cara is here as my friend. She is not here as a reporter. Just my friend, here to support me."

With reluctance he continues, "Sure." He escorts us into a room, where an older man with glasses and thinning hair is seated behind a desk. After introductions, Dr. Thompson says, "Karen, I'm very sorry for the loss of your daughter. I can't imagine how heartbreaking this must be. I performed Bonnie's autopsy the day after she was discovered."

"Thank you. Can I see the report now?"

"Yes, if you wish. I need to caution you that—"

"I understand. It's okay."

"I'll leave you three for a while," says Sergeant Marrs.

Dr. Thompson hands me a thick stack of pages. I start reading.

Manner of Death: Homicide

At no point have I been informed of the official cause of death. I never saw a piece of paper that formally ruled it accidental, nor, until now, anything officially calling it a homicide, either. I have not even been allowed to see the death certificate. It's as though I'm not even part of the investigation of my own daughter's death.

I continue to read through the report. Certain phrases stand out, activating a mix of fury and sorrow.

. . . multiple blunt trauma injuries to the head . . .

Slowly, the picture I have been dreading but needing to fill in for the past six months emerges. I am so sad for my baby and so murderously angry at the person who took her away.

But it is still better than having to guess.

. . . left index finger shows a palpable fracture . . .

I learn what for months have been the absent details of what happened to my daughter in the last minutes of her life. Bonnie had fought the monster who eventually overpowered her and stole her existence.

On the posterior scalp, extending from the right vertex of the skull posteriorly and distributed fairly uniformly over the back of the head with a slight right-sided predominance are a collection of 11 lacerations . . .

In my mind, I am remembering the segment of my police academy training on abuse of children. I remember trembling inside as I looked at the images and listened to the cases, wanting to plug my ears. Now I am reading a report detailing how my daughter was assaulted, brutally beaten, and killed.

If the decedent was still alive at the time she entered the water in which she was found, hypothermia and/or drowning may have contributed to the death.

"There is one other piece of information," Dr. Thompson tells me. "Critical information. I'm sorry to have to share it with you; however, it will prove useful in trying to find out who is responsible for this."

I don't respond, but I don't break eye contact with him, either.

"Bonnie had minor tearing in her vaginal walls."

"Does that prove rape?"

"In a trial, the defense would argue that small tears of that type can be caused by rough consensual sex or a lack of lubrication. Those things are true, I'm afraid. I wouldn't be able to deny them on the stand."

Inside, the mother in me breaks down in a combination of raw sadness and righteous fury. On the surface, the detective in me continues to meet Dr. Thompson's eyes, asking for more.

"There is only one piece of positive news that comes out of this, as I said."

Bonnie's mother wails inside. The detective continues to stare, demanding information.

"Whoever did this to your daughter left behind his DNA."

———

To use the word *lucky* regarding anything in this horrible situation seems odd—but we *are* lucky, in that, by now in the mid-1990s, we have reached a point where DNA evidence can help us in a way it couldn't before. When Dr. Thompson tells me the killer left his DNA inside my daughter, it makes me sick to my stomach but also excited. There is a possibility of finding this monster. It will never bring Bonnie back, but it might bring her the justice she deserves.

"Karen," says Dr. Thompson, "there are pictures from the crime scene and the autopsy as well. I can show you these, but they may not be easy to handle."

"I'd like to see them."

Dr. Thompson takes a manila envelope from his files and places it on the desk. Cara squeezes my hand.

Dr. Thompson removes a series of pictures from the envelope and begins to spread them out. I feel as though I might stop breathing, but I force the air to continue in and out. Cara comes closer, placing her hands on my shoulders.

Bonnie's corpse on an examining table. Close-ups of her broken knuckles and scraped hands. Her bludgeoned head, parts of it shaved to expose the lacerations. I get the sense that these aren't the worst of the pictures, but Dr. Thompson insists he is showing me all of them.

I raise my reddening eyes to him, fighting to keep it together. "What could have caused the head injuries?"

"It's hard to say. Probably not the fall, since it's the bottom of the back of her head, and that area is usually protected. From that we can assume that it was a blow the killer administered directly."

"Using what?"

"That's difficult to say. It could be any number of things."

"Doctor," I say. "Tell me straight up what you think our chances are of convicting the person who did this if we find him. How strong is this evidence?"

"You know I can't say that. I can only make assumptions of probability."

I ask Dr. Thompson dozens of questions about the way in which this monster raped and killed my daughter and what evidence the autopsy provides that might help bring him to justice. Dr. Thompson answers me the way he is trained to: carefully. After an hour and a half, I have asked all the questions I have, at least for now. I can feel my emotions starting to overwhelm me. It is time to go home. I want to see my kids.

"Thank you for your time, Dr. Thompson."

"Certainly," he says. "Again, Karen, I'm truly sorry. I hope this will come to the right conclusion for you and your family."

Sergeant Marrs escorts me and Cara to the door, then pauses. "Needless to say, we have to ask you to keep this under your belt.

Please don't tell anyone anything about that report, including your family. All information regarding the case has to be managed with extreme care."

I find it remarkable that Sergeant Marrs and the rest of the troopers consider it a conciliatory gesture to let me see the autopsy report on my own daughter. Worse is that they don't understand the impact of telling me I can't speak to others about this. They don't understand that, when one loses a child, virtually nothing can help one survive, much less heal. The only thing that can provide some measure of sanity is the feeling that progress is being made—and the only thing that can validate that feeling is the communications of it to others. At least Cara knows. That's one person I can talk to.

Keeping it in, on the other hand, intensifies the grief that's already there. It isn't Sergeant Marrs's fault. He doesn't know that telling me to keep this and everything else to myself leaves me with no alternative but to replay it over and over in my head. He doesn't know that it means I will lie in the bathtub feeling as though I am experiencing every strike to Bonnie's head, reliving the pain and the attack she had to endure at the hands of some anonymous fiend who has so far eluded the radar. I now know the suffering she underwent, and the fight she put up. It hurts in a way I couldn't have fathomed.

Not long after, I receive another call from Sergeant Marrs.

"Karen, I have a bit of news, though we're not yet sure whether it's anything significant. Some tips have come in that are worth following up on. One of them has to do with a young man who worked with Bonnie at Sam's Club. It was someone she apparently had complained to her supervisor about. Do you have any knowledge of this?"

"No." It would have been against Bonnie's nature to paint a negative picture of anyone. "She never told me about any problems she was having with anyone there."

"We've learned that he obtained her phone number off the company computer. Do you know whether she'd been receiving calls from anyone repeatedly, or perhaps being harassed by phone?"

"No. If it was happening, I didn't know about it. Can we pull up Gary's phone records to see?"

"That on its own wouldn't be significant. It would only mean that Bonnie received telephone calls from an individual her mother didn't know about. Unfortunately, that would not be uncommon. We're going to continue digging. I'll let you know what we find out as soon as I can."

Sergeant Marrs hangs up before I can ask more questions, but I call right back. "Are you going to test him? Do you have his DNA?"

"Listen, Karen, you have to trust me to give you information in the right way. That means only information which is relevant, and only when I have it. We will bring him in, and we will run his DNA against the sample. We will go as fast as we can, as always."

"When are you bringing him in?"

"As soon as we can."

It is spring of 1995. Samantha, nearing her thirteenth birthday, is in her bedroom, doing her homework. Knocking on the door and entering the room, I realize that most of my conversations with her and her brothers in the past months have involved my asking them questions like a detective, trying to uncover information they might have hidden away somewhere that they don't realize. This one is no different.

"How was your day, sweetie?"

"Good," she says, without looking up.

I kiss the top of her head. "What are you working on, math?"

"Yep."

"Looks like you're doing a great job. Hey, can I ask you something?"

"Sure."

"Did Bonnie ever say anything to you about a guy at work who was bothering her?"

"No."

"You sure she never mentioned anything about a guy calling her? Some guy who got her number?"

"No. She would never do that to Cameron."

"I know, honey. But sometimes, even if you have a boyfriend, other boys might like you and try to get you to like them. So I just wanted to know if there was someone like that at Sam's Club that you knew about, who liked Bonnie and was maybe flirting with her."

"I don't know. Hey, you have to sign my test from yesterday. I got ninety."

"I'm proud of you," I say, and kiss her again.

I don't bother asking Adam or Jason. Samantha and Bonnie shared everything. If she didn't know, the boys definitely wouldn't, either. Any secrets Bonnie might have had, she took with her.

It's about a month after my conversation with Samantha when Sergeant Marrs finally gets back to me. When he does, my breath stops for a moment. There is only one thing I want to hear.

Instead, I hear the opposite.

"I'm sorry," says Sergeant Marrs. "We took his DNA, but it wasn't a match. I recognize how hard this is. Please understand that part of the reason we want to share only significant information is to help you avoid the natural ups and downs that happen anytime you're trying to catch a perpetrator of a crime. It's very important to try not to get too excited about possibilities. As you know, we will check out everyone worth checking out, but we want to make sure you're keeping your expectations where they should be."

"My expectations are that you're going to find out who killed my daughter."

"There's another young man. Someone else who worked with Bonnie. We're going to test him as well. We've learned from talking to Bonnie's supervisor that there was a meeting the morning she was murdered, and this person's name isn't on the sign-in sheet."

When Sergeant Marrs had mentioned the first colleague of Bonnie's, I'd let my hopes rise. As he describes this potential new suspect, they stay where they are, just as he'd instructed.

"It's at least enough for us to bring him in for questioning," he tells me. "I'll let you know if anything comes of it."

I almost want to say *Don't bother.* I'm starting to understand why detectives are so reluctant to share information with the families of victims. They want to do anything possible to avoid building expectations.

I later find out that Sergeant Marrs told potential suspects that a cigarette butt had been found at the scene and that DNA was retrieved from it. This was a ruse to get people to volunteer their DNA—especially if they didn't smoke—on the assumption that they would be easily eliminated as suspects.

"Can you tell me his name?"

"No."

"I could ask around, see if the kids know anything . . ."

"We'll check him out as fast as we can, Karen."

Exasperated, I hang up the phone. When I turn around, Jim is there.

"Bad news?"

"The only good news will be if they ever catch the guy. Every other kind of news is bad."

"Listen, Ken and Valeri are coming up for a visit next week. How about we take the boat somewhere? It's been a while."

We both know it's more specific than that. We haven't taken the boat anywhere since before our trip to Florida last September. Jim isn't just saying we haven't taken the boat anywhere lately; he's saying I haven't done much of anything in the past eight months other than search, and suffer.

"We could sail from Seward around to Whittier. Just for a week or so. You could be back in hours if you needed to be."

It's a similar argument to the one he'd used to convince me to travel to San Blas six weeks after Bonnie's murder. I realize he's doing it out of concern—and maybe because he's tired of watching me obsess—but I'm still hesitant. In my mind, every hour not spent investigating is an hour wasted. Plus, I'm still paranoid about leaving the kids.

"Think about it, okay? I don't want to stand here and tell you it would be good for you. But it would."

Two nights later, I'm saying goodnight to Adam when Sergeant Marrs calls.

"Hi, Karen. I'm sorry to keep repeating the same script, but we checked out the young man I told you about earlier in the week, and it turns out he was in fact at the meeting. He just hadn't signed in. Other people vouch for his attendance. It's another dead end, I'm afraid."

"Do you have more than just their confirming his alibi? Can't you bring him in and test him anyway?"

"We did bring him in. We took his DNA. It isn't a match. He's clean. I'm sorry."

I walk into the living room. Jim is working through some chords on his acoustic guitar.

"Okay," I say. "Let's go."

Packing for the trip, I feel different than when I packed in a spontaneous rush for Mexico two seasons ago. Seward is two hours from Anchorage by car; Mexico is ten hours by plane. I spent the entire Mexico trip fighting the restless anxiety of being too far from my surviving kids. This time, at least, I'll still be close. We'll start from Seward, where the boat is docked, and sail around to Whittier. The salty air used to feel invigorating on my skin. It used to make me feel alive. Maybe it can again. We've even talked about docking in Whittier for the summer and venturing out from there on day trips. We usually sail out of Seward and know that area well by now. But Whittier is for us still mostly uncharted territory.

A week later, when I see Ken and Valeri emerge from the terminal, a strange feeling comes over me. As we greet them and exchange hugs, the feeling intensifies. It isn't Ken's fault. I haven't seen him since last September, when we flew down to Florida, planning to celebrate their wedding, and instead came home to bury my daughter. Ken will always be the person who told me about Bonnie. He is the same sweet, cheerful person as always, but when I see him, I envision him holding out the yellow Post-it and saying *I'm sorry for what I'm about to tell you* with his eyes. I wonder whether I will ever be able to look at him again and not feel what I'm feeling now. When he asks me how I am, I say, "Fine," because saying more will be useless.

The next morning, the four of us drive to the Seward Marina. There, resting quietly in its slip, sits our thirty-seven-foot 1978

Crealock, *Sea Monkey*. It looks lonely to me, like a racehorse that hasn't been let out to run.

It feels good to get back on board. Though I had never sailed in my life until we bought the boat nearly two years earlier, the movements and actions have already become familiar, and reassuring. Doing is good; thinking is painful. Jim and Ken grew up on powerboats and are used to being on the water. Valeri, like me, is a relative novice, but she is happy to be part of the adventure and take on whatever simple tasks are assigned to her.

We imagine the trip will take about a week, though with sailing, you never know. Depending on the whims of the weather, you might have to pull in at any time. Not to mention you're never going more than a few miles an hour.

We cast off our lines, head out of the slip, and under motor power inch slowly out of the harbor, Jim at the helm. Once out of the harbor, Ken raises the main, and I pull out the genny. The wind fills our sails, and we start to pick up speed. The sense of freedom makes me smile. This has always been a moment I've relished—turning off the motor, watching the instant when the wind and the sails meet at just the right angle, and then feeling nothing but the sheer power of nature guiding you across the water. I will never be free of my own thoughts, but the simple energizing force of a moment like this takes me somewhere else temporarily, and I am happy to go. The sensation of the sea air on my cheeks and in my hair is something basic, natural, and good.

It is a straight shot down Resurrection Bay toward the Gulf of Alaska, and the winds are cooperating. As we move out of the harbor and down the bay, we adjust the sails to maximize the angle of the wind, then sit back and enjoy the seascape and the freedom of the water. The air is crisp and cool. We sit in our jeans and windbreakers sipping coffee and taking in the wondrous view.

A few days later, we turn the boat toward Prince William Sound, passing the islands that are now best known for the catastrophic *Exxon Valdez* spill in March 1989. I stare at the water reflecting the mountains on the far shore and feel a sense of calm. They seem to shoot straight up out of the water into the clouds, stretching forever into the sky.

Around Passage Bay, the wind subsides, and we motor up again. Here the breathtaking glaciers emerge, some peeking out of the water with the majority of their mass hidden below, others looming hundreds of feet above. Being among the glaciers has a stark, humbling effect that never lessens. The sun reflecting the sky-blue light of the glaciers is a sight unlike any other.

Sailing in Alaska can be treacherous for the uninitiated. They say the water is so cold that if you fall in, you'll die of hyperthermia before you can drown. In most areas, the water is very deep, two hundred feet in some places, six hundred in others. And the tides here are extreme, the water level sometimes changing as much as twenty feet in the space of four hours. One has to find a spot with the right depth while taking the tidal shifts into account. Each night, we drop anchor in protected coves where the water is about twenty feet deep at low tide, dropping more than one hundred feet of chain. We cook dinner on the portable grill and enjoy wine by the late sunset before finally falling asleep, usually well past midnight. In the morning, we rise to watch the mist rise off the water, drinking our coffee and appreciating our smallness amid the vast beauty. The more time I spend on the open sea, the better I understand the power of the water and the creatures who inhabit it. As we proceed through the Bay, we see the usual cast of characters—otters, bald eagles, puffins, seals, sea lions, whales—and we appreciate that this place is their home, and we are merely visitors.

"A bear!" Ken shouts. "There, in the water!"

I see the dot in the water that Ken is pointing out, but I laugh and tease him for thinking it's a bear. He may have grown up on boats, but he's still from Florida.

As we get closer, though, I am shocked to see that Ken is right. A brown bear is paddling along in the water with his mighty front legs, like a big muscular instructor demonstrating the dog paddle. We guide the boat closer and follow him. Soon we are only a few feet from the bear. He is more buoyant than one would imagine. His head and shoulders are above the water, hind legs tucked behind him, the pads of his massive back paws refracted just below the surface.

His brown fur glistening, the bear calmly turns his head, and his big dark eyes regard us directly. He doesn't seem concerned with our presence. We continue alongside him as he paddles further; then he casually scrambles up onto shore, powerfully shakes the water from his body, lumbers into the woods, and disappears. Ken smiles at me with exaggerated pride, and I laugh.

On our fifth night, as we search for a cove, the skies erupt. Sheets of rain pound the yacht. On Jim's orders, Ken, Valeri, and I stay belowdecks sipping hot beverages while he braves the elements, protected only by the canvas bimini over his head. The inflatable dinghy we tow behind us flips over, losing its seat. Soon, the rapid drumbeat of the rain slowly subsides, and the storm wears itself out.

With each day, I've felt myself relaxing a little. The uncomfortable feeling I had toward Ken wears off more and more. The dark moment when he brought me the news that my daughter was dead will always hang between us, but here, somehow, among the enormity and pureness of nature, I'm able to put it in a different place, and we enjoy each other's company in the simple way family should.

A week after leaving Seward, we are approaching Whittier. A half-hour from the marina, Jim radios the harbor master to get a slip number or to find out where to raft up.

"*Sea Monkey*," says a crackling voice over the radio speaker, "the Coast Guard has been trying to reach you regarding an emergency message."

"What's the message?" Jim says.

"I don't have that information, sir. I've only been told that they're trying to track you down."

With the force of a slingshot, I am back on the sailboat in St. Mark's, staring up at Ken's anguished face again as he holds out the cruel Post-it with the name and number of an Alaska State Trooper. In my mind, I'm certain I am about to receive news that one of our other children has had an accident and is dead. I feel my breath start to catch and my stomach knot.

Jim hails the Coast Guard on the radio.

"U.S. Coast Guard, U.S. Coast Guard, U.S. Coast Guard. This is the *Sea Monkey*, over."

"*Sea Monkey*, this is the U.S. Coast Guard. I'm sorry, but we have been asked to relay an urgent message."

As Jim, Ken, Valeri, and I listen together, the voice tells us that Ken and Jim's father has died of a heart attack. Jim's eyes grow wide, and his mouth drops open. I wonder if I looked like that when Ken gave me the news about Bonnie.

"But we just spoke to him!" Ken says. Jim and Ken had called their father a couple of days earlier to wish him a happy sixty-third birthday. But the men in Jim's family do have a history of dying young. Jim's expression is matched by Ken's as they fall into an anguished hug. Guilt rises up in me because there is only thing I feel in response to the news: overwhelming relief.

Two other thoughts come into my head, both unexpected, each with its own strange and stubborn logic. The first is that I no longer want to travel, since nothing good can come of it ever again. The second is that I no longer want to be around Ken, since the last two times I have been around him, I have been informed of death.

Just as we did the previous September, we cut our trip with Ken and Valeri short. Once again, there is the need to rush back home to prepare a funeral. Maybe it's more natural this time—a parent instead of a child—but the pain on Jim's face is no less real than mine was, and beneath the private wave of relief, my heart is breaking for him.

The four of us look at one another in silence as Jim docks the boat. We leave it in Whittier, and head back to Anchorage. An hour into the drive, there is quiet among the four of us. Jim and Ken have hugged and shed tears. Valeri and I have given what support we can. There is nothing left to do but accept the pain that goes with being human. I sit in the passenger seat, staring out at the Alaskan wilderness.

———————

The buzz of my new cellular phone against my hip surprises me, since the signal in this area is usually sporadic at best. I scramble to pull the phone out of my pocket. In June 1995, it's still a novelty to me, as it is to most of my real-estate colleagues, all of whom need to be available to potential buyers at any hour. Sergeant Marrs greets me.

"Hi, Mike. I'm on the road back into town from Whittier." Part of me doesn't want to hear from him. I no longer want to hear news of promising leads or potential suspects. My expectations have again lowered, out of self-protection.

"Karen, recent steps in the investigation have surfaced the name of another young man who was in Bonnie's English class. There isn't much I can tell you now, other than there are some red flags that warrant further digging. For example, we do know that this young man was present when Bonnie's body was being recovered."

I know from my undercover work that killers, before anyone knows they've killed, will often show up at the very crime scenes they have perpetrated, out of perverse, morbid interest.

"Nothing is certain, as you know. I just wanted to call to let you know that there seem to be some pretty strong signs here, so we're going to investigate further."

I try not to be aggravated by the slow, methodical approach of the troopers, in such contrast to my own rabid search for information. I have listened to drunks who call in the middle of the night just in case they might possess a useful nugget. I have given time to psychics who tell me they know something. I listen to anyone who will talk. I take copious notes, combing them later for the right piece of information that might unlock the truth. I have shared all these bits and pieces with Sergeant Marrs.

"Listen, Mike—"

"We'll get back to you as soon as we know more. I'm so sorry, Karen."

I do little for a few days, or maybe it's a week. I'm no longer sure how long the peaks and valleys last. I have stayed mostly in my room, alone. I have called Jason, Samantha, and Adam to tell them of the latest suspect. I have kept the conversations short, for there is less and less to say.

Then, on consecutive days, I receive two different phone calls. The first is from a retired surgeon in town named Dr. Arndt von Hippel, who calls to tell me he was at McHugh Creek the day of Bonnie's murder, and saw her. He invites me to his home to talk.

When I get there, he offers me a seat, prepares two cups of tea, and tells me that he was jogging at McHugh Creek on the morning of September 28, 1994. At one point, he says, he was jogging up the trail steps, and saw, coming down the steps in the other direction, two guys and two girls, young, college-age, smiling and joking. One of them in particular, one of the girls, had looked particularly nimble skipping down those steps, and he had commented on it to her, remarking how easy she made it look. She had returned the comment with a smile and continued on with her small band of compatriots. A short time after the murder, Dr. von Hippel tells me, he had seen Bonnie's picture in the paper, and recognized her as the girl to whom he'd made the comment at McHugh Creek. When he saw my picture as well, he says, he noticed the similarity in the shape of our eyes.

Upon realizing that the girl he'd seen in the papers was the same girl he'd seen at the creek, Dr. von Hippel says he called the troopers but received no reply. So he called a second time, and then a third. Finally someone called him back and took his information. Whoever he spoke to, he tells me, thanked him and said they'd be in touch if there was anything else to discuss.

"That was the last I heard from them," Dr. von Hippel says. "So I wanted to contact you. To let you know."

"Thank you," I say.

After leaving Dr. von Hippel's home, I call Sergeant Marrs.

"Yes," he says. "I recall the conversation with Dr. von Hippel. We have his information. If anything comes of it, we'll certainly let you know." It's the response I've come to expect, but it gets me steamed anyway.

The next morning, my phone buzzes, showing an unfamiliar number for the second time in two days. I answer.

A woman identifies herself as Bonnie's English teacher. "There's something I'd like to talk to you about," she tells me.

Shortly thereafter, we meet up in a coffee shop. On the desk in front of me is a stack of photocopied papers, which she has pulled out of an envelope. The top sheet is filled with barely legible scribbles.

"I asked my students to write in a daily log," she explains. "Grammar and spelling didn't matter. It was just to get them to write."

I pick up the stack of pages, some of which are marked with a sticky tab. The black handwriting is scribbled and ragged.

"I know they told you the DNA isn't a match, but I thought you should see this regardless. I wouldn't feel right if I didn't show it to you."

On the sheets of paper I hold, I read the student's angry and violent journal entries describing his troubled state of mind.

"My God," I hear myself say. I think: *This is the guy.*

I thank the teacher and take the journal to a forensic psychologist whom I'd seen testify in murder trials. He reads the journal and tells me it makes no sense to have eliminated this suspect, at least not without further investigation. I ask him if he'd be willing to call the troopers and tell Sergeant Marrs the same thing. He says he will.

It's a few days later, late evening, when Mike calls me, dismissing the potential evidence of the journal entries.

"Karen, we can only go on what the DNA tells us," he says. "Plus he has an alibi, and someone to corroborate it."

"What if it was more than one person?" I ask. "The DNA

didn't necessarily have to come from the killer. What if it came from the accomplice?"

"If there were more than one person, someone else would have talked by now."

"How do you know?"

"Karen, it isn't a match," Mike says. "We have to eliminate him. I'm sorry. There's nothing more to say."

7

Spring comes to Anchorage in 1998. Three years can seem like forever, or like barely any time at all. This period has felt like both to me. In one sense, the days stretch out endlessly, filled with hope that I'll wake up from the terrible dream and hug my daughter again. In another, they blur together in a montage of unanswered phone calls and frustrating conversations.

I have continued to be a thorn in the troopers' sides, pushing them constantly and getting nothing in return. I have gone directly to the commander of the unit and insisted that they alter their protocol, since the current approach hasn't yielded anything of use. They tell me they are doing plenty, but I see zero evidence. I continue to try every avenue possible to elicit information, separate from the troopers. With Sandy Cassidy's help, we continue to print bumper stickers, take out ads, keep Bonnie's face on the buses, and solicit donations to increase the reward fund. Every September 28, we put a special announcement in the paper. We put notices in the church bulletins and ask people to continue to pray.

For months after Bonnie was taken from my life, I considered whether or not to go back to my volunteer undercover police work.

I'd attended the monthly departmental meetings and listened to the briefings, but each time I thought I could get back out on the street, I was wrong. It took me over a year, but eventually, I was able to face it, and went back. My civic duty now seemed more important to me than ever.

I felt like a rookie on the job, having forgotten so much. My instincts were rusty, and my confidence was shaken. Worse yet, my first night back on patrol, I ended up covering a murder. It felt surreal. The victim was an older man. Had it been a child or a young woman, I don't think I could have handled it.

———

The temperature starts to rise and the snow begins to melt into little rivers—a period Alaskans refer to as "breakup." It is midmorning on a Monday when Sergeant Marrs calls. Rain is hitting the windows, distracting me further from the work I'm already having trouble doing. In the past three years, I've spoken to Sergeant Marrs less and less. Leads have been exhausted, and the information has slowly dried up. The conversation has slowed to a trickle, and now, essentially, to silence. There are other cases to pursue and other crimes that need solving. Like so many others, Bonnie's case has gone cold.

"Hello, Karen," Marrs says. "How are you?"

This isn't a question that is possible to answer, but people feel obliged to ask it. I give the generic answers that are expected in response—"fine," "okay," "not bad"—and which hopefully strike the right balance between respect and truth. People know how you're really feeling, but asking is their way of showing they care. I understand that and try to remember it, instead of resenting them.

"Karen, listen, there's some news I want to share with you. We don't know what it is yet, but it's worth pursuing. We have a DNA match."

My insides freeze. Sergeant Marrs waits for me to reply. When he realizes I can't, he continues.

"I know we've had false leads in the past, so I didn't want to call you about this development until we ran the test first. The individual in question was a bus driver on Bonnie's route. Not the regular driver—a guy who filled in sometimes. We've done some further searching and have discovered some odd things about him. Reports of his having tried to proposition young girls. Teenagers. One of them was the daughter of another driver."

I know better by now than to allow any feeling of hope, but it rises in me nonetheless. I recognize I will have the same response even if a hundred leads turn out to be false.

"He was a substitute teacher as well, and got fired for saying certain inappropriate things in class."

"Do you have him?" I ask. "Is he in custody?"

"It isn't quite that easy. He's since moved out of state."

"Where?"

"California. A town called Davis—small place outside of Sacramento. University of California has a campus there. I and one of my colleagues are going to fly down there tomorrow to question him. I'll contact you once we return and let you know what we're able to find. Naturally, we don't want to get too excited."

I think about the school paper Bonnie wrote that she never got to turn in. It was due the day she was killed. She had read it to Samantha the night before, and Samantha had told me about it a few weeks after the murder.

It was an English exercise. The theme Bonnie had chosen for the paper was "Saying Good-Bye." In it, she wrote about loss, and what it meant to have had to say good-bye to some of the important figures in her life. Her close friend Katie, who had died as a result of a drunk-driving accident. Her biological dad, Gordon, who had never really been part of her life. Her boyfriend, Cameron, gone away to college.

I hesitate to tell the kids about this new development. I know how hard the emotional swings have been on me. How much harder might it be on them? But it would be worse not to let them know. I call Jason, then Adam, and, finally, Samantha, to tell them the news. I call Jim as well, even though we aren't really together at the moment. A period of on-again, off-again has taken hold with us—we keep breaking up for a month or two and then getting back together, probably because neither of us can find anyone else, or have the energy to try. We've even bought a home together, something a little bigger, closer to downtown. Despite this gesture of commitment, I think both of us know we aren't ideally suited. Yet we keep coming back to each other.

The kids' hope is tempered, like mine, but it pushes through with the same insistence. I can hear it in their voices. I hear myself telling them to stay cool and expect nothing. We have to expect nothing, I tell each of them, yet at the same time, I hear the voice in my own head saying something very different.

Up on the hillside, just below the Chugach Mountains, I have a seventy-acre listing that includes a cabin. The property rests at the top of a familiar hiking trail, fifteen minutes from my house, in the middle of a cleared-out wooded area. I've been up to it twice before, first a few months ago to inspect the land with its owner, and again more recently to show it to a potential buyer, who liked it but eventually backed down because of the lack of accessible water.

Spring is the season when people embrace change and newness, which is true for real estate as well. I drive the fifteen minutes to the bottom of the hiking trail, armed with cleaning products and gardening tools. I'll enjoy the hike and the warming air, spruce the place up a bit, take some pictures, and update the listing to woo the optimistic spring buyers.

I get out of the car and wait, smiling in anticipation of the hiking partner who will accompany me today. A few minutes later, I see Jason's car come over the rise. As he pulls up alongside my car, I see Traci, now his wife, in the passenger seat, and the wonderful little face of my travel companion, facing backward in his car seat.

Austin, not yet one, is Jason and Traci's son, and my first grandchild. He squirms adorably as Traci helps me fit the carrying pack onto my back and pulls his pudgy little arms and legs through the appropriate holes. Once he's in and secure, he's happy, his little head looking around to check things out from this fun new perspective.

Austin, born on May 5, 1997, has the dubious honor of being the first birth in our immediate family since the last death. It's only natural that this unblemished new life made me take stock—in all the normal ways one does when going from being a parent to a grandparent, and in all the dark ways one does when one has suffered the loss of one's own child. The joy and miracle of a grandchild seems extra precious.

I had never been afraid of death, but after Bonnie was murdered, death became something different to me. A daughter is not supposed to be taken before her mother. Bonnie's death was unfair and cruel, and I'd fought against it with everything I had in me for three and a half years. I fought it like a person trying to paddle a raft into the ocean with her hands, only to be beaten back every time I seemed to be making progress. I fought it at the expense of the love and attention my surviving kids deserved.

I'm not sure how much fight I have left. Initially, I'd been fueled by a seemingly inexhaustible mix of sadness, rage, and an insatiable desire to solve the mystery of who had brutally raped and murdered my beautiful daughter. Now, though, the fuel is running out.

I had seen myself as Bonnie's crusader. If the troopers wouldn't treat me as a partner, or at least a helper in the cause, I'd been determined to take it on myself. Over the last three years, encouraged by Sandy Cassidy, I continued to place posters and banners around town, put Bonnie's face on the sides of buses, and watch the reward fund grow. Bonnie's murder is still a topic of conversation in Anchorage. But despite the leads and the suspects, we have nothing.

I survive, but I am tired. I live, but I am defeated. I can't give Bonnie justice in this life. Eventually, I will join her in the next one. It's not that I wish to die, but the idea of it carries a certain peace and comfort. I wouldn't have to fight anymore. I could just be with her again.

All this time, I've convinced myself that my quest was to find the person who took her away. But that's really a distraction from the thing I truly want, which I'll never get: I just wish I could hold her again. See her smile. Smell her skin, hear her laugh, wipe her tears.

Traci asks me if I'm okay, and I assure her I am. Despite my inner gloom, I'm looking forward to the hike. No matter what else I've got going on inside, private time with my first grandchild is a pick-me-up.

Starting out, I feel good. Austin and I enter the wilds of the hillside, and the dark cloud that has begun to crawl over me starts to slide back and is replaced by something different. It isn't quite hope, nor is it exactly a reigniting of the rage and sorrow I'd felt in the weeks and months after Bonnie's murder.

But it is, somehow, a rejection of whatever depression I'd

started to feel. I can feel the sun on my face and the sweet breaths of this perfect new little human riding on my back. Austin's closeness is breathing something fresh and unexpected into me. I start to talk with him the way one does with a one-year-old. It's a one-way dialogue, yet still meaningful. I talk to Austin about the trees and the sky, the clouds, the air. He makes his little sounds in response, and I feel that we're having a deep talk. Grandparents say it all the time to their amused children when they bring their grandchildren home: *We had a great time together* or *We had a great little conversation.* They don't say it with any irony. They mean it. I'm having a great time, and a great talk, with Austin.

But as I start to proceed up the trail, something new starts to sneak over me. It's a very different feeling than the one of resignation I've started to feel so deeply in recent days. It's much stronger and more primal. It's fear.

As I look around at the wilderness, I no longer see the beauty of nature and the lushness of spring. I see danger. I think about the bears coming out of hibernation. I think about the number of moose in the woods around these trails. I consider Austin's vulnerability and the fact that I am carrying nothing in the way of defense other than the pepper spray attached to my key ring.

"Austin, honey," I say. "We need to go back." We are just a third of the way up to the cabin, but the fearful feeling has seized me. All my instincts tell me that I need to get my grandson away from here.

I turn and start walking as fast as I can in the opposite direction, back toward my car. Though I try to keep my voice light for Austin, in my mind I hear myself praying, something I seldom did before Bonnie's murder but have done every day since. *Dear God, please don't let anything happen to me or Austin. My kids have already suffered enough. Please.* It is rare for me to ask God for protection, but I'm not asking it for me. I'm asking it for Austin and my surviving children. They have been through enough.

We reach the gate by the road where my car is parked. I unstrap Austin from the harness, buckle him into his car seat, and drive back to Jason and Traci's.

"What happened?" Jason asks. "Why are you back so soon?"

I give him and Traci a simple version of what happened, telling them I'd felt fine for the first quarter-mile up the trail before starting to get unnerved. Jason, my oldest child, regards me dubiously. He knows how confident a hiker I am and that I am far from "bear-anoid." It's true—in my entire life, I can count on one hand the number of times I've felt anxious while hiking or exploring the wilderness.

But he also knows that I always listen to my instincts, and I can tell he understands that I felt something deeper while out on the trail with Austin. He chooses not to question me further as I lift Austin into Traci's arms. She tickles him. He coos and giggles. I take a drink of water and tell them I'm going to lie down.

"Thanks for taking him," Jason says. "I bet he loved it."

"We both did," I say, giving Austin a kiss on his cheek.

I walk into the living room and collapse onto the sofa, realizing that I've arrived somewhere new. The walk with Austin was a passage into another mental space. I won't ever give up on my quest to find out what happened to Bonnie, but since she died, I've been thinking about what I should do for her. As I hiked up and then raced back down the hillside with Austin, that perspective changed. Now I find I'm thinking about what Bonnie would have wanted me to do, and there is only one answer. She'd want me to go on. She'd want me to be there for her brothers and sister—and nephew. She'd want me to try to live.

I kiss my grandson good-bye and thank Jason and Traci for

my time with him. The nagging feeling of fear remains inside me, but I try to shake free of it and instead think about the smell of Austin's skin and his delighted giggles.

When I get back home and see that there's a message on my answering machine, I feel twin waves of excitement and fear. I play the message.

"Hi, Karen. This is Sergeant Marrs. I'd like you to please give me a call whenever you can. There's been a development in the case." Marrs's voice betrays nothing; it never does. I dial his number, my foot tapping the floor.

"Hello, Karen."

"Is it confirmed? Is he the guy? Tell me this is over."

"Karen, I don't know if you're aware. There's a new system out."

"What do you mean, a new system?"

"A new DNA system. The feds have just released it. It's more accurate. And it's mandatory for all testing."

"Of new suspects?"

"Of all suspects. New or existing."

"Mike, what are you telling me?"

"Even suspects who have been tested with the old system have to be tested again. Using the new system."

"So you have to fly down to California and test him again?"

Sergeant Marrs doesn't answer.

"Mike?"

"We already retested his DNA, Karen."

He wasn't a match. Another dead end.

"I want to see the new SeaLife Center. You're coming with me."

It is May of 1998. The new SeaLife Center in Seward, Alaska, on the shores of Resurrection Bay, is the state's only public aquarium and ocean wildlife rescue center, a result of money awarded to Alaska because of the *Exxon Valdez* spill. My friend and colleague Marci Bouchard, who's like a sister to me, can sense that I need a distraction, and she knows I rarely say no when she tells me she wants to do something.

Since Bonnie's murder, three and a half years ago, people have for the most part used kid gloves with me. They've tried to get me to leave the house, see people, do things. Since the release of the new DNA testing system six months earlier and subsequent ruling out of the former bus driver, I have been in despair. There is no longer any purpose in denying it: Bonnie is gone forever, and whoever took her away will be neither found nor punished. I want to tell myself otherwise, but I can't anymore. Jim and I remain in each other's lives, but as distant as we are present, sometimes a couple, sometimes not. I need someone like Marci. A few years younger than me, with no kids, Marci is available anytime, and sees no reason why I shouldn't be, too. Her tank never runs out, and she has no subtlety, which makes me appreciate her even more.

She and I drive the two hours north toward Seward. She does most of the talking, as usual. We're both underwhelmed by the center. After spending an hour there and checking out some decent Alaskan paintings and photos in the gift shop, we leave, giving the place a combined failing grade. We stop at a restaurant called Rays, have a drink, and head back home.

We take Marci's car, but she asks me to drive, and I'm happy to accept. Being behind the wheel is better than being a passenger—it forces me to focus on the road instead of thinking about anything else.

I am going about seventy-five when two cars come speeding around a blind curve, side by side. One of them is heading straight for us. I barely have time to register the fact that they must be playing chicken—and that neither is making an attempt to avoid us—before I'm forced to swerve right to avoid them.

The rest happens in what feels like extreme slow-motion. I see the two cars fly past as we are forced off the road and down onto a narrow, steeply sloping shoulder made of gravel and grass. Beyond it, out of the corner of my eye, I see a line of trees, and, past the trees, water. I know I need to get the car back onto the paved road to avoid sliding farther down the incline, and I immediately try to twist the wheel back up toward the road. But it's too late. As the left wheels hit the pavement, the car flips.

I hear the tinkling of glass all around me and feel the roof starting to crumple. I brace myself against the steering wheel and try to look to the side to see if Marci is okay. As the car continues to roll, I stamp one of my hands against the roof and the other against the door frame. Neither of us is screaming. It's more like we can't believe this is happening. The car bangs through a second and third flip as the sounds of buckling metal and shattering glass create an out-of-body symphony. A car flipping happens slowly and awkwardly. There's a lot of time to think.

With a final, resounding thump, we land—mercifully upright, though we are now straddling both lanes of the remote road. Marci's car is equipped with airbags, but they deploy only on frontal impact. I look at Marci and she looks at me, and we say the same words at the same time: "Are you okay?" Both of us are still strapped into our seats. Past the steep ditch at the side of the road, there is water. I don't remember the windows being down as we were driving. Then I realize they've all shattered from the impact of the crash.

"What should we do?" Marci says. "Should we get out quick?"

"No!" I answer. "Go slowly. As slowly as you can. We don't know if our backs and necks have been compromised. It might feel like we're okay, but you can't always tell."

Marci looks at me dubiously, but she also trusts the requisite emergency courses I'd gone through while being trained at the police academy, which I never imagined would pay off during a trip to the SeaLife Center in Seward. She doesn't move.

"That's why they always stabilize football players when they get injured and carry them off the field in neck braces. Careful."

"Okay," she says.

Instinctively I reach down for my cell phone, but am shocked to find it's still there, just out of reach of my fingertips. "I think I can reach it," I say. It's on the floor mat beside my foot, but I don't want to bend or stretch in the wrong way.

I manage to extend my arm enough to pinch the phone between my index and middle fingers.

Miraculously, the phone works. Even more miraculously, I get a signal, which is unusual for this area. I dial 911 while keeping one eye on the road we are now blocking in both directions. I give the dispatcher our location and a description of the car that ran us off the road—a light blue, older-model Bronco.

Five minutes later, Marci spots the ambulance coming down the road. We've managed to slowly maneuver ourselves out of the car, and a driver coming in the opposite direction has pulled over to help. He asks if I'd like him to take some pictures. I ask him why I would want him to take pictures. For insurance, he says. I thank him and say sure, why not. He takes pictures of me and Marci while the medics get out of the ambulance and start to ask questions to assess our condition. While they do, Marci says to me, "Damn good thing you were driving instead of me. I'd have slammed on the brakes and we'd both be dead now."

As the volunteer medic begins to attach the C-collar to my neck, my cell phone rings. The medic hands the phone to Marci, who answers. I hear her say, "Your mom and I were in an accident.

We're okay, but she can't really talk right now." On the other end, I hear my daughter Samantha's voice, rising. Marci assures her we're okay and will be home soon. I feel a wave of guilt. I remember that Samantha's friends have a belated fifteenth-birthday surprise party planned for her, and in minutes, one of them is going to arrive at the house to bring her to another friend's house around the corner, where the party guests will all be hiding out. Now she's been told by Marci that we were in an accident and I can't talk.

Moose Pass Volunteer Emergency Services takes us back to the hospital in Seward to be examined. Once there, I manage to get cell service again. I call Samantha, who tells me that when she got to her friend's house, they all jumped out and yelled "Surprise!" In response, she cried, "My mother's been in an accident!" and burst into tears.

I tell her I'm okay and apologize to her for ruining the party. I ask her what made her call me in the first place. Nothing in particular, she says. But it isn't the first time she's called me spontaneously in a time of need. Over the past three and a half years, we have both developed the sense that whenever I could use a little support, somehow Bonnie sends her sister a message to get in touch with me. Months earlier, Samantha had called me out of the blue at two in the morning to tell me she loved me. I'd been awake, thinking about Bonnie and crying desperately.

We're released from the hospital. Marci had asphalt from the road in her elbow that needed to be scraped out, but I've somehow managed to escape without a scratch, as though a guardian angel was protecting me.

———————————

More years pass, with further challenges to be met. Adam, my youngest son, struggles with impaired vision. I recall watching him at age ten, in his hockey gear, so proud to strap on the goalie equipment and be the last man standing after all others had failed. I remember the regular shutouts becoming games in which he would allow a few goals, then a few goals becoming more than a few, followed by the complaints of blurred vision, which soon became severe. I remember finding out from the ophthalmologist that he needed corneal transplants in both eyes, and that even with the transplants, it was no sure bet that Adam would ever regain his vision.

We put him on a donor recipient list for corneas, a list I didn't know existed. It took seven years before we were notified that a cornea was available. In 1998, Adam underwent a transplant in his left eye. He stayed awake for it, and when it was done, he could see—not with perfect clarity, but better than before. When his name came up again, he consented to repeat the trick, though he asked to be put under that time. The operation was far less successful, however, and the donated cornea didn't take. Adam is considered blind in his right eye.

I travel back to the day when he got the first transplant, at eighteen, and then the other a year later, just before the twentieth century became the twenty-first. I was worried about what the new millennium might bring my son. I am a mother; I worry even when I know there's nothing I can do. Adam in his sweet positive way would tell me things were fine, but I continued to worry. How would he make a living, who would he meet, what path would his life take?

And curveballs kept coming. Adam had dated a girl named Jennifer at Service High School, who toward the end of their senior year suddenly left Anchorage for Waco, Texas. She hadn't wanted anyone, including Adam, to know she was pregnant. When Jennifer gave birth to their daughter, Jayleigh, in July 2000, she tried to give her up for adoption, but Family and Youth Services told her she was obligated to inform the father. They called Gary's house and asked if he knew Jennifer. When he said he did, they told him she'd just had his baby. Gary informed them they must be referring to his son.

When Adam heard the news, he flew down to Waco to meet his daughter, then called me saying, "Mom, she's so beautiful, and so smart!" He was already hooked.

Meanwhile, my oldest son, Jason, worked to achieve his youthful ambition of becoming a paramedic. After we'd moved to Texas for Gary's job with BP in the late 1980s and got moved around year to year, Jason had moved from high school to high school—a different one every year—trying to fit in among peers with deep southern drawls and Confederate flags draped over the fronts of their houses. But he never took his eye off his ultimate goal.

When we came back to Alaska, he participated in a program called Medical Explorers, volunteering every Saturday for eight hours in the emergency room of Humana Hospital in Anchorage, watching and learning the ropes. Jason's drive and ambition, like Bonnie's, Samantha's, and Adam's, often surprised me, even though they reflected my own.

Jason finished high school in Anchorage when we returned, then went on to the University of Alaska Anchorage, and Kenai Peninsula College, always working various jobs, never wanting to be dependent on me, Gary, or anyone else. After marrying Traci in April 1995, he got a job at Toys R Us and earned a series of promotions—a result of his natural work ethic and, with Austin's birth in 1997, the growing responsibility of being a husband and father.

The promotions meant Jason was moving up in the working world, but they also delayed the schooling he yearned to complete toward the aim he so badly wanted to achieve. He applied to both the Anchorage Fire Department and the Anchorage Police Department, hoping one or the other could serve as an indirect route toward the paramedic career he knew he was supposed to have. He followed in my footsteps by getting hired on by APD, but quickly realized it was neither the job for him nor truly a route, indirect or otherwise, toward the job he really wanted.

Within another two years, in March of 2001, Jason and Traci's twins, Tanner and Logan, were born, and their family moved two hours southwest, from Anchorage to Soldotna, where Jason enrolled in a firefighter academy. In the meantime, he sold insurance to provide for his family and save money toward the goal of returning to school full-time.

Jim and I are out for dinner at a nice restaurant in Seward, eight years into our on-again, off-again relationship, when he finally proposes. I tell him, "You're not taking my breath away; you're taking my appetite away." Things between us are far from perfect, but they're good enough. I don't understand why he thinks our tying the knot is suddenly going to transform the relationship. But I hear myself say yes anyway.

8

The end of 2001 nears its close in a nervous hush. It is only two months since the planes hit and the towers came down. There is hardly a person among the three hundred million citizens of the country not replaying the images in their heads again and again, not still feeling whatever they felt upon hearing the news and seeing the surreal footage. We are sharing profound fear and confusion. I have spent the past seven years trying to get answers about the person taken from my life. Now, thousands of Americans are demanding the same. I see my own despair reflected back on me every day, in the eyes of an endless parade of devastated strangers.

The entire country was awash in overwhelming grief, and it seemed my pain had had its time and was now unimportant in the grand scheme. I must figure out a way to keep living while accepting that I no longer had a right to expect the phone call telling me justice would be done. It would not, and I would have to learn how to accept this truth.

I watch the president tell us we are going to find out who did this. He wants to deploy soldiers. It seems like he doesn't care where the soldiers are sent; he just wants to send them. In his words, there seems to be false confidence, but I can understand his need to say something. The nation won't accept silence or inaction.

In the days after Bonnie's murder, I had been hopeful. In the ensuing weeks and months, sporadically optimistic. In the years that followed, and with each lead and each suspect cleared by DNA, my hope dwindled until it was almost gone. I'd always had a close relationship with God but never felt it necessary to participate in organized religion. It has only been in the past couple of years that I've tried to attend church most Sunday mornings. My parents always taught me that if I did something wrong, God would know, and at some point I would pay the price. It was the same for everyone, they said—eventually, there's a reckoning. Bonnie has been gone for seven years, but no reckoning has come. Whoever stole her has not had to account for his deeds, and I have never stopped asking why.

As the president concludes his remarks with that dumb crooked smile of his, the phone rings. It's Wayne Lienhart, Janice Lienhart's husband. Janice has become uncharacteristically absentminded in the past few months, scheduling a meeting for one place and then going to another, getting times wrong, and generally acting scattered. A few weeks ago, Wayne had informed the organization we'd set up, the Friends and Family of Bonnie Craig, that Janice was unable to handle the responsibilities of treasurer any longer, but he hadn't said anything more. We all knew there was more, though.

Wayne asks me to come by the house. As I arrive and enter the room, he walks over to me. He and Janice's sister Sharon are there, and Janice is in bed.

"She isn't able to respond to much at the moment," he says. "She doesn't recognize most people, so please don't be offended."

I'm stunned to see the woman I've known for years looking so frail. Janice is a vegetarian and a health nut, always eating weird concoctions and health drinks, always staying trim, always filled with energy. I have never seen her rest or take a break. Now, her eyes appear a thousand miles away.

I take Janice's hand and talk to her about nothing. I believe she's listening. I lean down toward the bed and give her a hug, nearly recoiling at her thinness. After a while, I get up to leave.

"Thanks for coming," Sharon says. "Obviously, we don't know how much she hears, but I think she's in there. We're still waiting on some test results. I want to make sure we have your contact information, because I don't know how or where Janice kept it. Would it be under Foster or Campbell?"

I'm still using Foster, though Jim and I have now split up, less than three years after getting married. We've split in legal terms, anyway, though we still slip in and out of each other's lives. The day we got our divorce, he asked me to go with him to Australia. We travel well together. We were just really poorly suited for cohabitation.

"Knowing Janice," I said, "it would probably be under Bonnie. That's what she used to call me accidentally."

A small sound comes from the bed, and we all turn. It isn't much, but it seems to be the hint of laughter. We smile in amazement. She has heard us.

I plan to visit Janice again the following week, but before I can, Sharon calls to tell me that she is gone. Tests later reveal that Janice's brain was undergoing rapid deterioration as a result of Creutzfeldt-Jakob disease, a form of mad cow disease.

She was only sixty-two. She and Wayne had been married for four decades. They had five grown children and seven grandchildren. I think about how, and why, some families seem to get hit with one tragedy after another. I wonder whether Janice would say she had lived a full life. I wonder whether this woman, who pioneered the victim's-rights movement in the state of Alaska, would say she left Earth with any regrets. I take my copy of *When Bad Things Happen to Good People* off the shelf at home and read it, again.

It is my father who calls to tell us the news that my brother, Andrew, has died, in February 2005. One of Andrew's friends, after not being able to reach him, asked the landlord to open the door to his small apartment, and found him there. The friend was too late, Dad tells us. Andrew had already stopped breathing.

Sadly, we aren't surprised. My oldest and only surviving brother had battled health issues and psychological demons his entire life. He'd finally lost.

When I was a child, I'd regarded him as larger than life, stronger than Atlas, smarter than Einstein. Then as a teen, he'd started smoking pot. Others did it and seemed to be able to function, but with Andrew, it had a dulling effect. Whatever ambition he'd had vanished. He became listless, content to remain living with our parents for as long as they'd let him, constantly borrowing money from them, and from me, without ever paying it back.

When I was thirty, I'd stopped lending him money or buying him things (which he'd only pawn anyway). Tough love was the only option I felt could help. He had been prescribed lithium by the doctor, though it never seemed to do any good. The word *depression* was thrown around, but none of us really knew what it meant or how to help.

We were heartened when he married Anna and they had Alannah in 1993, then Aaron three and a half years later. He had the proverbial nuclear family. If anything could bring Andrew out of his fog, I thought, it would be fatherhood.

Instead, work—or the lack of work—seemed to overwhelm him. The first time he tried to permanently escape, using pills, they pumped his stomach, keeping him around for his wife and kids a while longer. I didn't understand how he could commit such a self-ish act, though I could never bring myself to ask him about it. I was too angry, and too confused. When he came out of the hospital, it was Anna I asked. She told me Andrew had said he felt he was doing everyone a favor. It made me angrier. To outside eyes, he was an engaged and willing father, happily shuttling the kids to karate and swimming, overseeing their homework, playing chess with them, patiently teaching them and loving them. But by the time we receive the call from my father, Anna, at the end of her rope, had asked for a divorce. Unable to keep a job, indifferent to her, withdrawn from all relationships except those with his kids, Andrew had been mired in gloom; now he'd seized what he felt was the only way out.

Almost two years later, in June 2006, it is my mother in decline—suffering from something her doctor tells me is called "failure to thrive."

"It's common when someone has lost a child, especially due to tragic circumstances," he tells me. "In lay terms, we refer to it as loss of the will to live."

I fly from Anchorage to Ontario to be with my father. My mother's downward slide in the wake of Andrew's death is not surprising, nor is the speed with which it has occurred. I know what it has taken me to try to survive having lost one child. She has now outlived two of her three children and one granddaughter. Part of me wonders how she held on as long as she did.

In the two years since Andrew's suicide, I noted her becoming more and more depressed, through my father's reports and my occasional visits. She went hardly anywhere, did hardly anything. I witnessed her memory start to fade as I would take her for lunch and listen to her ask, again and again, "Is Andrew coming, too?"

"There's something else," the doctor says. "Something separate from her . . . spiritual constitution."

"What is it?" I ask.

"We've discovered she had cancer."

"Cancer?"

"Yes. I'm afraid it wasn't apparent before."

"How could it not have been apparent?"

"She came in a number of times complaining of mild discomforts or reduced appetite, but never with anything that warranted testing of the sort that would reveal such a thing."

As humans, we are built to endure. The amount of pain we can suffer yet still survive is often astonishing. But it takes its toll. My mother is seventy-five years old, give or take, when her spirit finally gives out. She never told us how old she really was, other than joking that she was perpetually thirty-nine. The autopsy reveals cancer all over her body.

In December of 2006, I stand on the frozen ground of Settlers Bay Golf Course, in Wasilla, gazing at my daughter Samantha, now twenty-four, beside her husband-to-be, Ryan. Samantha looks rugged and beautiful in her wedding dress made of polar fleece. She and Ryan have been dating for eight years, ever since meeting in high school. They're both good kids. Ryan will soon finish his degree in construction management and begin heading up projects for a local construction company. Though Samantha doesn't need anyone to take care of her, I believe he loves her and will do his best to try.

Samantha and Ryan look at each other, the shared glow of their commitment in their eyes. I haven't been good at making this kind of commitment work. Maybe they'll be better.

My sons have also had their own ups and downs with commitment. Traci and Jason have split. Nine-year-old Austin, along with his five-year-old twin brothers, Tanner and Logan, spend alternate weeks between the two parents.

Although his daughter Jayleigh's arrival brought my son Adam greater purpose in life, I'm also grateful for Trina, a girl from Anchorage and a positive, kind soul like him, who took the worry out of me and replaced it with hope, first as his girlfriend, then as his wife. The first thing that impressed me about her was the way she accepted and cared for Jayleigh, who was only an infant when they started dating. Zoie, born in July 2006, their first child together, expanded that feeling. My baby boy has hit his stride. I still worry for him, of course. The cornea transplants were successful as far as preventing his going blind, but compromised vision limits one's choices. But he shows me that there is always a way to move forward. Sometimes the most important lessons come from the actions of your own kids.

Watching Samantha exchange vows with Ryan, I remember her sitting down at the kitchen table five years earlier and telling me she was going to Nebraska for a year of college. It would be different, she'd said, and cheaper. She wanted to go somewhere where she had only herself to depend on, and the University of Nebraska at Omaha was the perfect place to fill that order. The truth was, Bonnie had never wanted to go to UAA, either. She'd wanted to follow Cameron to Berkeley, in California, but I'd once worked for a rape crisis center in Berkeley and didn't feel it was safe there.

Samantha came back from her year in Nebraska a confident and responsible young woman full of new energy and focus. She resumed her communications degree at UAA but also got a job as a case worker at Clare House, a shelter for homeless women and children in Anchorage—I recall watching the change in her, seeing her discover what she truly wanted to do. She enrolled in Emergency Medical Training 1 and started to research the steps needed to get into medical school. She was disappointed when she couldn't get a job with the Anchorage Fire Department, but I was impressed when her disappointment turned to resolve, resulting instead in a position with the Anchorage Police Department, as a Communications Clerk II—in other words, a 911 dispatcher. She told me this path was actually better suited for her, the job was busier, more fast-paced, more challenging.

Bonnie would have been proud of her younger sister's attitude and tenacity, and she would have been thrilled for Samantha on her wedding day. I feel Bonnie's spirit as we cheer when the ordained family friend announces that Samantha and Ryan have become man and wife. Around me there are decorations of blue, silver, and white. We dance, hug, and eat pizza. The bride and groom, laughing, lie down and make angels in the snow.

A week later, on Christmas Day, I say good-bye to the kids and drive to the airport with my friend Belinda. She is a person of few words but bursting with energy and humor. The kind of person you want to spend time with.

Belinda and I first met at Fortune Properties in 1993, then later became best friends while colleagues for Dynamic Properties in 1995, a year after Bonnie's murder. Belinda later moved on to Northern Trust, but we're still in the same game, and still best friends. And 2006 has been a very good year for both of us. The market is healthy, people are optimistic, and it's a good time to be in real estate. Just as one has to ride out the downs, it's worth celebrating the ups.

"Let's go on a trip," Belinda had said to me in late September, right around the anniversary of Bonnie's murder. Real estate in Alaska slows to a crawl between Thanksgiving and January. "Why not reward ourselves a little?" It wasn't the first time Belinda had suggested something similar, leading us to Mexico and Hawaii on previous vacations. "Let's go wherever our miles can take us. We've worked hard this year. We deserve it."

Our criteria were simple: somewhere warmer and sunnier than Alaska, and, preferably, somewhere neither of us had been before. We booked a flight to Shanghai, then realized that, while it was certainly warm there in the summer, it was not especially so at this time of year.

We unfolded the world map and decided to keep the flight to Shanghai but then fly to the Philippines, where it was always warm. After some more discussion, we set a three-week itinerary: Shanghai, Hong Kong, Macau, Philippines, home. I was able to allow something inside that felt like excitement.

Despite a few hiccups along the way (we somehow don't realize we need visas to get into China until we're already checking in for our flight, leading to a madcap dash to the Chinese Embassy), we enjoy our time in Shanghai. Belinda is an easy travel companion, bothered by little. What others experience as frustrations, she sees as lighthearted adventures. We spend a few days in China, then a few more in Hong Kong and Macau. We are amused at the fascination with which people regard us. Some go as far as to ask, through gesture, for a picture with us. Belinda tells me it's because I'm the only fool in China wearing open-toed high-heeled sandals in winter.

On New Year's Eve, we board another plane and journey the two hours from Shanghai to Manila. This time our papers are all in order, and there are no delays. From our room on the thirteenth floor that night, we see a giant fireworks display erupting on every corner. As 2006 turns into 2007, the entire city lights up. The fireworks show is spectacular and seems to last all night. We join the revelers in the streets as it all unfolds. Citizens and tourists shout and cheer as one, their voices giving expression to the excitement of possibility. A New Year is a new chance. Thirteen times now I have watched the numbers turn over and held out hope that one of them will bring something new. It hasn't happened, and I know it never will. I give thanks instead for the surviving children I have, the wonderful families they have begun, and the daughter I had the privilege to know for her eighteen years of life. Near dawn, Belinda and I return to our room and go to bed.

From Manila, we journey to a beautiful resort called El Nido, on Lagen Island. Our itinerary calls for a few days at El Nido followed by a few days at a less-expensive resort called Club Paradise. We spend the daylight hours snorkeling, diving, and exploring the other islands dotting the area, and evenings relaxing by the pool, enjoying drinks, and walking along the shore or dining on the beachfront. We chat with the casual ease of close friends. The topics don't matter, nor does the hour.

I try to stay as unplugged as possible from my cell phone and my laptop, and I more or less succeed. Rather than try to stay on top of the time differences between our destinations and Alaska, I check messages only every few days, instead of constantly, like at home.

On our second morning at Club Paradise, on the fifth of January 2007, I linger in bed until late morning. I take a long shower, then put on my bathing suit and beach cover-up. Belinda, who always sleeps later than I do, will meet me down by the pool whenever she gets out of bed.

Before leaving the room, I allow myself one check of the laptop, a three-pound VAIO convenient for travel. I scroll down through the list of messages, trying to focus only on those that demand immediate attention and forcing myself to ignore the others. There are thankfully only a handful, and I convince myself that most of them can wait. I'm about to turn the power off and turn for the door when I notice a message from someone I don't recognize, with a one-word subject line that makes my heart skip a beat: *Bonnie.*

> Karen,
> My name is Tim Hunyor, and I am an Investigator with the Alaska State Troopers, Cold Case Unit. I know that you are out of the country, but it is important that I talk to you, as we have new developments in Bonnie's case.
> Can you please call me or send me a telephone number where I can call you.

In the message signature for Investigator Timothy A. Hunyor of the Alaska Bureau of Investigation Cold Case Unit are several numbers where he can be reached, including an after-hours number.

For a moment, I am frozen, forgetting where I am. It has been more than twelve years since my daughter's murder. Twelve years of unending anguish and countless empty leads. I know better than to get excited by a random e-mail from yet another trooper, but even against my better judgment, it is impossible to suppress a new rush of hope. Still, I've been down this road so many times already, only to be disappointed and further saddened.

None of which, however, stops me from rushing to the front desk, my head muddled. "I need to make an urgent phone call," I tell the young Filipino girl at the desk. She is confused at first, but soon she understands, at least enough to hand me an old-fashioned cell phone the size of a small brick from behind the desk. I ask for instructions on how to dial Alaska. She seems amused by such an unusual request, which I can understand—I can imagine how seldom that question is asked.

I screw up the first couple of tries to call Trooper Hunyor, then finally get the combination of international and country code right. I hear ringing, but the call drops. On my second attempt, I hear a crackling voice on the other end, but I can't get him to hear me. I keep trying. We get as far as his saying hello, my saying "It's Karen Foster," and a few words cutting through the static, but no further.

The Filipino girl advises that I wait a few minutes and try again. I do, but the connection is still poor, so I reply to his e-mail instead with the details of where I'm staying.

"I tried calling you," I write. "I don't have a number where you can reach me, so I'll just keep trying back to reach you." I give him my itinerary and tell him I'll try back in about an hour. After sending the message, I race back to the room. Belinda has gotten out of bed and is rubbing the sleep out of her eyes. I tell her about Trooper Hunyor's message.

Her eyes widen, then meet mine. "Oh, my God," she says. Her words mean two things. First: *I hope*. And second: *Don't hope*.

"Do you want to go home?" she asks.

"There's no sense in doing anything yet," I say. "The only thing to do is wait." Belinda takes my hand and looks at me with affection and sympathy. I appreciate both.

We head to the beach. I lie back on the chair and stare out at the ocean. Belinda asks me if I feel like talking, though she knows it would be purely for the purpose of distraction. As she's asking, another e-mail pings.

Trooper Hunyor apologizes for being unable to hear my calls, and again requests that I call him regarding updates in Bonnie's case.

> In short, we have some information about an individual that is in prison in New Hampshire and we are trying to do some background on him. I would like to talk with you and let you know what we have so far.

I rush back to the front desk, this time with Belinda beside me. The Filipino girl hands me the phone without a word. I try again to get a decent connection, but it's as spotty as before. In frustration, I start typing on my laptop once again, explaining the small island's lack of landlines. I suggest we try Yahoo Messenger, though I really don't know how to use it.

For the rest of the day, there is no response from Trooper Hunyor. I wonder whether my message went through. I check my sent folder half a dozen times and see that the message says it's been transmitted. Belinda tries her best to keep me occupied. We go for a walk through the resort. We have dinner. We stay up talking in the hotel room.

By midnight, Belinda dozes off. I stare at the VAIO as long as I can keep my eyes open. Soon I recognize that I need sleep, so I switch off the lights and try to rest. Instead I lie awake, trying to resist hope or optimism. I try different mind-emptying techniques I have acquired over the years. Tonight, none of them work. In the darkness, fear creeps over me. Identifying a killer is far from the same as putting him away. The justice system is not about fairness or truth. It is a game.

––––––––––

When I wake the next morning, Belinda reminds me to call my son Jason. It is his thirty-third birthday. I know what kind of connection I'm going to get. From the front desk, I get through, but I don't know if Jason can hear me, since all I hear from the other end is dull crackling. I tell him I love him and wish him a sweet day. As I'm about to hang up, I hear, "Mom?"

"Honey!" I say. "You're there! Happy birthday, Jase. I love you so much. I feel bad that I'm not with you today. What are you doing for fun?"

"Well, the boys are with Traci at the moment. I'll see them a little later." My son is keeping his voice positive for me, but I know he is feeling lonely. "How's the trip?"

"Great. Listen, Jason, I have some news. Potential news. I got an e-mail from a trooper, someone I don't know, saying he wants to talk to me about a development in the case. I have no idea whether it's anything, so there's nothing for us to get excited about. But he wants to talk right away. As soon as I find out what it is, I'll let you guys know."

There is a loud crash, and Jason yells.

"What's the matter?" I ask.

"That was weird," he says. "You know that vase?"

I know exactly the one he's referring to. It holds broken pieces of pottery and glass that he and Bonnie had found during a trip we'd taken when they were kids. He keeps it on the top of his fridge.

"That's what you just heard."

He doesn't say anything for a moment, and I think I know why.

I can picture the spot where the vase was always kept, right in the center, with lots of space around it.

"Did you move it?" I ask him.

"No—I didn't," he says, his voice starting to break. "It was where it always was." Jason checks the top of the fridge. The dust outline where the vase had sat is undisturbed. "There's no way that thing could have fallen," he says. He doesn't say the rest: *on its own.* We both know he isn't alone. Bonnie is there with her brother.

Belinda and I spend the next day much the same way we spent the evening before—her trying to distract me. We lie by the water. We walk the beach. We go diving. We have lunch in the café.

Finally, as we're heading back to the room, a new message from Trooper Hunyor appears in my inbox.

> Karen,
>
> I wanted to let you know about the new developments in Bonnie's case. I do not know if you have heard about CODIS so I will try and explain it.
>
> CODIS is a national database for DNA profiles. It was developed by the FBI, and several states enter DNA profiles of people who are incarcerated in their state Correctional System. During a search of the CODIS System, a match occurred between the DNA profile obtained from Bonnie and an individual in the New Hampshire system. What we are doing now is a background on this individual. We determined he was in Alaska at the time, and we are going to start talking to people who know him. We wanted to let you know about the match. When you get back in town, I would like to sit down

and talk with you. We do not want word to get out to the press just yet, as we are still in an investigation process.

I am sorry to have to tell you over the Internet, but with the phone system it was hard to make the connection. You can call me anytime. I will check my e-mail over the weekend and answer any questions that I can. I look forward to meeting with you when you return.

Tim

Two days ago, I was a real-estate agent on vacation with her best friend celebrating a successful year. Today, the detective inside me has come storming back to the surface. I write a long e-mail to Trooper Hunyor, with lots of questions. I pause, my thumb held over the Send button. Belinda sees my hesitation and asks the reason for it. I lie, telling her I'm just considering whether I've covered all the right questions. The truth is I am worried that in asking so many of them, I might draw from Trooper Hunyor the same reaction I've received from all the other troopers over the years—annoyance, avoidance, or both.

I convince myself that Trooper Hunyor is different, even though I have no reason to believe it. I press send.

Thank you for this information. I don't know about CODIS and am glad to hear about it. I have some questions and wondering if you have answers to any of them. Who is the guy and how old is he? Where was he working at the time of the murder? Did he work at Sports Authority? Or some business over by Sam's Club? Whereabouts did he live? What kind of vehicle was he driving? Do you know if he went to the university or was in any of Bonnie's classes? Or going to UAA? Did he hang out with that student who had written the journal?

What is he in jail for? How long has he been in there and when is the earliest he could be released? Was it a 100 percent match on the DNA?

Are you familiar with Bonnie's case? I know there's a lot to read. Were you with the troopers when she was killed?

Sorry for all the questions. Thanks. I will let you know my dates and would like to meet with you as soon as I am back.

Look forward to talking soon,

Karen

The weekend passes with no response from Trooper Hunyor. I am frustrated with myself. I have turned him against me just as I inadvertently did the other troopers. They thought then that I was sticking my nose in where it didn't belong, and Trooper Hunyor has obviously formed the same opinion. Belinda does her best to keep me occupied. When she wakes in the morning, I lie and say I, too, slept great.

I am swimming in the ocean early Monday afternoon, January 8, 2007, when Belinda waves me to shore. I have brought the VAIO with me to the beach and asked Belinda to tell me if she sees a number appear in the inbox.

Karen,

The guy we are looking at is Kenneth Dion, and he was born in 1969. He is in custody for robbery and received 6 to 15 years, so he will be there for a while. I am familiar with Bonnie's case. I met you during the initial investigation. At the time I was an investigator assigned to CIB [the Criminal Investigations Bureau] in Anchorage. I transferred from Fairbanks AST [Alaska State Troopers] in August 1994. In Fairbanks I worked in the Investigations Unit. I retired as a sergeant in

2000, and they asked me to come back as an investigator in 2002. I was assigned to the Cold Case Unit in March 2006. I can tell you that it is a good match. But we are still doing background on him, so there are a lot of unanswered questions.

Tim

A name. A DNA match. A living person, in jail for another crime, known to have been in Alaska at the time of the murder. Belinda sees the look in my eyes, and I can see her concern in response. The last thing she wants me to do is start to feel hope. But she shouldn't be worried. It is not hope I feel, and it is not relief. What I feel is sick.

9

After I exchange e-mails with Trooper Tim Hunyor, I'm desperate to speak to the kids, but I know I won't be able to get through. I e-mail them instead. Adam will be thrown. Jason will be composed. Samantha, who has just returned from her honeymoon in Costa Rica and Panama, will be ecstatic.

I keep the e-mails brief and direct, telling them only what I know, which is technically very little but has still unleashed an avalanche of emotions inside me. For more than a decade, I have imagined someone calling me and saying the words, "We have him," or a hundred variations of that simple statement. The same number of times, I have imagined my reaction of sheer joy, coupled with a sense of closure and finality.

But I feel nothing like closure. I feel stark fear. Not fear of the killer—fear that, like so many others who have done bad deeds, despite being found and accused, that Bonnie's killer might still get away with it. The mother in me feels a twinge of something approaching relief and hope, but the detective is concerned only that we might not have sufficient evidence to convict the man who raped and killed an innocent eighteen-year-old girl in broad daylight.

I ask Trooper Hunyor if I should come home. I am hoping he'll say yes. Instead, he tells me that there's no reason to rush back, since they are only starting the process to extradite Kenneth Dion from New Hampshire. I ask him a second time, suggesting that maybe there is something I can do to help. He gives me the same answer, telling me it's best if I enjoy the rest of my vacation and then meet with him upon my return.

Of course, it's impossible for me to "enjoy" anything. I spend restless hours by the pool, my head spinning, and then more restless hours in bed. Despite Belinda's constant assurances that it will all work out, I stay hopelessly distracted for the rest of our trip. I wake up in cold sweats every night and am on edge throughout the day. I feel guilty that I'm ruining Belinda's fun. The kids e-mail me back enthusiastically, their words full of optimism, and I counter with reminders that we still have a long road ahead before the man will even see an Alaskan courtroom.

Trooper Hunyor sends another e-mail asking me to keep a tight lid on the information he has shared. Other than informing my kids, as well as Gary and Jim (and Belinda, who already knows), I am not to tell anyone that Bonnie's killer has been identified. The exposure of such information prior to trial could be disastrous, he tells me. I trust Trooper Hunyor and believe what he says. At the same time, all I want to do is talk to someone—if the phone had been working, I'd probably have called half a dozen of my friends in the media by now—and my kids are desperate to do the same.

I think about the weeks immediately following Bonnie's death, when I would repeat the words "It was murder" to anyone willing to put a microphone in front of me. My unwillingness to zip my mouth, and the campaigns taken up by Janice Lienhart and Sandy Cassidy, out of nothing but kindness, to help prove that my daughter *was* murdered. Maybe more public dialogue could help bring forth witnesses who know something about the man incarcerated in New Hampshire. But our system says you only get one shot at a trial, so I e-mail the kids back telling them not to share this information with anyone other than their spouses, whom they're allowed to tell. Not another soul, though, no matter how much they might want to. Until the start of the trial, we are on a strict gag order. If we go to the media, it can give the defense ammunition—either for a mistrial, cause a change in venue, or other possibilities—any of which could endanger our chances at a conviction.

I don't include the thought that those chances, in my mind, are already slim. I know in my heart, or maybe I just need so badly to believe, that the DNA match is real, that we finally have the killer. But I don't trust the legal system to deliver, and privately I still feel that the troopers have messed up so much of the case that to get a conviction would be a miracle, DNA match or no DNA match. There will be technicalities. Lost evidence. Unreliable witnesses, if any witnesses can be scared up in the first place. The detective in me feels skeptical. The mom, scared.

———————

What Trooper Hunyor doesn't tell me is that, in late November 2006, before Belinda and I flew halfway across the globe, he and a fellow trooper had flown across the United States, from Alaska to New Hampshire, to question Kenneth Dion. I won't hear the specific content of this taped interrogation for another four years, but in it, the detectives learned valuable things about Kenneth Dion. *"Your name has come up in a little investigation we're working on,"* Tim Hunyor says to Dion on the tape. *"The case happened in September of '94. It was a pretty high-profile case. Did you read the news or listen to the news, read the newspaper back then?"*

"Oh, yeah, all the time," Dion answers.

"Okay. You probably heard about the situation, then, about a young girl named Bonnie Craig."

"Bonnie Craig . . ."

"Eighteen-year-old college student."

"I can't recall. I can't remember."

"Okay. Did you ever meet someone called Bonnie or anything like that?"

"I have no idea."

"Let me show you her picture. Y'know, that might bring some memories back. Do you ever recall, y'know, maybe meeting her through someone else, maybe one of your friends or anything?"

"Her?"

"Yeah?"

"Eighteen years old?"

"Mm-hm."

"Hell, no. My wife woulda killed me. For some reason, I got a bad memory. I forget things. Faces I'll remember. I've already forgotten your name."

"Y'know, and the sad thing about it, later on that day, her body was found at McHugh Creek."

"Whoa, whoa, whoa. What are you trying to say?"

"Well, like I said, I'm just down here investigating because your name has come up."

"Why would my name come up?"

"That's what I'm trying to figure out. Did you get to travel the state quite a bit?"

"A little bit. I been up to Denali a couple times with friends from the military. I've been to, maybe, Valdez a few times. I like it there."

Dion tells Trooper Hunyor that he and his wife, Tammy, went out a lot. They went dancing, had good times. But he says he had a bad cocaine habit and an ingrained temper. He liked to brawl in bars.

"I grew up fighting all my life," Dion tells Trooper Hunyor. *"I was one of the top fighters when I was seventeen years old— youngest rated in the top ten in the world in men's full contact."* He is a fifth-degree karate black belt, he claims, and plans to return to Alaska and open a martial arts school.

"There was one time that I had a lot of my weapons in the car when I first moved back up there with my brother," Kenneth Dion boasts.

"What kind of weapon did you have on you?" Trooper Hunyor asks him.

"It was just a sai, martial arts weapons, that's all. Sai—it's a prong-like, a fork, almost. I had nunchucks, three-sectional staff."

His marriage to Tammy didn't last, Kenneth Dion says. *"That's the worst thing I've ever screwed up in my life, is that marriage right there,"* he will tell the troopers. *"Loved her to death."*

Ten days later, on January the eighteenth, 2007, Belinda and I pack our suitcases and board the plane for the flight home. I turn to her once we're in our seats and ready to take off. "I'm sorry if I ruined the trip."

"Don't be silly," she says.

I smile at my friend.

"We can talk as much or as little as you want," she says, placing her hand on mine. "You look tired. You probably want to sleep."

She's right. I am so very tired. Seconds after she makes the suggestion, my eyes close.

Embracing the kids as I arrive out of the terminal, I feel the exhilaration I've been trying to suppress. I can't help but be swayed by the looks on their faces and the sounds of their voices. Samantha, who got malaria in Costa Rica and spent most of her honeymoon miserable, smiles and cries. The boys act more stalwart, but there is euphoria in their eyes.

I say lots of things to try to rein in their hope, but it's no use. They believe their sister will finally receive justice. How long it takes doesn't matter. I smile at them, and we just keep hugging and kissing each other. It's all I need right now.

I call the troopers' office as soon as I arrive home in late January and tell the receptionist I urgently need to meet with Trooper Tim Hunyor. The earliest chance would be Tuesday, she says, the day after tomorrow.

I go into the office the next morning and find it impossible to focus. I imagine Kenneth Dion, in prison in New Hampshire. I imagine him on an airplane to Alaska. I imagine him walking into a courtroom in Anchorage, to finally be put on trial for the act he committed.

Being told they have the man who killed Bonnie has put me into a fresh tailspin. My obsession, slightly faded by time, has been revitalized, and with it the insular focus that prevents me from seeing or doing anything else. I am perpetually distracted, living for the moment when I will be told that the man has crossed into Alaska and awaits his tribunal. I try to do the things normal life requires: work, eat, spend time with my children, stay mentally and physically fit. To those around me, I have maintained a certain level of health. I have great friends. I do things. I'm successful in my work.

But now there is a man in custody, a man about to be put on trial for something I know he did to my daughter and my family, but something I will have no ability to try to prove. I will be just a member of the gallery, an observer, as lawyers, a judge, and a dozen arbitrary members of my community decide whether the man is innocent or guilty. I will sit and watch it play out, helpless, just as helpless as I was thirteen years ago when I was told my daughter had accidentally fallen off the edge of a cliff and plunged to her death.

———————

That Tuesday morning, I meet with Trooper Tim Hunyor, a thickset man with a trim mustache and a midwestern accent. I thank him for his involvement in the case and ask about their progress in getting Kenneth Dion to Alaska. Due to security, Hunyor stonewalls me. He can't disclose that information. He reminds me not to say anything to anyone about the fact that a man in custody has been identified as a DNA match, that to do so would pose a serious risk to the success of our case. I thank him and leave.

At home, I find the number for the New Hampshire Troopers' headquarters and call them. I ask to be put in touch with a senior official. I plead with him to expedite the transfer of Kenneth Dion. After verifying that I am who I say I am, he tells me they are doing everything they can to make the process as quick as possible. Hopefully, it won't take more than a couple of weeks to get Dion up to Alaska, he says.

But January quickly turns to February, and February to March. I stay on Trooper Hunyor, whose calm, kind demeanor never changes. If he's annoyed by me, he doesn't show it. Sergeant Marrs has retired. In his retirement blurb in the newspaper, he said he wished he could have solved Bonnie's case.

Still, I don't understand what's taking so long. What can possibly be so hard about getting a person from one state to another? I find it more and more difficult to focus on my work, and it's showing. Selling real estate has always come easy to me. But I now struggle each day to get to the office, much less execute my job. Two things are critical for success in my field: initiative and follow-through. I have neither. I put up a good front, fooling those around me, but my internal energy is different. I go through the motions of my role but accomplish nothing. Periods of drought are not uncommon for Realtors, but this is different. In 2006, I earned north of two hundred thousand dollars. In the first quarter of 2007, I earn seven hundred and fifty.

I am at a conference with the Surviving Parents Coalition. We are at a "family roundtable" organized by the Department of Justice. The roundtable consists of murder victims' family members, and survivors of abduction and rape. We go around the table sharing the event in our lives that brought us here. My story is only one among many. For a whole day, I listen to gut-wrenching stories of survival, pain, loss, and family devastation. Some of those in the room report having been lucky to see their child alive again. Some speak of children still missing. Most speak of a child or loved one who has been murdered.

In the room, at the table, there are not just parents. There are siblings, too, and their agony is just as great. They tell their stories of grief and pain. In a way, their psychological and emotional ordeals are even more difficult than those of the parents, since they typically have had to deal with both the loss of a sibling and the inadvertent abandonment by a parent obsessed with their deceased child.

At the end of the day, all of my tears spent, I call Samantha, Adam, and Jason and apologize to each of them in turn. I tell them I'm sorry not only for the pain they have surely endured but for my inability to be there for them. Of course, the death of their sister Bonnie was unbearable for me. But I'd never really understood the depth of their loss, or the need they'd had for their mother.

The week after the murder, Adam and Samantha had stayed at Gary's, which I'd felt was the right decision. I realize now that it wasn't. I should have kept them close at my side and hugged and kissed them every night and day. I had spoken to them from a practical view, warning them that their friends wouldn't understand or know how to react, and that they might avoid them or respond awkwardly or inappropriately. Gary had sent them back to school the following Monday, a decision I wouldn't have made, but by then I had already sunk into my fixation on catching the killer, and my own pain. It became my sole mission, at the expense of my duties to them as a mother.

They never demanded anything of me. They were the ones who gave me strength and sympathy. It shouldn't have been that way. I should have been the rock for them. They had to find their sympathy from others. They had to struggle to reclaim some kind of normalcy entirely on their own while growing up overnight, their childhood and their innocence stripped away. No doubt they heard again and again how difficult it is for a mother to lose her child, and they must have felt obligated to put aside their own pain to give of themselves so I could go on.

I tell them I am ashamed. I apologize over and over, seeing now that they gave me room and left me alone with my grief and obsession, because I gave them no other choice. They lost me, for years. After an event that changed their lives, too, I abandoned them. I cry into the phone. I tell them I'm sorry. I can't get those years back. But I'm here now, I tell them. Each of my children says the same thing to me. *Don't worry, Mom. It's okay. We knew you were there. We always knew.*

Toward the middle of April 2007, I receive a call from Trooper Hunyor.

"Hi, Karen. Sorry this has taken so long, but I have some news. They're going to begin with the pretrial hearings. The wheels are in motion."

"You mean he's been extradited?"

"That's going to take a little bit longer. I know you and I would both like it to be a fast process, but I'm afraid it usually isn't. Extradition can take a while. We'll all have to be patient. However, the process can start without him. They can do the indictment without him being present. I'm going to put you in touch with a woman named Katie Paakki, who works with the district attorney's office, and Pat Gullfusen, the state prosecutor. All of your questions can go through them in terms of the proceedings."

I call Katie Paakki and ask to meet with her. She is the gatekeeper, young and direct. She tells me that all of my inquiries can be placed to her and she will relay them to Pat, who works out of Juneau.

"Indictment is set for April twenty-seventh," Katie tells me.

"Does that mean the gag order is lifted?" I ask. "Can we talk about it?"

Katie pauses. "No. Not until after he's indicted."

Kenneth Dion is in jail and can't hurt anyone else's child. But as more days pass, more evidence may be lost, and more memories may fade. Witnesses may die or start to forget. Investigators who worked the case may become unavailable. We are already depending on people who will need to comment on a time, and a place, thirteen years in the past. No one can blame them for having moved on and forgotten whatever information they may have once had. Time is against us.

I phone or e-mail Katie daily, asking for updates. She normally gets back to me after two or three days, usually to advise me to be patient, things take time. When I ask if she can have Pat Gullfusen call me, I am told that he is working on another case.

On April 27, 2007, I drive with my son Adam to Anchorage's main courthouse, where in the first years after Bonnie's death, I'd sit watching one murder trial after another, absorbing everything I could in the event that it might be useful in the trial I hoped would eventually bring her killer to justice. A decade has passed since I sat on these benches, listening to lawyers make arguments that would either set the accused free or land them in prison.

My ex-husband Gary and our daughter Samantha meet us there. Anxiety rushes through me in a new way, and with a new power. I look down and see that my hands are shaking. We are here, exactly where we have hoped to be for years, and now that the moment is truly at hand, my emotions are more heightened, more raw, than they have been at any time since Jim's brother Ken looked down at me in the boat.

The courtroom is crowded, the gallery full. Some of the people sitting among us are there to defend themselves or enter a plea in open court. Others are there to support the defendants scheduled to appear before the judge. Attorneys, legal aides, and other assistants shuffle stacks of papers waiting for their cases to be called. We sit in the back row of the gallery. No one knows who we are. Though one doesn't wish for attention in the situation we have found ourselves in, attention sometimes provides hope. Here we feel like four people among the great unwashed masses, and that makes us believe that Bonnie's case will be considered the same— just another file to push through as fast as possible.

Katie Paakki slips into the courtroom late. She's already told us that Pat Gullfusen will not be attending in person but will be connected by phone when Kenneth Dion's case is called.

Twenty-six cases are scheduled to be heard today, including Bonnie's. The first few cases are called before the judge. Soon I lose track of the case numbers. They all seem to merge together. Numbers are called. Men in orange stand, things are said, and they sit again. Their pleas of guilty or not guilty are entered by the people in suits representing them. My head swims.

Finally, our case number is read. I hear Pat Gullfusen's voice come through the overhead speaker in the courtroom like some strange overlord. Katie has informed us of the charges laid against Dion: first-degree murder, second-degree murder with intent to cause serious injury, second-degree murder with extreme indifference, and first-degree sexual assault. He is not being charged with kidnapping because we've passed the ten-year statute of limitations on that charge.

I wait for the judge to state these charges, but he doesn't. The word *murder* is not uttered. I hear him say something that sounds like, "The charges are waived." I think I must be dreaming.

The judge asks if Kenneth Dion has money for an attorney to represent him. Someone from the public defender's office says he does not. The judge says a public defender will be appointed for him. He says there will be a pretrial conference on October thirty-first and the trial date will be set for December seventeenth. He calls the next case number. Katie Paakki exits the courtroom.

I chase Katie down, Adam and Samantha trailing me. "Katie!"

She stops. "What is it?"

"What was that?"

"What was what?"

"He didn't read the charges. How come?"

"Oh," says Katie, "they waive that in the interest of time."

"Well, do we at least know how he's going to plead?"

"Oh, no. The judge just enters a default plea of not guilty for now, since he isn't yet represented."

I don't know what to say. I have stayed up all night praying that Kenneth Dion would plead guilty and spare us the hell of a trial. Katie turns and leaves. We have been processed. Behind us, others continue to file out of the courtroom as well, a crowd of anonymous regular people marshaling hope, even in the face of evidence to the contrary.

With Kenneth Dion's name now public, the media starts to dig, and information about him begins to surface. I learn from an article in the *Anchorage Daily News* on May 1 that he had been in jail two months before Bonnie's murder, then out on parole at the time of her death, before being sent back to jail again two months later for parole violation.

The journalists have done their homework. The article lays out a long rap sheet accumulated by Dion over the years, including eighteen convictions, ten misdemeanors, and eight felonies. From the age of eighteen, with the exception of a three-year period from 1999 to 2002, he never went more than a year without committing a significant offense.

I feel my mission shift. Kenneth Dion has been indicted, and, as Trooper Hunyor said, the wheels of justice are now in motion. I can't do much to influence the outcome. But I can do something to try to help other mothers, other siblings, and other families avoid the nightmare we have endured. I realize that if Kenneth Dion's DNA had been collected on his earlier arrests, Bonnie's murder could have been solved in months, perhaps weeks.

I rechannel my energy, switching from detective to lobbyist. I do some homework and learn that there are more than five thousand DNA samples waiting to be processed and input into CODIS in Alaska alone. In 2007, the entire database contains less than 11,000 samples. I go to the Alaska Scientific Crime Detection Laboratory and talk to people there, all of whom deny there is an issue. No one is admitting to the problems created by the backlog.

I phone people in D.C. until I am directed to someone who is part of the fight, a woman named Lisa Hurst. I ask her if she's aware that Alaska doesn't collect DNA on felony arrests.

"Yes, I know," she says. "Only six states do. Maryland, Virginia, California, Texas, Kansas, and Minnesota."

"It could have made a difference in my daughter's case. It could have made a difference of twelve years."

"I know," she says. "There's no law that says an individual citizen can't try to introduce a new state bill." She encourages me to contact lawmakers and get them to introduce a bill requiring the collection of DNA on all felony arrests. "I can send you some information to help."

Despite there being just sixteen days left in the current legislative session, I run with this, bringing it to Governor Sarah Palin and Senator Hollis French. I argue for the need to collect DNA on all felony arrests, telling them we can't wait. That people will be murdered and raped because we didn't take action.

In twelve days, we get the bill passed, and Governor Palin signs it into law in June 2007.

I am at the office, staring at my computer screen, inspecting listings. The year 2007 has not been a good one for me, careerwise, and it's been months since I have generated a dollar. Belinda has tried to spur me, but nothing is happening.

The phone rings. I absently pick it up.

"Karen? It's Tim Hunyor. I'm calling to let you know that Kenneth Dion has been extradited from New Hampshire. He's here, Karen. He's in Alaska."

Knowing that Dion has crossed into my home state, where I believe he violated and murdered my daughter, causes something to happen inside me. Though I've never laid eyes on the man, the knowledge that he is only miles away feels like picking up a bad scent. I feel newly desecrated by his presence.

———————

It's nearly the thirteenth anniversary of Bonnie's murder by the time I lay eyes on Kenneth Dion for the first time. We are back in the courthouse, this time for the first pretrial hearing. I recognize Dion from pictures, though his red hair is now shaved close to his scalp. He walks in wearing a suit and a vaguely agitated look. I feel so much hatred and revulsion toward this man that in a way I feel nothing at all. My skin crawls and my insides grow cold. I am squeezing Samantha's hand harder than I want to. I feel both exposed and anonymous, and both feelings are uncomfortable.

Lawyers exchange information. The judge asks questions. The man accused of killing my daughter stares forward, revealing nothing.

———————

In mid-October 2007, I receive an unexpected call from the Alaska Scientific Crime Detection Laboratory, informing me that the National CODIS Convention is being held in San Francisco at the end of the month and asking if I'd agree to be their keynote speaker. I'm told that there will be probably about five hundred attendees from law enforcement across the nation. They want me to share the story of Bonnie's case. They'll be happy to fly me down.

Two weeks later, I find myself standing at a podium in a large banquet hall. Jim has accompanied me on the trip, since it's one of our on-again periods, and we're always at our best when we're not at home, anyway. In front of me sit rows of CODIS personnel, crime-lab specialists, prosecutors, district attorneys, and law-enforcement officials.

I lean toward the microphone. "You are the new heroes of justice," I say. They are silent.

I have told my story many times over the past thirteen years, but never to this large a group and never to a room of people who could make so significant a difference in the lives of others.

"My daughter, Bonnie, was brutally raped and murdered on September 28, 1994. She was eighteen years old."

Some of them scribble on their pads, some quietly sip their water. There is no way of knowing whether my message is getting through or if it matters to those listening. When all is said and done, all I can do is speak from the heart.

"She didn't do drugs. She wouldn't even think about alcohol. She started Students Against Drunk Driving in her high school. She participated in a peer-counseling group for other students. She played violin in the school orchestra. She wanted to be a social worker or a psychologist. She wanted to go to UC Berkeley with her boyfriend, but I told her it was too dangerous there, so she enrolled at the University of Alaska. She was the first girl on her high school wrestling team. Her goal was to never get pinned, and she didn't."

I tell them about the evil Post-it, my being told that her death was a hiking accident. I tell them about our blended family, my four kids, Jim's three, and about how they all had to struggle with the loss of a sister and the absence of a mother who was alternately obsessed with the investigation and paralyzed with grief.

"It feels like your guts have been ripped out of your body. You can't function. At first, even making a cup of coffee was a difficult task. My mind would be racing one moment and go blank the next."

I tell them about how I pestered the troopers. I tell them about my work with the Anchorage Police Department and my fear that it was retaliation.

"I worked with Anchorage PD, but Bonnie's case was in Alaska State Troopers' jurisdiction. I'm sure many of you can understand my frustration. I knew all the investigators with APD and trusted them. I wanted them to be working on the case. I was overwhelmed with the guilt that it could have been because of the last drug bust I worked on. It was something I would have to wonder about until the case was solved."

I tell them about my fear that mistakes were being made and clues missed.

"Originally, I thought the murderer would be caught within a week. Then a month. Then I was sure it would happen during the holidays. Deadline after deadline passed with no answers."

I tell them about Sandy Cassidy contacting me out of the blue and pushing me to keep Bonnie's case in the public eye. I tell them about the posters, the bumper stickers, the flyers, the bus signs. The candlelight vigils and memorials. The media coverage. The reward fund, which started at five thousand dollars and went up to fifty, but still didn't help.

"On the third anniversary, we had new signs made: *Someone is getting away with murder.* Every anniversary since then, every birthday, every time I go to a graduation or wedding, the pain hits hard. The grief is overwhelming. Certain songs on the radio, certain locations in town, certain memories—they all bring back the pain."

I tell them about Bonnie's colleague from Sam's Club, dismissed as a suspect when his DNA didn't match the sample taken from her body. I tell them about the young man in Bonnie's English class and his vicious journal entries. All the suspects over the years, all those interviews, all the swabs taken and tested. The bus driver from California, the DNA match, all of us jubilant that the case was finally solved. The state demanding that further DNA testing be conducted, and the new results eliminating him.

"Investigators and crime-lab analysts were dumbfounded. It was not our man. The years passed, and the case became cold."

I tell them about the DNA Identification Act of 1994, which authorized the FBI to establish a national DNA index for persons convicted of serious felonies. Four years later, it finally became operational. By late 1999, ten different states, including Alaska, were uploading suspects' DNA profiles to the national index on conviction using the new technology. I tell them ten states isn't enough. Neither is twenty, thirty, or forty. More important, although it won't be long before all fifty states are collecting DNA on conviction, I emphasize that we need to get them to do so on felony arrest. When children are taken from their families, there is a ripple effect that never ends, and a pain that has no bottom. England enters their DNA profiles in two days. Our goal should be at least within a few weeks. It's a start. No one should get away with murder. With collection of DNA on arrest and the proper maintenance of the database, they won't.

"Thank you," I say. I see pairs of hands come together. I hear the sound of applause, and I see many people in the audience standing. I have told them my story. And it seems they have heard.

Back home, I start pushing for a new crime lab. I meet with the mayor of Anchorage to get him to agree to donate the land. I launch AlaskanCitizensforJustice.com to generate support. I e-mail all of the state senators and representatives and call key players on the judicial and finance committees. I organize a joint press conference with Victims for Justice, STAR (Standing Together Against Rape), and Alaskan Citizens for Justice so that the public will realize the crime lab is the foundation of our justice system and that the current one is underfunded and underresourced. I go on radio and TV. I speak about the overcrowding in the current building and the inability to get rid of the current backlog. I tell them that the lab can at present process only the most serious crimes, and usually only as they come to trial. Funding isn't the issue. A general fund exists, fueled by revenue from the oil companies. The issue is a lack of resources and space. They're busting at the seams.

Slowly, people start to return my calls. Discussions get scheduled. I know by now that things don't happen overnight, if they happen at all. It takes time, persistence, then more time and more persistence.

It is two years after Kenneth Dion's indictment, a year and a half since the first pretrial hearing. The trial date has been continually pushed back, and the reasons are increasingly frustrating. Initially, the trial was set for September 2008. The judge had given both sides more than a year to prepare, so there would be no reason to change the date. Then September 2008 was changed to January 2009, and January to May. The public defender needed extra time to go through the files. More information was needed on the DNA evidence. The judge's family vacation. A change in defense attorneys. A few days earlier, the initial judge assigned to the case was arrested for drunk driving and withdrawn.

To make matters worse, after the initial defense attorney is taken off the case, the new one discovers a conflict and has the case turned over to the Office of Public Advocacy. We're starting from scratch. Andrew Lambert, now the third attorney assigned to represent Kenneth Dion, tells the judge that the previous two attorneys did basically nothing, and he is going to need another year to prepare his case.

My body and mind are a mess the night before each scheduled hearing. I feel on the verge of tears or hyperventilation. It is a terrible buildup of anxiety, usually for the sake of five or ten minutes of disappointment. I see Dion once more, in orange prison garb. He attends only when forced to, his typical absences making everything seem even less real.

My friends have done everything they can to lift my spirits. I get together with my girlfriends. We go shopping, eating, hiking, camping, white-water rafting. I even train for a marathon. It all helps, but only temporarily. It's strange to me that now—with the case at hand, even if it is delayed again and again—feels like the right time for me to leave Alaska. As I stare at the map, I feel a pull I haven't felt before. During the last fifteen years here, I've thought about moving many times. For the past five, I've been talking about retiring to Naples, Florida, where you can park your boat in your backyard. Now I've been offered a position in Florida that I feel I can't turn down. That I don't want to turn down.

This chapter of my life has presented its purpose. I will continue the part of the fight that I can wage for my stolen daughter, but given the chance to fight it with greater strength and support, I can't say no. If I can help one other family avoid going through what we have gone through, it will be worthwhile.

A month earlier, while attending a meeting of the Surviving Parents Coalition in Boca Raton, Florida, in mid-February 2009, I'd met Hank Asher, a wealthy Floridian who had made a fortune in data mining. Hank had donated a quarter of a million dollars to help the SPC lobby for laws to protect children. I learned that, in the days after 9/11, he'd helped the federal government build a database to identify possible suspects, which had been instrumental in uncovering multiple figures who were involved in the plot. Hank was highly involved with the National Center for Missing and Exploited Children and worked closely with John Walsh, of *America's Most Wanted*. I never asked Hank why he was so invested in the protection of children, and he never offered to tell.

I had volunteered to come down to Tallahassee when I'd heard that the DNA bill was stalled in the state judiciary committee. Other members of the SPC from Florida joined me there, like Drew and Joyce Kesse, whose daughter Jennifer had vanished three years earlier, and Hilary Sessions, whose daughter Tiffany had disappeared at the age of twenty. Parents who had no answers but would never give up.

Hank also invited Martha Bennett, an attorney from a century-old law firm with a strong track record of lobbying success. Martha introduced me and the other parents to the key players on the committee, and she attended when each of us in turn addressed the judiciary committee, telling them about our respective cases and the importance of DNA collection on felony arrest.

As I waited for the cab to take me back to the airport, Martha told me Hank was hoping I could fly down to Boca to meet some of his team. I did. While there, I visited Flint Waters, a man with whom I had walked the halls in Washington, D.C., visiting senators and trying to get support for the Child Protection Act.

Flint, now working for Hank, had created a program to help identify which computers worldwide were downloading child porn, and he was working with law-enforcement officials all over the country. Hank had created an organization called TLO, The Last One. When I asked what it meant, he said he didn't want to rest until every last pedophile was behind bars. I told him I agreed, and Hank asked if I'd be interested in coming to work for them.

The offer was clear-cut: move to Boca and help fight the battle, at grassroots. Hank would pay, and I would fight. I would push for legislation to protect kids and get all fifty states to collect DNA on all felony arrests—thereby helping other families avoid what mine has gone through for fifteen years.

Kenneth Dion may be in jail, but the wheels of justice move like molasses. With Flint's help and Hank's backing, I could get in front of the people I'm now trying to get to by phone and e-mail. I would travel to different states and lobby for collection of DNA on arrest. I would stand before committees and bodies and tell them my story. I would attend bill-signing ceremonies with governors and senators. I could utilize the media in a way I can't do here, because it might affect the upcoming trial, even potentially leading to a change of venue. I would make my voice heard—more than it could ever be heard from Alaska.

"I have no choice, guys. This is a chance to really make some change," I tell my kids in March 2009. We sit in my living room, and I tell them I am moving across the continent to continue fighting the fight on Bonnie's behalf.

"You know I've been working to get the DNA bill passed into law in Florida, but it's not going anywhere. They can stall forever, just like with Bonnie's case. Florida is critical. If we can get it passed there, it makes it a lot easier to work on the other states, especially in the East. It makes more sense to be there full-time than to keep going back and forth."

"The trial is going to happen eventually," Adam says. "What will you do?"

I look at my children. Though I will always see them as my

kids, they have not really been kids for a long time. Jason will soon be closer to forty than thirty. Adam is twenty-eight; Samantha, twenty-seven.

I look at Adam as he waits for me to answer the question. "They've offered to fly me back to Alaska for the trial and the pre-trial hearings. I'm not accomplishing anything here. We're gagged again until the trial starts." I also point out that I'm worried about how much longer my dad will be able to live on his own and how much easier it will be for me to get to him from Florida than from Alaska. "I need to be able to visit him more often than I do now."

"We understand, Mom," says Samantha. "You're doing the right thing."

"We'll come visit once or twice a year; you'll come home once or twice a year—it'll work," Jason says, echoing Samantha's support. "Plus there's Skype, Facebook. You still won't be able to get rid of us that easily."

We share a laugh. Samantha walks over and hugs me tightly. Jason and Adam do the same. We can all feel someone else in the hug, too.

It is my third day in Boca when I receive a call from Adam's wife, Trina. She knows to tell me first that my son is alive before telling me anything else, but I can tell from her voice that the rest of the news is not going to be pleasant. He was rear-ended, she says, out of nowhere. The impact was large, the car accordioned, and the injuries to his neck extensive. He's in the hospital now, she tells me, stabilized, drugged, but alive. She knows the minimum I need to hear.

I tell Trina I'm getting back on the plane, but she insists other-wise. He's badly injured, but there is nothing I can do by rushing back. It is eerily reminiscent of my conversation with Trooper Hunyor telling me they found the person who killed my daughter but that my coming home right away would accomplish little. Nothing can fully prevent bad things happening to people, and some of those people are your own children. You can't protect them every hour of every day for their entire lives. You would like to, but you can't.

The next morning, Trina calls back. Adam has suffered two torn discs and a torn ligament in his neck. Rehab is going to demand hours, and it is going to be hard—at least, if he wants to be able to lift his daughters normally. Adam, in a drug haze, gets on the phone, expresses his love, and tells me if I spend my time worrying about him instead of getting on with it, he won't forgive me. He tells me I have a job to do in Florida. He has a beautiful supportive spouse, the smiles and laughs of his daughters, his brother and sister and their families, and my support from afar. It's all good, he says. Everything's fine.

As soon as I hang up with Adam, the phone rings again. It's Jason.

"Hey, Mom."

We briefly discuss Adam's accident. Jason is a good brother who has been there before for Adam, and he will be there to help again now.

Behind the conversation about Adam's accident, I hear something else in his tone. Something positive, like a smile. Like pride. Though I am listening to the voice of a thirty-five-year-old man, I hear in it the voice of my son, sweet and determined, enthusiastic for all the possibilities that might come.

"I did it," he tells me.

My firstborn has reached a goal he's been striving for since he was a teen: getting his paramedic degree.

"I just finished the last exam," he says.

"I'm so proud of you," I said. "You've worked so hard for this. You've known you wanted it for a long time. What's next?"

"I start an internship at Cypress Creek next month. It's just north of Houston. Once I finish that, I'll be a paramedic. We'll come back to Anchorage."

I hang up the phone smiling and picturing my eldest son hanging out with Texans. Jason, like Samantha, is drawn unavoidably to a career whose sole purpose is to help others. I don't know how much of this has to do with what happened to Bonnie, and it doesn't matter. All I feel is pride. Though Bonnie is gone, she imbues her brothers and sister with a strength that can't be taught and that continues to surprise me, even though I have seen it in action now for years.

The phone rings a third time. As if materializing out of my head, it is Samantha's voice. In her tone is the opposite of the pride and contentment I heard in Jason's. In her voice, there is only sadness. I know what it's about. We've talked openly and frequently about the troubles she and Ryan have been having. They've been at odds over both the little things and the big things. The signs have become unignorable. High school sweethearts don't automatically translate into compatible spouses.

I've never been anything but honest with my daughter, and we both know that, having ended three marriages myself, it would be hypocritical for me to tell her to hang on.

"I'm sorry, honey. Does it have to do with Bonnie's case?"

"No," says Samantha, sniffling. "I wish it was. I'm not just talking about supporting me through the trial. I'm talking about supporting me in life. It just isn't going to happen. We're just different."

"Everybody's different," I say. "The question is how much." In her silence, I hear the answer. Ups, downs. They're part of every

Bonnie, age 2, wearing the coat I bought her for Christmas. *(Paul Fletcher)*

Bonnie and her older brother, Jason, as ring bearer and flower girl at my wedding to Gary Campbell, June 21, 1980, in Calgary. *(Gary Campbell)*

Adam, Samantha, and Bonnie dressed up for Halloween in Midland, Texas.

(Karen Foster)

Family photo taken in May 1987 in Midland, Texas.

(Karen Foster)

Family portrait with me, Gary, and the kids in 1989.

(Sears Portrait Studios)

Bonnie and her boyfriend Cameron Miyasaki at Portage
Glacier, in the summer of 1994.   *(Cameron Miyasaki)*

Bonnie in Mexico on a family vacation in 1994.

(Karen Foster)

Above and right: Aerial shots of McHugh Creek and waterfall, where Bonnie's body was found.

(Courtesy of the Anchorage District Attorney's Office and the State of Alaska Office of Special Prosecutions and Appeals)

Alaska State Troopers searching the crime scene in 1994.

(Courtesy of the Anchorage District Attorney's Office and the State of Alaska Office of Special Prosecutions and Appeals)

A leaf with a single drop of dried blood on it, found at the top of the cliff from which it was initially thought Bonnie fell while hiking.

(Courtesy of the Anchorage District Attorney's Office and the State of Alaska Office of Special Prosecutions and Appeals)

In January 2007, Alaska State Trooper Tim Hunyor, now retired from active duty and living in Ohio, was the first person to inform me that they'd found a DNA match—though it would take until May 2011 before the case went to trial.

(Timothy Hunyor)

Kenneth Dion's 1994 Alaska driver's license.

(Courtesy of the Anchorage District Attorney's Office and the State of Alaska Office of Special Prosecutions and Appeals)

Kenneth Dion in December 2006, when investigators first flew down to New Hampshire to interview him.

(Courtesy of the Anchorage District Attorney's Office and the State of Alaska Office of Special Prosecutions and Appeals)

Kenneth Dion seated between defense attorneys Leigh Ann Bauer, left, and Andrew Lambert, right, in October 2011.   *(Bill Roth/Anchorage Daily News)*

Assistant Attorney General Paul Miovas outlining the state's rape-and-murder case against Kenneth Dion.

*(Bill Roth/*Anchorage Daily News)

My son, Adam Campbell, kissing my head as our family received news of the verdict.

(Anchorage Daily News)

Sharing a group hug after sentencing. From top: Adam, his friend Kelly Cannon, me, Jason (in the middle), and Samantha with her back to the camera.

(Anchorage Daily News)

Me with my grandchildren! Although they never met their aunt Bonnie, they've all been shaped in positive ways by Bonnie's life. Back row, left to right: Jonas, Logan, Jasmyn, Jayleigh, me, Tehya, Tanner, and Austin. Front row, left to right: Lucas, Emme, and Zoie. *(Karen Foster)*

Above left: From left to right: Jim's son Jesse, Samantha, Jason, and Adam, at Jason's wedding in October 2013. *(Karen Foster)*

Above right: Every year on March 30, Bonnie's birthday, the family celebrates with a birthday dinner, and my granddaughters Jayleigh, Zoie, and Emme go to her grave to wish their aunt a happy birthday and bring her flowers. *(Adam Campbell)* life. I hold the phone close to my face and tell my grown-up daughter I love her. With time, I tell her, everything's going to be all right.

———————————

In late fall of 2010, eighteen months after moving down to Florida, I get a call from a hospital in London, Ontario, telling me that my father has been admitted with a kidney issue. In addition, the doctor tells me, he seems progressively disoriented. I get on a plane to Canada.

Within minutes of seeing my father, I realize he can no longer take care of himself. There are moments in which one's parents seem to age overnight. It has happened. I talk to him about a retirement community or assisted-living facility. He is lucid enough to tell me he isn't having any of it.

There is only one option. In November, I pack up my condo in Hillsboro Beach, putting most of my things into storage, and throw as many items into the car as it will hold. I drive the two days north and arrive on Dad's doorstep. The child taking care of the parent. Part of life's cycles.

10

I t seems strange to finally be here, on May 10, 2011, starting Kenneth Dion's trial for the rape and murder of my daughter, Bonnie Craig, on September 24, 1994.

We are sitting in Anchorage Superior Court just before nine o'clock in the morning. Acting for the plaintiff, the State of Alaska, are Assistant District Attorneys Paul Miovas and Jenna Gruenstein. Miovas is clean-cut, almost military in presentation, very polite and proper, and to the point, yet he also exudes a kind and empathetic aura.

With our agreement, Miovas and Gruenstein had initially offered the defense a plea deal of seventy-five years. It would have spared us the torture of a trial, ended this hell earlier, and still ensured that Dion would spend his life behind bars. There was no reason for him to take that deal, of course. At nearly forty years old, the difference between another seventy-five years and another ninety-nine—the maximum sentence for first-degree murder—is no difference at all.

The defense attorneys are Andrew Lambert and Leigh Ann Bauer. Lambert is an aggressive defense attorney and a known showboater. Presiding is Judge Jack Smith, whose short wispy hair matches his mustache and Van Dyck beard.

This is Paul Miovas's first murder trial as Alaska's assistant district attorney in charge of cold-case homicides, but I feel confident in him largely because of how much he's communicated with me and my family, which already surpasses what the troopers and our previous prosecutor managed. As soon as he took over the case last July, when the original prosecutor had health issues, Miovas had asked us to meet with him and Jenna Gruenstein to discuss the case. He'd let us know we would be included as much as we wanted to be, even welcoming our input on the potential jurors. In most cases, family members are relegated to spectators, and certainly not involved in any important decisions. It impressed me when Miovas said, "Karen, I know how active you've been all these years regarding Bonnie's case, and I'd like you to be involved in this process. We can decide together on jurors. I value your insights."

I had anticipated feeling nervous on this day, but I can scarcely believe just *how* nervous I am now that the trial has really arrived. The man accused of killing my daughter is going to be tried before a jury of his peers, and they are going to put him in jail or set him free. He has served his time for armed robbery in New Hampshire and now stands to become a free man should the jury have a shred of doubt about the prosecution's case. We are focused and intent, ready to take notes, observe, contribute. Paul and Jenna have made us feel like we're part of the team. Still, during the trial proceedings, we will be at a remove, unable to do anything but watch it unfold.

I take a seat on the spectator benches alongside my father, my children, and a group of potential jury members. From an original jury pool of a hundred and twenty or so, the lawyers have whittled it down to thirty-eight. It is from this group that, through the process known as voir dire, fifteen people will be chosen, and then from that fifteen, a final dozen, to decide Dion's fate.

Judge Smith calls out each individual's name, and one at a time, people rise and walk toward the stand. They raise their right hands and swear to tell the truth, the whole truth, and nothing but the truth, so help them God. They settle themselves into the chair, and Miovas asks them questions. Trooper Tim Hunyor is in attendance, too, sitting quietly at the prosecution's table.

Many potential jurors list reasons they'd prefer not to be picked for trial. Some describe vacations they're planning. Others are in the midst of divorces. Some are taking summer classes at UAA. A man expresses concern that he stands to lose customers from his one-man business. A young woman has a trip scheduled to go see her grandmother, who is dying of cancer. A woman whose father is an assistant pastor at a church down the road says she feels uncomfortable sitting in judgment on people because only God has the right to evaluate our lives.

Jobs, families, lives. Sitting here, it becomes clear to me that our democratic system—though I believe it's the best thing we've come up with so far—is fragile. It asks us flawed humans to form views of each other's acts and the motivations behind those acts, and then it asks other flawed humans to pronounce consequences. Bonnie's fate is already written. Kenneth Dion's fate will be written by the courtroom skill of a couple of lawyers and a random group of a dozen fellow human beings.

It also reminds me that everyone has problems. We all have lives to manage. These people are not so different from me. They are dealing with the same thing I and my family have been dealing with for the past sixteen and a half years. They are just trying to get through the day.

By the following morning, almost exactly twenty-four hours later, the group of fifteen jurors has been chosen (the final twelve will be selected after the trial, before the verdict). Paul Miovas and Jenna Gruenstein have incorporated feedback from me and my kids about which potential jurors we'd like to see kept or discarded. We feel pleased with the selection, though of course it's impossible to know what people will think and believe once they start to hear the two versions of the story.

I take my seat in the gallery with my father, Jason, Samantha, Adam, and Trina. A number of friends, acquaintances, and colleagues are there to support us as well. Kenneth Dion is brought in wearing a suit and tie, his reddish hair neatly trimmed, and takes his place alongside his defense attorneys, Andrew Lambert and Leigh Ann Bauer. The bailiff removes Dion's handcuffs. The word *LOST* is tattooed across one set of his knuckles; *SOUL* across the other. I don't know whether Dion has recently added these or whether he's had them for a long time. Either way, it's accurate.

Judge Smith orders the jurors called in. They file in quietly, looking serious. The judge addresses them, explaining how the trial will be conducted: opening statements from both sides, followed by the prosecution's presentation of evidence and calling of witnesses (which the defense may or may not do as well), then the closing arguments, each side telling the jury what they believe the evidence has proved and suggesting what conclusions they believe should be drawn.

Judge Smith continues, telling the group to consider only the facts presented to them. They must resist being influenced by sentiment, prejudice, passion, or public opinion. They must base their verdict upon a fair consideration of the evidence. They must remember that objections or requests are not evidence, nor are his rulings to allow or reject them.

They are not to decide any issue by simply counting the number of witnesses testifying for one side or the other. They are to consider that no one can see or hear the state of mind with which another person's acts were done or omitted, but what a person does or fails to do may indicate that person's state of mind. They must not read, listen to, or watch any newspaper, radio, or television reports concerning the case.

"The indictment reads as follows. Count One, Murder in the First Degree; that on or about September 28, 1994, at or near Anchorage in the Third Judicial District, State of Alaska, Kenneth M. Dion, with intent to cause the death of another person, caused the death of Bonnie Craig, date of birth March 30, 1976. Count Two, Murder in the Second Degree; that on or about September 28, 1994, at or near Anchorage in the Third Judicial District, State of Alaska, Kenneth M. Dion, with intent to cause serious physical injury to another person, or knowing that his conduct was substantially certain to cause death or serious physical injury to another person, caused the death of Bonnie Craig, date of birth March 30, 1976. Count Three, Murder in the Second Degree; that on or about September 28, 1994, at or near Anchorage, in the Third Judicial District, State of Alaska, Kenneth M. Dion, acting either alone or with one or more persons, committed or attempted to commit Kidnapping or Sexual Assault in the first degree; and in the course of or in furtherance of these crimes, or one of them, or in immediate flight therefrom, he or any person caused the death of Bonnie Craig, date of birth March 30, 1976. Count Four, Sexual Assault in the First Degree; that on or about September 28, 1994, at or near Anchorage, in the Third Judicial District, State of Alaska,

Kenneth M. Dion engaged in sexual penetration of Bonnie Craig, date of birth March 30, 1976, without her consent."

The jurors are listening intently. I know that there is a lot they won't hear. I would love to stand up and tell them that this trial isn't going to be about the truth, that many facts about Kenneth Dion will never come out in court. The fact that he'd been arrested and convicted of assaulting other women. The fact that he was an admitted junkie. The fact that he was serving time in jail in New Hampshire. Nothing prejudicial against the defendant is permitted in a murder trial. Only the facts of the case at hand matter. Information will be strategically presented or withheld as each lawyer tries to convince the jury to see Kenneth Dion in one light or another. Court isn't that different from the way we argue in real life: sneakily.

"At this trial," says Judge Smith, "it is the job of the lawyer for the state to present evidence to prove the charge against the defendant. According to the law, the defendant is presumed to be innocent of the charge unless the state can present enough evidence to prove the defendant guilty beyond a reasonable doubt. The distinguishing features of a criminal trial are what are known in the language of the law as the presumption of innocence and the burden of proof beyond a reasonable doubt. The law presumes a defendant to be innocent of a crime; thus, a defendant, although accused, begins the trial with a clean slate, with no evidence favoring conviction. The presumption of innocence alone is sufficient to acquit a defendant, unless you are satisfied beyond a reasonable doubt of a defendant's guilt after careful and impartial consideration of all the evidence in the case. That you be satisfied beyond a reasonable doubt of a defendant's guilt is the burden of proof. It is not required that the prosecution prove guilt beyond all possible doubt, for it is rarely possible to prove anything to an absolute certainty. Rather, the test is one of reasonable doubt. A reasonable doubt is a doubt based upon reason and common sense. Proof beyond a reasonable doubt must be proof of such a convincing character that, after careful consideration, you would be willing to rely and act upon it without hesitation in your important affairs. A defendant is never to be convicted on mere suspicion or conjecture. The burden of proving the defendant guilty beyond a reasonable doubt always rests upon the prosecution. This burden never shifts throughout the trial. A reasonable doubt may arise not only from the evidence produced, but also from a lack of evidence. Since the burden is upon the prosecution to prove every essential element of the crime charged beyond a reasonable doubt, a defendant has the right to rely upon the failure of the prosecution to establish such proof."

Some of the jurors look at Kenneth Dion. They have listened closely to the judge's words, and they understand that, at least right now, he is guilty of nothing.

———————

Judge Smith says we are ready for opening statements. He invites ADA Paul Miovas to begin.

"Thank you, Your Honor," Miovas says, standing and buttoning his suit jacket. "Good morning, ladies and gentlemen. Before I do my opening statement, I want to basically thank you. You've heard a lot through jury selection, but now we are going to basically tell you what we think the evidence is in this case. This is not the opportunity for me to stand up here and argue the case to you, ladies and gentlemen. That's not what Mr. Lambert and I are going to do at this point. We're just going to tell you basically what this case is about. The judge has given you some instructions, and I'm just going to add one additional thing to what the judge has told you about this process. This process is about one thing, ladies and gentlemen. We are seeking the truth here. That's what this court-room is about. That's what we're doing here. We're making sure that Kenneth Dion gets a fair trial, and you as jurors are seeking the truth about what happened in this case."

I am happy to hear Miovas bring up this point. Most trials I have observed seem to have little to do with the truth or what's fair.

"I have a lot to cover, so be patient with me. I'm going to try to do this in an hour. There's a lot to cover. You have to understand, ladies and gentlemen, what we're dealing with here is a situation that took place September 28, 1994. Sixteen and a half years ago. I want to give you a good enough road map in my opening so that you understand when you hear through the witnesses, the testimony, and evidence, that you understand kind of how it all pieces together. I think both parties just ask that you be patient with us and listen to the evidence as it's presented."

There is a projection screen set up at the front of the courtroom. Miovas is holding a remote in one of his hands. He clicks a button, and a picture comes up on the screen. It is a picture of a smiling eighteen-year-old girl with her head tilted slightly, a gleam in her eye.

"Ladies and gentlemen, this is Bonnie Craig."

"I want to tell you a little bit about Bonnie Craig in 1994 so that you understand the context in which this evidence is coming," Miovas says. "Bonnie was an eighteen-year-old UAA student. She was a freshman. She graduated from Service High School in 1994. She lived here in Anchorage, and she had started going to Service High, and she had the intent to study psychology. Bonnie went to class two days a week, Monday and Wednesday. She took a full load of core classes, and she would start school at seven o'clock in the morning and go to class until about four in the afternoon. In addition to that, she would often stay late at school. She would go to the computer lab. She would correspond with her boyfriend. You're going to hear about that. She would study. She'd stay and study in study groups. You're going to hear about that. And basically, she took her studies very seriously."

Miovas has told me that a likely defense ploy will be to try to paint Bonnie in a negative light. So he's going to try to show the real picture of my daughter first.

"Now, she wasn't just a full-time student. Bonnie also had a full life outside of her studies at UAA. She worked. Most people are going to say she worked part-time, but I want you to understand this, ladies and gentlemen. Bonnie worked at Sam's Club. She generally worked every Saturday and Sunday. She worked Tuesday when she wasn't in school, and then she either worked a Thursday or a Friday. Four days a week, seven and a half hours, about thirty hours a week."

As Miovas describes Bonnie, my heart glows with pride. She didn't study hard out of obligation or pressure. She studied hard because she wanted to study hard. She didn't get a part-time job because I gave her an ultimatum. She did it because she wanted a job.

I remember walking Bonnie's route the week after she was murdered in the futile hopes of finding clues. Miovas describes Bonnie's typical school day—how she got up at about five o'clock in the morning on Mondays and Wednesdays, and how even though she was eighteen, she'd never gotten her driver's license, so relied on rides from her dad or her friends, or, for the most part, on public transportation, on the bus system. She walked about two and a half miles to catch the bus to school.

"These weren't her only obligations, work, school. She also looked after her little brother and sister. She had a twelve- and a thirteen-year-old brother and sister, Adam and Samantha. Adam and Samantha, basically, at this point, were old enough to take care of themselves, but still needed a little supervision when the parents were at work, and that was Bonnie's responsibility. And in fact, when this occurred, one of the things that Bonnie had been doing that week was watching Adam and Samantha while her parents were both out of town. That's not all. She also babysat for different friends. You're going to hear from a friend of hers named Wendy Goodrich who worked with her at Sam's. Wendy had a child, whom Bonnie would watch whenever Wendy needed. So she's watching her brother and sister, she's working full-time, she also watches the kids of a coworker."

I think of two things: Bonnie's diligence in all things, and her dedication. Just as I'm thinking about the latter, Miovas brings up the part of her life to which she was most dedicated before she was taken away.

"And then one of the largest aspects of Bonnie's life that you're going to hear a lot about during the course of this trial is she had been dating Cameron Miyasaki for about a year and a half. They started dating in their junior year. Cameron, because he's a very bright young man, he got into Berkeley—University of California, Berkeley—and had left a couple of months prior to Bonnie's death. This is 1994, so you have to realize that we don't have a lot of the technology we have today. Bonnie would go to her computer lab at school, at UAA, either Monday or Wednesday after her classes or Friday when she was doing extra studying or stuff for extra credit, and set up an appointment to talk to Cameron down at Berkeley. All of this is going on. You have to understand, it left very little time for Bonnie to do anything outside of her work and school commitments, and her commitments to her family."

Bonnie was killed on a Wednesday; Miovas talks about how

she'd packed lunch for her twelve-year-old sister, Samantha, the previous Monday morning—a rice cake, a couple of carrots, an apple, some Starbursts—and wrote her a note, and how Bonnie stayed late to study that night with a couple of friends at the university. How on Tuesday morning, she made sure that Adam and Samantha got breakfast before they were picked up by their middle-school bus, then herself headed to work at Sam's Club. How she left her little brother and sister a note on Tuesday saying she'd be home later than they would, but that she'd buy them a pizza if they cleaned the house. Gary returned that night from his trip to New Orleans, around ten P.M. The next morning, Samantha heard Bonnie get up around five as usual, heard her run down the stairs, and leave for school. Miovas talks about her two-and-a-half-mile walk to the bus stop. About the psychology test that morning to which she never showed up.

September 28, 1994, had been a crisp, sunny day in Anchorage, and McHugh Creek had been busy. It was one of those places people went to on that kind of day. A lot of people were out, enjoying the weather. One of those people was a young woman named Jennifer Braunschweig, who, while she was exploring and photographing the area in midafternoon, happened to notice something unusual in the water—a body, floating facedown. In those pre-cell-phone days, Jennifer had no way of calling from the scene, so she ran back to her car, drove to a weigh station, and called the Alaska State Troopers. The investigation began.

Miovas shows a photograph of McHugh Creek. He mentions that McHugh Creek was not a big, messy crime scene. Bonnie was found floating in the waters of the creek, dead. At the top of the cliff, twenty feet upstream from where she was found, was some disturbed vegetation and a leaf with a drop of Bonnie's blood. A single drop. That's it.

I hadn't known about the leaf with the drop of blood on it until more than sixteen years after the murder, when Miovas took over the case. He disclosed to me that they had found the leaf right away, while shooting the initial video of the crime scene. The troopers had withheld that information from me, just as they'd withheld so much else. Alongside my resentment toward the troopers, however, was a sense of relief and excitement. Before, all we had was the DNA sample that showed sex had taken place between my daughter and Kenneth Dion. But the leaf suggested something much bigger. It meant she was already injured before going over the cliff.

Miovas talks about the injuries the troopers discovered when they removed Bonnie from the water. Eleven lacerations, all the way up the back of her head, going in multiple directions. Blood blisters on her knuckles. Abrasions on the side of one hand. Lacerations all over her fingers. He foreshadows the approximate timeline that will later be explained in more detail, suggesting that my daughter was murdered sometime in the early hours of September 28, 1994.

Kenneth Dion sits and stares ahead, wordless. I imagine he is pleased knowing that Miovas isn't at liberty to tell the jury about how he was in and out of jail during the period in question. Dion knows Miovas can't tell the jury about how he broke his parole and was put back in prison. The jury hears only part of the truth.

"The judge has given you instructions, and you're going to be asked to plug the facts in to what you have, use your reason and common sense, and seek the truth in this case, ladies and gentlemen. That's what this process is about. In the end, I'm going to come back before you, and I'm going at that point to argue to you what the case is about. In these scenarios, ladies and gentlemen, you as members of our community, you've all been selected to speak for our community. You speak for Bonnie Craig, you speak for the court system, you speak even for Kenneth Dion, and the state. You speak for everybody. That's your role here. And in the end, I'm going to ask you to speak the truth, and hold this man guilty because he killed Bonnie Craig on September 28, and he is guilty of doing that. I'm going to ask you to hold him accountable. Thank you."

Judge Smith tells the courtroom that the defense needs more than an hour for its opening statement, and we're left with less than that today. We're adjourned until morning.

———————————

The next day, I sit in the same spot on the same wooden bench. The same fifteen individuals take their spots in the jury box. They are strangers, but strangers about whom we know plenty from the voir dire process. The lawyers and the judge assume their familiar places. The man who I'm certain killed my daughter sits expressionless in his pressed shirt and dress pants. He knows that in a few weeks he may no longer be wearing a prison jumpsuit or walking with his hands cuffed together. He has served his time for the armed robbery in New Hampshire that the court will never hear about, and earned his parole.

"Good morning," says Andrew Lambert, lead counsel for the defense. He reminds me a little of Dustin Hoffman. Lambert is a short, slight man who wears an earring and who, when he first started practicing in Anchorage, was known for being the first defense attorney to sport a ponytail. "For seventeen years most of you have heard that Bonnie Craig was murdered and sexually assaulted. Seventeen years later, you're going to learn that Bonnie Craig was not murdered, and she was not sexually assaulted." My father squeezes my arm in support. Samantha's hand squeezes mine a little harder. I am sick to my stomach, repulsed by the thought that they expect anyone to believe Bonnie would have anything to do with this loser. He was a junkie. He was married. He had an infant girl. And they are purposely tarnishing Bonnie's name, making her into a common sleaze. But none of that matters. This is a conversation, and all that does matter is which side of the conversation those people sitting on one side of the courtroom choose to believe.

"What you will learn during this trial is that Bonnie tumbled down a sloped, jagged, rocky cliff at McHugh Creek that's about thirty-five-feet tall, striking her head numerous times. It resulted in eleven lacerations to her head, and one of those lacerations included a skull fracture, caused her to die within about fifteen or twenty minutes of receiving that last skull fracture. What you'll learn during the trial is that Bonnie Craig and Kenneth Dion had sex. You'll learn that they had consensual sex. You'll also learn that there are no witnesses. There's going to be no witnesses and no evidence that's going to present Kenneth Dion's vehicle either along the route Bonnie Craig took that day or at McHugh Creek on September 28, 1994. The state wants you to use logic and common sense to assume because Bonnie Craig had certain events going on in the last few days of her life and Kenneth Dion's DNA was in her vagina, on her underwear and on the outside of her pants, that he must have murdered and raped her. But actually your logic and common sense are going to lead you to that Bonnie accidentally died, and Bonnie had consensual sex with Kenneth Dion."

Like Paul Miovas did yesterday, Lambert takes us through the few details we know about Bonnie's last morning. He talks about Samantha hearing her sister leave. "It's clearly Bonnie. They hear a door slam. They don't hear any voices. They hear footsteps going down the walkway, and that's all they hear. They never hear a car. They don't hear a horn. They don't hear an engine. They don't hear other voices, they don't hear footsteps, anything like that." Lambert mentions that there was one witness to Bonnie's commute that morning, a fifteen-year-old papergirl named Mandesa Byrd who recognized Bonnie from Service High School. Mandesa told the police that she was out delivering newspapers when she saw Bonnie at about 5:20 A.M. walking down Vern Drive. She accurately described Bonnie as wearing a jean jacket and a red shirt.

Then, one by one, Andrew Lambert lists the things that were not seen and cannot be known. He specifically makes note of no one reporting having seen an individual matching Kenneth Dion's description anywhere nearby. "Now, what we don't have Mandesa Byrd seeing, and what we don't have the police knowing, is that at that time as she sees Bonnie walking past down Vern Drive and up Legacy, she does not see a redhead. This man had redder hair [in 1994] than he has now. Mandesa Byrd does not see a redheaded man, at the time would be about a twenty-four-year-old adult, in the neighborhood. What's more important also is that Mandesa Byrd does not see a 1991 black Ford Tempo. That is the car that Kenneth Dion had at the time. She doesn't see either of those."

An Anchorage citizen named Eric Behr on his way to work saw what he thought was a young girl in a blue jacket carrying a backpack, but did not see a redhead or a black Ford Tempo in the area. The driver on Bonnie's bus route said he knew Bonnie but can't recall whether she got on the bus that morning or not. The bus driver on the route a little farther on said he thought somebody matching Bonnie's description got on his bus. But he wasn't sure. Two other witnesses said they saw Bonnie, or someone who looked like Bonnie, talking to two males, both with black hair, driving a gold or yellowish Toyota or Datsun. None of the hikers at McHugh Creek that day who spoke to police reported having seen either a redhead or a 1991 black Ford Tempo.

After putting in the minds of the jurors the things that weren't seen, Lambert then lists the things that were seen, so that he can use them as evidence to contradict the state's timeline, which suggests that Bonnie was murdered early in the morning. In particular he cites the original testimony of Dr. Arndt von Hippel, the retired surgeon and a regular jogger through McHugh Creek, who said he saw Bonnie bounding down the trail steps around ten in the morning on September 28, with another girl and two males, neither of whom were Kenneth Dion. As Lambert speaks, I remember sitting in Dr. von Hippel's house a couple of years after the murder, sipping tea and listening to him tell me that he'd seen a girl he was sure was Bonnie during his morning jog through McHugh Creek on the morning of September 28, 1994. At the time, I'd considered it potentially valuable information. Now, it's information that might help the defense's case.

"Dr. von Hippel described her hair as being kind of short and brownish," says Lambert. "And when asked what she was wearing, he said she was wearing a blue denim jacket, which she was. When asked did she have anything on her collar, he said, you know, there might have been, you know, some of those denim jackets have sort of a fleece collar. I remember something whitish around her collar. Bonnie had a white scarf on. When asked what color shirt she had on, he said I can't remember the shirt color. But what kind of pants did she have on? She had on like white jeans or khaki pants. Bonnie Craig had on white Zena jeans. What kinds of shoes did she have on? She had on either whitish kind of tennis, hiking shoes or something that's sort of a hiking thing, but it seemed appropriate for hiking. Bonnie was wearing white Nike tennis shoes. Dr. von Hippel described Bonnie's clothing because Dr. von Hippel saw Bonnie alive, well, and happy at 10:00 A.M."

———

As Andrew Lambert describes the investigation conducted by the troopers at the crime scene, all the fear and frustration I felt nearly seventeen years ago comes back in full force. The troopers searched for three and a half hours, he notes, and found nothing but some slip or scuff marks and a leaf with a drop of blood on it, neither of which were ever photographed. Video of the crime scene was shot, but then lost. These were bad mistakes, Andrew Lambert admits— the unfortunate result of an investigation led by a deputy who shouldn't have been in charge. The guy who should have been in charge, the trooper in charge of that unit, Sergeant Mike Marrs, had been out of town that day. Sergeant Marrs had had to assign supervision of the scene to a younger deputy, Corporal Robert Baty. And Corporal Baty had assigned another deputy, Curt Harris, to the scene. Andrew Lambert doesn't wish to put down Detective Harris. He just wants the jury to know that almost nothing was done right, and as a result, any evidence that might have been of value is, sadly, not available.

This information is all new to me. I knew only that Sergeant Marrs had been out of town at the time of the murder and that responsibility had been delegated to others. Until now, I never knew the names of those who'd carried out the examination of the scene.

As Lambert calls into question every aspect of the procedure, my horror resurfaces. I feel waves of dread that the initial investigation—or the lack thereof—will make it impossible for us to get a conviction now. Lambert doesn't even mention everything

I know is missing, like the original interviews that were supposed to have been recorded but were not, instead yielding a series of blank tapes.

What we're left with, Lambert tells the jurors, is a series of witnesses who saw no redhead and no 1991 black Ford Tempo. We're left with no drag marks, no tire tracks, no signs of ligature. The police searched the surrounding trails, he tells the jurors. They searched outhouses. No footprints, no hair, no fingernail scrapings. They searched the culverts from Potter to Girdwood. No clothing, no fibers. There is evidence that Bonnie and Kenneth Dion had sex. There is evidence that Bonnie fell from the cliff. And there is Dr. von Hippel, says Lambert, who saw Bonnie "happy, joyful, having a good time with two guys and a girl that are not that guy over there."

Andrew Lambert gestures toward Kenneth Dion, who continues staring forward. I hear Samantha whisper "Shhh" in my ear. I realize I've begun to cry.

———————

Lambert expertly tells the jurors plenty while telling them nothing. That's the point of conducting an effective defense, after all: as Judge Smith said in his opening instructions, it is not the responsibility of the defense to prove innocence. They need only create doubt.

We know Kenneth Dion's sperm was found inside Bonnie, Lambert says, but we have no way of knowing exactly how long it was there. We have one drop of blood, he says, where we would expect blood everywhere. We have injuries that imply a beating with a weapon like a tire iron, yet we have no weapon. We have a number of experts making guesses that amount to nothing.

And nothing is all the defense needs.

"So, ladies and gentlemen, at the end of the day, you're going to have no choice in this case not only to find Ken not guilty, but to tell everybody here he's innocent. She died accidentally. She was not sexually assaulted. We're sorry, everybody, for the last seventeen years, but you made a mistake. Thank you."

11

Samantha is the first witness to be called by the prosecution. ADA Paul Miovas asks her to spell her name for the court and confirm that she works for the Alaska Police Department as a 911 dispatcher and is Bonnie's little sister. Samantha sits upright and says these things with pride.

We know what course her testimony will take and what Miovas's purpose is in calling her. He wants the jury to hear from the person whom Bonnie was closest to, the little sister she cared for so deeply and with whom she shared her secrets. He asks her about our complicated family life, Bonnie's dedication to school and to her siblings. He knows Samantha is more than happy to speak of her sister's virtues.

He asks her about every detail of Bonnie's routine. He wants the jury to get the full picture of Bonnie's dedication to her family, her friends, her boyfriend, and her studies. He knows that's all he has. So he pushes hard, ensuring that, through Samantha's eyes, the fifteen strangers in the jury box will come to understand the nature of the girl who was murdered in cold blood. When Miovas is done asking his exhaustive questions, Judge Smith calls a ten-minute break.

———

Defense attorney Andrew Lambert wastes no time in his cross-examination of Samantha.

"Are you married?" he says.

"No."

"No, you're not married?"

"I am not married."

"Okay. I thought you had been married and . . ."

"I had been."

"Okay. So you're divorced now."

"That's correct."

"Okay. I wanted to make sure because I heard you say Campbell was the last name and I thought you had a different last name, and I wanted to make sure I addressed you correctly."

I know what he's doing. I suspect that he couldn't care less if he addresses her correctly, that he's simply trying to cast Samantha in a negative light by mentioning her divorce. He is indirectly telling the jury that she may not be reliable.

Lambert asks Samantha to confirm our complex living arrangements at the time—Jason in his own apartment; Gary and I doing week-on, week-off with Adam and Samantha; Jim's kids also living in our house. Lambert's questions paint a picture of a family in disarray.

"And Bonnie turned eighteen I think on March 30th of 1994?"

"That's correct."

"And about a week after she turned eighteen, she moved out of the house, didn't she?"

"Yes."

"She moved in with her stepfather, Gary."

"That's correct."

Lambert takes Samantha through more back-and-forth about the relationship between Gary and Bonnie, then says, "All right. And some of that time Bonnie was kind of off doing her own things, too. She's eighteen years old and she's out doing other stuff, too." He keeps Samantha on the stand for a long time, using all the same details that Miovas had used to paint a picture of coherence and routine but instead depicting it as one of chaos and inconsistency.

I look at the faces of the jurors as Lambert finishes. I have no idea what they're thinking.

Judge Smith adjourns the courtroom, telling us it's as good a time as any to break for the day before resuming witness testimony tomorrow morning. This will be the pattern for the next few weeks. Knowing we have little in the way of hard evidence, almost all of the state's questioning goes to try to show the jury who Bonnie was. Nothing in the trial will prove that Kenneth Dion killed my daughter. Instead, it is up to the prosecution to convince the jury that a girl like Bonnie could only have ended up at McHugh Creek with a man like Kenneth Dion against her own will. They will call people to the stand to testify that Bonnie was a good girl who wouldn't stray, and the defense will work to undermine and poke holes in their stories. Typical defense tactics, but I can barely stand to see them in action.

The next day, the prosecution calls Bonnie's high school boyfriend, Cameron Miyasaki, to the stand. Cameron is thirty-four now, married. He walks to the stand in a dark suit and light-gray tie, looking somber. I have not seen him since Bonnie's funeral, nearly seventeen years ago. As he is sworn in and begins to answer Jenna Gruenstein's questions, I hear the same soft-spoken, kind-hearted young man Bonnie first introduced to us. He still wears his black hair parted in the middle, just like when he was seventeen. Underneath his thinning hair and slightly rounder face, he's still the same twinkly-eyed boy I first met when Bonnie started dating him in eleventh grade. Cameron was always quiet and polite, and it seemed clear that he cared deeply for Bonnie. They had actually first met as grade-schoolers, when we lived briefly in California. It was chance that brought both families to Alaska, and both kids to Service High School in Anchorage. I enjoyed the way her eyes would light up whenever she talked about him. As a mother, you don't care about much else.

Assistant District Attorney Jenna Gruenstein asks Cameron questions about his relationship with Bonnie. Cameron talks about their first date, a movie at Fireweed Theater. They fell for each other quickly, he says. They were very similar, and their connection was an easy, natural one. Gruenstein shows him a picture from the spring of 1994. Cameron smiles and says, "I remember this picture." It was before he moved to California for college, he says. They were picnicking in Portage, on the Turnagain Arm, forty-five minutes outside of Anchorage.

"On your way back from Portage, did you do anything?" Gruenstein asks.

"We stopped at McHugh Creek."

"Was there a particular reason?" she says.

"No," Cameron answers. "I think we knew the spot and I don't remember why exactly we stopped there. We sat on some rock and watched the sun and just talked."

Cameron tells the courtroom how the two of them would talk

all the time, about everything. About how they didn't stop talking, even when he was thousands of miles away.

When Gruenstein declines to ask Cameron further questions, Andrew Lambert pounces. He knows that our case rests on Bonnie's character and little else, and he wants the maximum possible reaction out of Cameron in order to cast the maximum possible doubt in the minds of the jurors about Bonnie. Cameron is in a nostalgic haze, the memories of his sweet relationship with Bonnie obviously preoccupying him. Lambert's only aim is to let Cameron know that Bonnie might not have been the girlfriend he thought her to be. To that end, the defense attorney cites excerpts from a letter Cameron wrote to Bonnie from Berkeley telling her he didn't want to ruin her college experience by forcing her to maintain the long-distance relationship.

"It's my understanding that you were unaware that Bonnie had exchanged phone numbers with another gentleman and had repeatedly been calling him, asking him to go out," Lambert says to Cameron.

"Yeah. I didn't know," Cameron says in response. He looks stung.

"And that you knew that Bonnie had gone to play pool one night with Lynn Catchpole at Hotshots." Lynn was Bonnie's best friend at the time. Hotshots was a local pool hall.

"I don't remember that now, but I see it here."

"But Bonnie failed to tell you about the three men she was playing pool with until the wee hours of the morning?"

"I don't remember."

"There's nothing in the transcript where she described playing pool with three men till the wee hours of the morning."

"No. No."

"And Bonnie didn't tell you about a study group that she had set up for Monday night with two other guys and a girl."

"Not to my recollection."

Lambert goes on like this, citing every example he can think of in which Bonnie was in the presence of other males outside of school or work. It doesn't matter whether they were friends with whom she was hanging out, fellow students with whom she was studying, or coworkers. Lambert just wants Cameron to picture Bonnie with other guys, and he wants the jury to absorb the reaction.

He even focuses on the intimacy between Cameron and Bonnie, asking questions about their sexual relationship: when they had sex, how often, where. I don't see the point, other than to try to paint my daughter as a sexual creature, and I don't understand why the judge is allowing Lambert to go down this path without demanding to know his purpose in it.

In her cross, Gruenstein tries to reverse the damage, directing focus back to the solidity of Cameron and Bonnie's relationship. She points out that Cameron still has the ring Bonnie gave him when they were going out. "How long did you wear that for?" she asks him.

"Years," Cameron says, smiling and wiping away tears. "We were very serious about one another," he said.

"What were your feelings toward her?" says Gruenstein.

Cameron smiles self-consciously, swivels in the chair, and looks to the floor. It is clear he's picturing her, remembering. He sniffles, tries to speak, then exhales. Collects himself again. Shakes his head once, sniffles a couple of more times. After thirty seconds, he finally squeezes out the words.

"I loved her . . ."

He tries to choke out the word *forever*.

At the break, Paul Miovas rushes over to me and says there has been an unexpected development—a big one. They have found the video of the crime scene, thought to have been lost long ago. Someone at the Alaska State Troopers' office, after reading an article in the *Anchorage Daily News* about the trial and Lambert's opening statement, knew where the crime scene video was and retrieved it.

It's good news and bad news, says Miovas. The good news is that it could help us counter the argument that the police mismanaged the investigation; the bad news is it could be grounds for a mistrial. Hold your breath, he tells me.

In the meantime, the trial resumes. Miovas briefly calls to the stand a man named Robby Martin. In September 1994, Robby was seventeen years old, and one of the members of the study group Bonnie had arranged on the Monday evening before her death. The other members of the group were Marvat Obeidi and Justin Devlin.

Robby testifies about a conversation that occurred afterward as he and Justin gave Bonnie a ride home. She talked about her boyfriend in California, Robby recalls, stating that she'd seemed very devoted to him. She said she wanted to get some schooling done at UAA and then figure out how to move to California. They were definitely serious, Robby says. Seemed like a nice relationship.

Lambert declines the opportunity to cross-examine.

Bonnie had many friends. She drew people in. One of her closest friends at the time of her death was a lovely girl named Lynn Catchpole, who'd also attended Service High School.

Today, Lynn Catchpole is Lynn Witte, and as she approaches the stand, I marvel at how the changes in her are as profound as the changes in Cameron are slight. She has grown from a teenage girl into a thirty-four-year-old woman with a family of her own.

"There's been reference to you possibly being Bonnie's best friend," Miovas says. "Would you agree that you're her best friend?"

"Yes."

"At that point in her life."

"Yes."

"What was Bonnie's long-term plan as far as Cameron living in California?"

"I know that she had wanted to go down to California and be with him and go to school there."

Lynn testifies about the event Andrew Lambert referred to, the late-night pool game. Lambert had achieved what he wanted, freezing Cameron while at the same time starting to build a negative portrait of Bonnie as a wayward girl, but the night Lynn describes is much more innocent. She said that she and Bonnie had gone to a school dance and then went to the local pool hall. While they were there, three guys approached them asking if they could split the table. All three were in the U.S. Army, out on a weekend pass. Lynn later dated one of them.

"I want you to explain, in your terms, the dynamic that existed between those three guys and you and Bonnie while you're shooting pool."

"Obviously, I was the single one since she wasn't. They were, I mean, they were very nice. They were just talking to us. They weren't hitting on her, but they were talking to her, you know, and obviously she had a boyfriend. I kept mentioning Cameron and they got the hint."

Lynn answers a few more questions, clarifying that Bonnie had not been flirting with the guys, was not interested. Miovas asks

Lynn about Bonnie's relationship with Cameron. She tells the court that Bonnie couldn't wait to e-mail him on her days at school; that she was figuring out how to install an early version of Instant Messenger in order to have ongoing dialogue with him; that she was serious about her plans to be with him in the future. Miovas asks if Lynn ever went to McHugh Creek with Bonnie, or if Bonnie ever talked about it as a place she liked to visit, and Lynn says no. Miovas points out Kenneth Dion and asks Lynn, Bonnie's best friend, if she has ever seen him or heard his name prior to the trial. No, Lynn says, she hasn't.

Miovas, having done his job, sits down. It is a game of cat and mouse. One side tries to build her up; the other tries to drag her down. As Bonnie's closest confidant and most frequent companion before she was murdered, Lynn has demonstrated that Bonnie was loyal to her boyfriend and serious about her future, not the promiscuous eighteen-year-old the defense would like to portray.

Judge Smith invites Andrew Lambert to begin his cross. Lambert stands, buttons his jacket, and takes a few steps toward the stand. He looks at Lynn and says, "You weren't with Bonnie on September 28, 1994, were you?"

"No, I was not."

"So you can't say this man murdered her, can you?"

"No, I cannot," says Lynn, her eyes immediately misting.

"You can't say this man raped her, can you?"

Lynn's breath catches as she fights the onrush of tears. "No, I can't."

"You can't say this man kidnapped her, can you?"

"No, I can't." The sadness unleashes itself. Lynn begins to sob.

"That's all the questions I have," says Lambert, and he sits back down.

Next to be called is my ex-husband Gary, whose most recent transfer for BP has been to Oman. He has flown across the world to testify for Bonnie and to help support Jason, Adam, and Samantha.

Miovas asks Gary about his business trip to New Orleans, the one he'd left for on the Friday before Bonnie's death. He asks him about the sailing trip to Florida that Jim and I took to be at Ken and Valeri's wedding. He asks Gary to confirm that Bonnie would sometimes watch her younger siblings, Adam and Samantha, alone and that he trusted her. He asks Gary to confirm that Bonnie had neither a car nor a driver's license.

I get the feeling Miovas is scrambling. He asks Gary over and over about Bonnie's routine, her diligence in taking the bus, her distress on the rare occasions when she'd be late for class and need a ride from him. He asks Gary about Bonnie's blue backpack, her key ring. Gary also mentions the wallet and purse Bonnie would usually carry with her. Now I get where he's going.

"Okay. We're going to hear from some of the investigators about this, Mr. Campbell, but I want to ask you. Of the items you listed just now, and I heard you say a blue backpack, a purse, a wallet, the Texan Instruments calculator, books, and a key ring, do you know what, if any of those items, were ever found at your house that the police never recovered?"

"Never found any of them," Gary says.

"Okay. So all of those items we listed there, completely gone; we never found any of them."

"I have no idea where they're at. They were never found at my house."

Miovas asks Gary the same questions he asked Samantha about the days and nights leading to Bonnie's murder. In particular, he solicits details about Gary's return from his business trip a day earlier than expected. Gary takes him through it all—how he came home, gave the kids the gifts he'd bought them, and how he woke up at seven the next morning to find Adam and Samantha still home but Bonnie already gone, which was normal. Gary went to work, then picked Samantha up from soccer practice after school. He was not alarmed by Bonnie's absence because he didn't expect her home from school until later in the evening. It was at around ten P.M. that Alaska State Troopers came to his house.

"I don't want to drag you through this too much, but tell me the circumstances," Miovas says. "As troopers show up at your door, what happens? How does this thing take place?"

"They call me out to the porch and I close the door and they tell me that Bonnie has been found and that she's dead."

"And where are Adam and Samantha when this is happening?"

"They're inside the house, I believe, sitting on the stairs."

"What was your reaction when they told you this?"

"I was devastated. I recall my legs giving out. I ended up on my knees."

After confirming that Gary had never seen or heard of Kenneth Dion prior to the trial, Miovas concludes his direct. On the surface, he seems to have accomplished little in calling Gary to the stand, but I recognize that this strategy is the only option available. He is going to bring up as many people as possible who knew Bonnie, from her boyfriend to her father and sister to her friends, and slowly paint a composite picture of her for the jury. The prosecution's questions vary little, since what jurors need to be convinced of is, at bottom, simple: that Bonnie was a good girl. A loyal girlfriend. Someone who had her head on straight, kept to her routine, and who wouldn't have had any spare time, let alone inclination, in the last seventy-two hours of her life to have had a secret tryst with the dead-eyed brute sitting a few feet away.

In cross, Andrew Lambert asks Gary what he knew of the conversations and e-mails between Bonnie and Cameron in the weeks leading up to her death. Gary says he doesn't know the specifics, only what Bonnie told him, but he recalls Bonnie's frustration at Cameron's practical side coming out and telling her not to come to California just to be with him.

"Now, were you aware in the week before Bonnie's death that she was calling—that she had exchanged her phone number with a young man named Joe Barr and had called him numerous times, asking him out?"

"I'm not aware of that," says Gary.

I'm not aware of it, either. In fact, I've never even heard the name Joe Barr before. What I do know is that Bonnie had lots of friends, both male and female, and teenagers spend a lot of time on the phone making plans to go out. The blatancy of Lambert's attempt to smear Bonnie's character makes me crazy with indignation.

"Are you aware that Bonnie actually called him on Saturday, September twenty-fourth, to talk to him about going out?"

"No, I'm not aware."

"I would assume you're not aware that on September twenty-seventh, the night before she died, that he called her that night?"

"Uh-uh."

"Or that she called him that night?"

"I'm not aware of . . ."

"Asking her out? Now all of these missing items of Bonnie's we've talked about, right?"

"Yes."

"You're not aware—you can't say there's any connection to Kenneth Dion having any of those missing items, can you? You have no personal knowledge of that, do you?"

"I have no personal knowledge."

"And whether or not you've heard or seen Kenneth Dion prior to 2006 doesn't mean that Bonnie may have known or seen Kenneth Dion in 1994, does it?"

"No, it does not."

"Thank you. That's all the questions I have."

Miovas questions witness after witness at length in the effort to portray Bonnie as a decent, responsible girl who couldn't have had a connection to Kenneth Dion, only to have Lambert pose a handful of questions in response that cast doubt on all of it. This was my worst fear, and it's coming true. You can talk about a person's character and their habits until you're blue in the face. But a trial, and its outcome, comes down to what you can prove.

Jenna Gruenstein calls to the stand Wendy Goodrich, a former coworker of Bonnie's from Sam's Club. With Wendy, Gruenstein keeps her questions simple; she asks about Bonnie's personality, her studies, even her hairstyle. She has Wendy confirm what she'd told troopers when they'd first interviewed her, how in September of 1994, Bonnie had babysat Wendy's two young kids the Saturday before she was murdered and that Wendy gave Bonnie a ride to work the following morning.

"Do you recall when you brought Bonnie to work with you on Sunday, did you also work on Sunday?" Gruenstein asks.

"Yes, I did."

"Do you recall anything about Bonnie that day?"

"She was just really ready to go to work and bubbly," Wendy says. "Like always."

"No further questions."

A murder trial is like a boxing match. I think we've won this round, but the members of the jury are the only ones who know how they're scoring it.

Jenna Gruenstein next calls Marvat Obeidi, a former fellow student at UAA who was working toward a degree in social work at the same time Bonnie was studying psychology. Since both were in the social sciences, some of their classes overlapped. Marvat took a psychology class with Bonnie, she says, and a Spanish class with Justin Devlin.

Gruenstein asks Marvat about the study session she had referred to in her original testimony to the troopers, the session that took place on the evening of September 26, 1994. Justin Devlin was one of the people there, Marvat says, as well as a friend of Justin's (Robby Martin, who had already testified) and Bonnie Craig.

"When you were studying," Gruenstein says, "how prepared did Bonnie seem for this test?" The test she is referring to was scheduled for two days later, September 28. Bonnie would never show up to take it.

"Oh, she was very prepared. I remember she was very calm and collected and just from what I saw and what I observed, she seemed to be a really good student, just head in the books, and was just on a mission to get a good grade in the class."

Judge Smith asks defense attorney Andrew Lambert if he has any questions for cross. Lambert stands slowly and raises his chin slightly. He doesn't step out from behind the defense table.

Lambert looks at Marvat. "You don't have any idea what Bonnie was doing on September 28, 1994, do you?"

"No."

"You don't have any idea why she might not have been in school that day?"

"No, I don't."

"Okay. Thank you."

You throw punches; you take punches. Back and forth it goes. You try to be the last one standing.

Jennifer Larsen, née Braunschweig, had been in her early twenties and had only lived in Anchorage for a few months when she went to McHugh Creek on September 28, 1994. I'd met Jennifer once before this trial. While I was at the IRS office downtown, standing in line, a man had approached me and said, "Excuse me—are you Bonnie Craig's mom?" When I told him I was, he hesitated, then said, "My friend is the one who found her body."

I asked him for the friend's number, then called. Jennifer had introduced herself and, with sadness and compassion, told me the entire story of that afternoon. She told me that, looking back, she was upset with herself for two reasons. First, she'd been taking pictures during her hike, but when she saw Bonnie's body, she freaked out, and stopped doing so unthinkingly. Second, she felt she should have gone down into the water, where Bonnie lay. Instead, she went to hail the troopers. When they arrived, they asked her to help put up yellow police tape to block off the area.

I had thanked her and told her she hadn't done anything wrong. More pictures wouldn't have changed anything, I told her, and her going down to the water wouldn't have, either. In fact, it could have put her in danger. But Bonnie would have appreciated what she had done, I said, particularly the way she had sprung into action. Getting help had been the right thing to do.

"I was out exploring," recalls Jennifer on the stand. She now lives in Lynnwood, Washington, and has flown the four hours here to Anchorage to testify. "It was one of my first times out since I'd been here exploring on my own. Everyone kept telling me to get out and see Alaska, so I took a drive down to Portage and stopped in Girdwood and then was on my way back into town, and I decided to stop off at the creek and explore a little bit."

Paul Miovas hands Jennifer a laser pointer and brings up to the screen an aerial photo of McHugh Creek from September 1994. He asks her to take the jury through her route that day—where she had parked, the trail she'd taken past the dirt lot, past a hairpin turn that leads to the top of the cliff. She had to peek around a rock to get a look at the lovely waterfall, she says, but when she followed the waterfall down to the water below, she spotted something unexpected, and horrifying.

"I think a lot of people's natural inclination is to maybe go touch somebody," says Miovas, "see what's going on, see if they can help, render aid, that sort of thing. Did you do any of that?"

"No," says Jennifer.

"Was it pretty obvious to you that the person was beyond the rendering aid part?"

"Yeah. I actually considered it, but I didn't see any movement and it—the person looked deceased, and I didn't have a very good feeling at the time, so I started to go call for 911 and then I decided to go back one more time and check, but again, I saw no movement and the fact that the face was in the water, I figured at that point they're—it was too late, obviously."

Cell phones were rare in 1994, so Jennifer went in search of a payphone. "I just got in my car and went to the first place I could find a phone. I didn't really feel comfortable getting people at the park, even though there were people there. I just felt like it might not be a good idea to have other people down there, so I—the first place I saw was the Potter weigh station, so I went there and asked them if I could use their phone and I—to call 911."

"And you said that there were—and I want to make sure that I don't misstate this—there were maybe four or five cars in the parking lot when you were there originally?"

"Yeah."

"Can you describe your car in the parking lot?"

"Yeah. I drove an older '84 Honda Prelude. It was navy blue."

"Okay. Do you remember anything about any of the other cars that were parked there?"

"No."

Miovas asks Jennifer if she's an outdoor-type person. No, she says, she's a city girl.

"You hike any kind of, I guess, sketchy trails or anything like that?"

"Not normally, no. I was really nervous because everyone kept telling me to be careful of bear and moose and everything else. I think I had heard afterward that there was maulings and stuff."

"The trail you hiked along at the bottom of the cliff area, did anything concern you at all, or make you feel like it was a dangerous trail?"

"No. It was pretty flat, as you can see."

"And the ones—how about the ones up top that you walked on? Anything dangerous or treacherous about those trails?"

"No, it was just flat from what I can recall, just flat dirt surface."

I don't know whether I'm smiling or crying. It might be both. Finally the topic has been raised—my daughter, an athletic girl, the first girl on the Service High School wrestling team, wouldn't have accidentally slipped off of a flat trail and stumbled off a cliff-side. Anger rises in me again. It isn't enough for this monster to have stolen my daughter's life. He isn't even human enough to admit his deeds and accept the seventy-five-year plea deal. Instead, he has to drag Bonnie's name through the mud in order to try to save his own hide.

"Did you ever go back to McHugh Creek after that day?" Miovas asks.

"No."

Miovas passes the witness to the defense.

"It was the first time you were out exploring alone?" Andrew Lambert asks.

"Yes."

"Turned out to be not such a good exploration, right?"

"Yes."

"Now as you get out of your car there and you walked across the road here, and let's just focus on the road, you didn't see any trails of blood along the roadway, did you?"

"Not that I recall, no."

And so it goes—Lambert repeatedly asking if she'd seen blood anywhere, Jennifer admitting that she hadn't; him pointing out all the areas of the trail that weren't flat, her saying she didn't remember.

I realize I'm staring at Jennifer, trying to will her to resist Lambert's manipulations.

"I'm sorry," Lambert says at one point, after taking Jennifer through a long discussion about the trail. "I'm not trying to be a pain."

Oh, give it a rest, I think. That's exactly his intent. But I worry that the jury may be buying it—all of it. Lambert tends to make self-deprecating jokes about his lack of ability with the laser pointer and computer, which makes some of the jury members smile. I feel sick.

"I'm going to back up, down to the parking area a little bit," Lambert says after a while. He's on a roll, and I believe he's enjoying it. "I think you said that there were four or five cars there. You described yours, but the . . ."

"That's from what I can remember. I mean, that's . . ."

"Right. And the other ones you can't describe?"

"No."

"So you cannot tell this jury there was a 1991 black Ford Tempo there?"

"No."

"Okay. Now, when you went hiking, it's fair to say you never saw a redhead hiking around there?"

"No."

"And when you were hiking, you didn't hear anybody—you didn't hear an argument anywhere?"

"Not that I can remember."

"You didn't hear any fighting that was going on?"

"Not that I can remember."

"You didn't hear anybody yell or scream?"

"Not that I can remember. There was a lot of people, so there was a lot of voices. I couldn't—I couldn't tell you."

"And as you got out and you're in this upper parking lot, and you're in the upper parking lot up there, in that area that you're walking around, the time you're up there, you don't see any blood trails or blood drips on the ground up there?"

"Not that I can remember. I don't think I would have thought it was blood, but I don't know that I would have, you know."

"Sure. I mean, but if you had seen something sort of reddish in a drip line, you know . . ."

"Surely, yeah. No. No."

Stop agreeing with him, I think. *Stop it.*

"Okay. And then this flat area up here where you were, going in and out of the trees, that area, when you were up there, you didn't see any ground disturbance, as if someone had had a fight up there? There's nothing in your statement about it, is there?"

"No."

"Nothing at your grand jury testimony about it, is there?"

"No."

"You didn't see anything that looked like a body had been dragged across the ground?"

"No."

"There was nothing in the dirt indicating anything had been dragged, right?"

"No."

"There was nothing indicating that debris had been moved because a body had been dragged through it, like leaves and twigs and things like that?"

"Not that, I mean, I wouldn't have looked for that, so I—I can't really speak to that. No."

"You didn't see anything that looked like someone had been trying to cover up the ground, as if something had happened there and they had piled things on top of it to make it look like you couldn't see it?"

"No. I . . ."

I want to stand up and say *You've made your point.* But Lambert isn't done. He points out that Jennifer Larsen was asked by the first trooper at the scene to help put up police tape, since no one else had arrived yet. The jury hears a very persuasive story: a dead girl was found in a creek at the bottom of a cliff, no signs of foul play nearby, followed by a highly unprofessional crime scene investigation. My heart sinks.

Miovas takes a few minutes to do his cross on Jennifer Larsen, and, at least to my ears, accomplishes nothing. He asks her more questions about the route she took up the hiking trail and the angle she had to use to see Bonnie. He elicits a few more details on the help she gave putting up the police tape. He mentions the fact that Jennifer at first thought the body was that of a man. I don't know what purpose any of this is meant to achieve, and I can see in the faces of the jury members that they don't know, either.

———————————

It is getting late in the day when ADA Paul Miovas calls Elaine Enriquez to the stand. Elaine was a few years older than Bonnie, but they'd moved in similar circles—from Service High School, which Elaine also attended; to Sam's Club, where she also worked; to UAA, where she and Bonnie had a theater class together and took the same psychology class, though at different times.

Miovas asks Elaine about a set of psychology notes she and Bonnie had exchanged on the night of September 27, 1994.

"What I'd like you to do is tell the jury a little bit about that," Miovas says. "When it was, and what you guys did."

"It was in the evening, and I had asked her about a study guide that I needed and she had asked me about my notes, and so we made the switch-off, and after work we agreed to go to [photocopy them], and then I was going to drop her off back home."

"And after you did that, did you go take the test the next morning?"

"Yeah. I took the test at the theater, yeah."

"And did you expect Bonnie to show up for the test?"

"Yes. And she didn't, and that weirded me out. She never showed up, and she's not like that."

"So you had exchanged notes the night before the test and went to take the test the next day, and she didn't show up for the test."

"Correct."

"And we have heard from another student that this is about midterms time during the school year?"

"I think so."

"All right. So you had, you said, a lot of tests. You had tests in almost all your classes in this time period?"

"I believe so. I think we were trying to close out a semester or something like that."

"All right."

"So we were all busy."

"And in fact, do you remember telling the troopers that you thought Bonnie might have had five tests coming up?"

"I remember saying that she had a lot of tests coming up."

"Okay. And you did describe her to the troopers as being stressed, and I want to make sure we're clear about this. But based on your perception and your interaction with her, what was the stress about?"

"College."

Miovas is trying to establish that there would be no way Bonnie would go out for a hike on her own that day, with or without anyone else. She was prepared and ready for her tests. He wants the jury to know that she was focused solely on her exams and not on having rendezvous with strange men.

Defense attorney Andrew Lambert has no questions for Elaine Enriquez, and Judge Smith releases the jury until the next day,

Tuesday, the thirty-first of May. "Remember, no research," he warns them. "You can't go to any of the sites. You shouldn't be forming any decision. Obviously you've only got part of the information. You need to wait until you have all of it."

Yes, I think to myself. *Please. Please wait until you have all of it.*

12

Happy memories of Bonnie come flooding to my mind.

I remember, when she was not yet two years old, buying her a wool coat with a red hood and white brim. It is warm and snug, and her eyes light up when she sees herself in her bedroom mirror with this new accessory. Wanting an excuse to take her out in it, I bring her along on a shopping trip, a shared excursion that always makes us both happy.

We sing songs together on the way home, and I unstrap her from her car seat and carry her inside, bouncing her up and down in my arms. She runs her hands over the fuzzy collar of her coat, her eyes twinkling with enjoyment, and I press my nose into her belly, making her laugh.

I open the front door and plunk her down inside the entrance, near our Christmas tree, which we'd decorated not only with tinsel and baubles but also fun items like chocolate ornaments. I return to the car for the groceries, and when I come back inside, Bonnie is standing there, looking up at me with a funny expression. Her hand is extended, and in her fingers she still grips the chocolate treat that she'd reached for . . . not realizing it was tied to the tree, which now lies horizontal on the floor. The mix of shock and innocence on her face makes me laugh with joy and love. I scoop her up, glad that her coat protected her and amused that she is a chocoholic just like her mother. We put the tree back up, and she eats the chocolate. She keeps her coat on the whole day.

I recall her at age five, full of energy and spirit, leaping out of bed every morning to hug and kiss me and ask me to play with her. We do puzzles, read books, play board games together. When she sees the bump in my stomach growing, she is overjoyed. She asks me if it's going to be a little brother or a little sister. I tell her I don't know, but she doesn't truly care. Adam arrives in the spring of 1981, healthy and round. Bonnie treats him like her own private Cabbage Patch Doll, cooing to him, tickling him, feeding him, teaching him everything she knows in her innocence. She tells me she wants to help change his diapers. I respond that she does enough for him and she doesn't need to take on that responsibility. They can be pretty nasty, I tell her with a smile. She doesn't care. She gets right in there. She takes it on. The next spring, she gets a little sister to go with her little brother. Two little siblings to play with, teach things to, and take care of. She dotes on them happily. I never have to ask.

Bonnie is only six, and I don't take her to movies often. But eight-year-old Jason has convinced me to take them both to see this one, about the cute little alien with the glowing finger and the boy in overalls who discovers him. They sit beside each other and stare in wonder as the boy and his siblings hide E.T. from their parents and try to help him get back to where he came from. Bonnie's big blue eyes grow even wider as the boy and his brother's friends ride their bikes across the face of the moon to get the innocent creature to the place where he can return safely home. In her fascination, she doesn't realize that Reese's Pieces are spilling out of the little orange bag now tilting in her hand. Jason notices, and laughs at her with affection.

We have just moved to Sugarland, Texas—Gary's latest transfer. I make it a goal to find a church with lots of kids, a Sunday school, and people our age. We start to develop a Sunday ritual of trying out different churches. On one Sunday, we end up at a small church on a property that looks like a big plantation. As we walk through the doors and sit in the pews, I notice there are no other kids, and everyone looks like a senior citizen. However, following the service, we are surrounded by parishioners. Within minutes, we feel like family.

We return to the church every Sunday. Bonnie and Jason both have their first communion there. They kneel at the altar, the bishop in front of them, saying prayers. He reaches for his miter, his headdress, and as he puts it on, a ribbon falls down the center of his face. We and the other congregants realize it's on backward. Both Bonnie and Jason break into giggles, and it becomes contagious to the rest of the congregation. The bishop tries to keep things serious, but it is too late. My son and daughter look at each other and share laughter.

I have just moved into my place up on the hillside. It's the last day of March in 1993, just past midnight. I run into Bonnie's room.

"Quick!" I said. "Grab your coat and boots! We need to get out of here! There's an earthquake coming!"

Bonnie jumps out of her bed and rushes to grab her coat and boots. I race behind her, grinning. We run out the back door to the deck. She is putting her boots on in midstride when my giggles get too loud, and she turns. "What's so funny?"

I finally burst out laughing. "Since when do we get warnings about earthquakes?"

Bonnie notices the clock on the wall and sees that March 31 has become April 1. "How could you do that!" she says, but she's already smiling. "I was really scared!"

My laughter comes harder. Soon, she breaks, too. We laugh together until the sun comes up.

Gary and I have split, and Bonnie has moved into the new home on Lone Tree Drive with me. It isn't an easy period for any of us, but the kids are handling it as best they can, and I have to admit I'm enjoying my private time with the little girl who has become a young woman before my eyes.

One of the first boxes we unpack contains the CD player. Bonnie knows that Miami Sound Machine is one of my favorite bands. When I'm not looking, she plugs the CD player into the wall. As I continue to pull out items, I hear the opening horns of "Conga," and I turn and smile. Bonnie is dancing and singing, making me giggle. She's getting half of the lyrics wrong. I join her, and we follow each other in an unbridled two-person conga line through the empty living room, the kitchen, and repeating the circle again and again as the upbeat music plays. I feel young and invigorated, and close to my daughter in a way I've never felt before. We sing and dance and perform our silly moves throughout the house, and the only thing I can think is, *I wish I could make this moment last forever.*

I walk into the Service High School gym preparing to hate what I see. I don't even like watching strangers wrestle. Now I have to watch my little girl do it. I am here because Bonnie tells me how much she enjoys the sport, and I know how proud she is that she's the first girl in the school's history to be on the team. But I don't like the sport; I find it somehow distasteful and grotesque.

As I enter, I see that there are three matches going on simultaneously—Bonnie has told me that they represent different weight classes. I take a seat on the bleachers and wait for her turn. I spot her talking and laughing with her teammates, enjoying the atmosphere. She sees me and waves excitedly. I wave back.

The match in front of her ends, and her coach sends her in. Bonnie and her opponent come together in the middle of the mat and shake hands. Then a chorus of cheers and shouts rise from the crowd, and I realize they are for Bonnie. The other two matches stop, and all eyes turn toward the middle of the gym.

Bonnie has told me again and again that her goal is never to get pinned. Her male opponent is bigger and faster than her, but she competes well, and he doesn't get her down on the mat. The crowd is cheering, "Go, Bonnie!" There are grunts and sounds from the mat. It ends in a draw.

When all the matches are done, I walk down from the bleachers to congratulate Bonnie. She has a tampon up her nose to stem the flow of blood, but she is grinning from ear to ear.

Back in the courtroom on May 31, 2011, I feel anxious but hopeful as Dr. Norman Thompson, the medical examiner I met with sixteen years ago to finally see the autopsy report, takes the stand.

The jury has seen a parade of witnesses who worked with Bonnie, attended school with her, or knew her from the neighborhood. Each of them has spoken about Bonnie's upstanding character and unimpeachable nature, only to have their words torpedoed by Andrew Lambert, for the most part by virtue of his simply pointing out that none of them have seen Kenneth Dion, his car, or any other evidence tying him to the events at McHugh Creek. But Dr. Thompson can talk about facts, and it is facts we need.

ADA Paul Miovas asks Dr. Thompson to briefly describe his career path, from his army stint to his biochemistry degree from the University of Colorado through his postings in Denver, Kansas City, and Lander, Wyoming, until, finally, landing at the door of the Alaska Medical Examiner's Office.

"I know it's impossible to give me an exact number," says Miovas, "but as you sit here today, how many autopsies do you think you've performed in your career?"

"Somewhere around a thousand," says Dr. Thompson. I notice that the members of the jury pay a little closer attention, and feel the day is off to a good start.

An ME's job when conducting an autopsy is twofold, says Dr. Thompson—to provide an opinion regarding both the cause and the manner of death.

"What was the cause of death that you determined for Bonnie Craig in this particular case?" Miovas asks.

"Bonnie had multiple blunt impact injuries to her head and, as a consequence, sustained brain injuries. In the circumstances in which she was found, it was possible that there may have been a component of, say, drowning or hypothermia. But overall the injuries to her head were sufficiently severe to explain death."

"Okay. And we're going to go through those in some detail, and I'm going to give you an opportunity to explain that a little bit further, but so that's cause of death. How about manner of death for Bonnie Craig?" There are five possibilities for listing the manner of death: undetermined, natural, accidental, suicide, and homicide.

"Based on the pattern of injuries and the investigation as I understood it at that time, but predominantly the pattern of injuries and the scene investigation, if you will, it seemed like a very comfortable conclusion for me to call this a homicide. I could think of no other explanation for this pattern of injuries [other] than to assume that they had been inflicted by another person."

I notice Andrew Lambert feverishly making notes. He looks uncomfortable for the first time in the trial. I wonder what questions he will ask in cross. Beside him, Kenneth Dion sits in a relaxed manner. He seems cocky, almost flippant. At some statements made by Miovas or Gruenstein, he shakes his head. At others, he scoffs visibly.

For now, I sit and listen as Paul Miovas spends the better part of an hour asking Dr. Thompson to explain the details of his conclusions regarding Bonnie's death. There was no evidence of drugs or alcohol in her, he says. No traces of cocaine or marijuana or other recreational substances. It was a severe head injury that led to her death.

As Miovas asks Dr. Thompson to review his conclusions, he shows various slides. Samantha closes her eyes or turns away as we are shown the body bag being unzipped; Bonnie being placed on the blue table, her clothes still on; views of her body from different angles, highlighting her injuries. The bruising on her right pinkie, the fracture on her left index finger—injuries that had to have come from two separate blows, Dr. Thompson notes. The broken, ragged fingernails along the fingers of her left hand. The seepage of blood staining her jean jacket. Her hair, soaked with blood, from after she'd been placed in the body bag and continued to bleed out, the cold waters of McHugh Creek no longer inhibiting the bleeding or washing it away.

"In one part of your report, you say that the injuries to the left hand are consistent with defensive wounds. Can you explain that conclusion and why you came to that conclusion?"

"A defensive wound is a term which basically implies that you have a pattern of injuries in a location, usually on the arms or forearms or hands, which indicate that there may have been an effort to put the hands, for instance, between the individual who's been injured and the injuring agent. Another way to think about that is if somebody points a gun at me and I put my hands up and a bullet goes through my hand, that would be evidence of a defensive act or a defensive impulse, and the wound that was caused in that circumstance would be called a defensive wound. It's not possible, when I use the term defensive wound, to say with certainty that somebody is trying to defend themselves, but wounds of this sort on the hand are certainly consistent with an effort to defend oneself."

"Okay."

Dr. Thompson notes that some of the injuries on Bonnie's hands were more than likely caused when she put her hands up to try to shield the blows.

Miovas glosses over the minor abrasions and bruises that were found on Bonnie's lower body, which could have come from just about anything. He asks Dr. Thompson to review them, but only in the interest of being thorough. He doesn't want to seem as though he's intentionally leaving anything out. He knows where he is heading, and so do I. There are moments when I'm not sure I can listen anymore, but I focus on the presence of my father on one side and my children on the other, and they buoy me long enough to stay present.

"Did you do what is commonly referred to as a sex assault kit workup on Bonnie?"

"Yes. Basically a sex workup is to try to obtain samples from locations which might retain sexual fluids or that sort of thing. So I'm looking for evidence of semen."

The jury is shown a series of slides. They are pictures of my daughter's anus and vagina. Dr. Thompson speaks in detailed technical terms about the most private parts of Bonnie's body. With the pointer, Dr. Thompson circles the laceration in Bonnie's vagina and notes, "You can see slightly pale margins of this laceration, a kind of a central red area. There's also some darker discoloration which was evidence of some bruising, which suggested to me that this laceration occurred while there was still heartbeat. While the decedent was still alive."

Miovas puts up more pictures, this time of Bonnie's head wounds. Dr. Thompson explains to the court how lacerations from blunt-force injuries look different from wounds inflicted by knives or similar objects. He discusses the injuries to the back of Bonnie's head, in particular one mysterious T-shaped slash that he says could have been caused by an object shaped something like a razor blade. He goes through the eleven lacerations one by one. They aren't incisions or puncture wounds. They are lacerations that go deep into the scalp, a series of them, like someone drawing red lines in a random pattern.

Miovas goes back to the picture of the central injury, the one at the base of Bonnie's skull. He asks Dr. Thompson if this wound alone, which fractured the skull, could be enough to cause death. Certainly it could, says Dr. Thompson, but it most likely didn't. Most likely, Bonnie survived that injury for a while—long enough for the swelling inside her brain to finally kill her.

I feel my mental strength waning as Dr. Thompson explains

to the court how he pulled Bonnie's scalp back to look at her skull and her brain, and how he removed her brain in order to examine the base of her skull more closely. Based on this examination, she might have been alive for an hour following the injury, he says. Maybe two hours.

My tears are coming furiously. I wipe them away as much as I can, but they won't stop. Against her will, Samantha has stolen a few glances at the slides. Dr. Thompson tells the court he has thought about this case for years, and his conclusion is the same as it was then: Bonnie's death was the result of a series of focused blunt-force injuries to the back of her head. No injuries to the body that would indicate the pattern one would expect from an accidental fall. I see how careful Dr. Thompson is trying to be; he is a professional, and he is not trying to sway the case in one direction or another. He is saying it because, as a medical practitioner, this is what the facts lead him to believe.

"Do you know what a sai is?" Miovas asks.

"I spent a year and a half in Okinawa, which claims to have developed that martial arts tool. It's a fork-shaped tool with a handle. The fork allows one to have a chance of defending oneself against an edged weapon, like a sword, so you can catch the sword in the fork."

"You know what nunchucks are?"

"Yes. Two elongated handles, sometimes metal, usually wood, tied together by a chain or string. They are typically said to be derived from a flail, which is a device for liberating grains from a sheath. So, the bottom line is, they are a potential weapon with two sticks joined together by a chain."

Miovas has mentioned the sai and nunchuks in previous days. They are the weapons Kenneth Dion boasted about keeping in his trunk.

"You didn't mention either of those items, but are those two items that would be included in the broad range of objects that could have caused injuries like those to Bonnie Craig?"

"Yes."

"Pass the witness, Judge."

––––––––––––––––––

Andrew Lambert has to work harder with Dr. Thompson than he did with the other witnesses, and he knows it. Still, he doesn't need to prove that Kenneth Dion didn't murder Bonnie; he just needs to plant doubt in the minds of the jurors.

So he talks about blood. He asks Dr. Thompson if he would expect lacerations of the type Bonnie sustained to bleed. If he would expect them to bleed a lot. He asks Dr. Thompson if he would expect blood to spatter from the impact of such blunt-force blows.

"When you have spatter, it shoots out in different directions, doesn't it?"

"Yes."

"All right. And so you're going to have blood droplets that are going to fall on the ground, most likely?"

"That would be a reasonable expectation."

"And you're going to have blood that's going to land on bushes?"

"That would be possible, yes."

"Leaves?"

"That would be possible, yes."

"Trees?"

"That would be possible, yes."

"Tree branches?"

"Yes."

"Pine needles?"

"Yes."

"Things like that?"

"Yes."

"And from eleven wounds, you would expect to see a fairly significant amount of spatter, potentially?"

"Yes."

If Kenneth Dion beat Bonnie Craig to death, asks Lambert, where is the blood? Where's the blood on the collar of her jacket? Where is the spatter? Where is the blood that would spray from the instrument of beating as it's swung back and forth? Where is the blood from Bonnie's body as she's carried to the cliffside? Where is the blood on the rocks? If Kenneth Dion beat Bonnie to death in his car and then dragged her up to the cliff, where's the blood in the parking lot or along the trail? If Kenneth Dion beat Bonnie Craig to death and she fought back, why are there no fingernail scrapings with Dion's DNA? Why is there nothing in the autopsy that shows that she scratched, bit, or fought him in any way? We have one drop of blood on a leaf, Lambert says. One drop. Why?

Lambert knows Dr. Thompson doesn't have answers to these questions. He doesn't care about the answers. He just wants the jury to hear him asking them.

Lambert isn't quite as persuasive as he was with the previous witnesses. It's obvious that he is now the one scrambling. He is trying to divert the jury's attention from the eleven lacerations and get them to focus on other things. He asks Dr. Thompson about the lack of fingerprints around Bonnie's neck, the absence of ligature marks, or of duct tape or other adhesive on her mouth. He asks Dr. Thompson about her broken fingernail. Could it have resulted from the fall? He asks Dr. Thompson about Bonnie's clothing, which was all put on correctly, apart from the one undone button. He asks complicated questions about bruising and inflammation with relation to cold water to try to inspire the idea that the injuries could have looked fresher than they actually were. He refers to the fact that no drugs or alcohol were found in Bonnie's system, asking Dr. Thompson to confirm that the lack of drugs or alcohol doesn't necessarily mean someone isn't involved in high-risk behavior. He asks Dr. Thompson to confirm that no two-by-four, tire iron, baseball bat, pool cue, metal pipe, jack handle, or sai with Kenneth Dion's blood has ever been found. He asks Dr. Thompson to confirm that the small tear in Bonnie's vagina could have resulted from rough consensual sex. He can't rule it out, says Dr. Thompson, but he's skeptical.

Andrew Lambert is good at what he does. But it's obvious to me that he's working mostly to distract the jury. Hopefully, they're thinking what I am—that Bonnie had eleven lacerations on the back of her head, which couldn't have been caused from an accidental fall down a thirty-foot cliff. It may not be Lambert's responsibility to explain them away, but he isn't refuting their presence very well, either.

———————

Dr. Thompson's testimony nears the end of its second full day as Paul Miovas performs his redirect. Lambert has asked Dr. Thompson endless questions about the manner in which blood forms, the rate at which it pools and clots, and the potential effects of cold flowing water on these processes. Miovas asks different versions of the same questions to elicit different versions of the answers. I wonder how much of this the jury has absorbed.

Miovas shows pictures, asks questions. Dr. Thompson, remaining as composed as he's been throughout, answers professionally, commenting on what's possible, what's reasonable, and what, in his opinion, is likely. Miovas asks him one last time to comment on those eleven lacerations Bonnie sustained.

"As I look at the injuries to the head, I see a remarkable similarity in terms of not so much their length, because they are of different lengths, but in their depth and the fact that they can get deep without some variation in which I would see, for instance, a fracture beneath one, a, you know, a very superficial injury to another. And, if I was looking at a fall, what I would expect is that the fall does not take place with the stereotypical similar amounts of force being applied because a fall is, by nature, uncontrolled. And so you have a fall—the first component of the fall may be three, six, eight feet. The second component of the fall is not likely to be that same distance. It might be considerably more or considerably less. But each impact would be different in terms of the angle of impact with the skull and in terms of the injuries that you'd see associated with it. So, if I saw eleven injuries to the head and they were all different in terms of depth of penetration, disruption of the underlying skull, marks on the skull, superficial lengthy scrapes, etc., that would be far more consistent with an accidental fall. The fact that they're all focused in this location makes me unable to draw a conclusion that this is an accidental fall because I'd expect to see far more injury elsewhere. And so the thing that makes the most sense to me is that there is force applied to the head, which is fairly similar from impact to impact. The most likely explanation for that remains application of force to the head in this focused area by the use of some kind of instrument. That can produce similar wounds of the number that we're seeing and distributed over the back of the head literally from one side to the other side. That makes sense. Any other conclusion that relies on all of these wounds being a consequence of a fall does not make sense."

"I want to ask you a very direct question. In your opinion, is it even possible, because we heard a lot of 'it's possible, it's possible, it's possible'—is it possible, based on a fall from that cliff, for the impacts that we've just outlined to take place on Bonnie Craig?"

"No, which is the point of my conclusions."

"Not only is it not reasonable, it's not even possible, in your opinion?"

"It is not possible."

"Thank you, Dr. Thompson."

13

Today, June 2, 2011, Captain Robert Baty is chief of police of the Cordova Police Department. In September 1994 he was Trooper Baty, serving as part of the Criminal Investigations Bureau, which would travel statewide to assist on the biggest or most complicated cases.

When the call came in on September 28, 1994, that there was a dead body floating in McHugh Creek at the bottom of a cliff, Baty was an acting corporal. Normally, his sergeant, Mike Marrs, would take the lead, but the sergeant was out of the office, so it fell to him. Corporal Baty organized a half-dozen-strong team to investigate, and assigned primary duties to Detective Curt Harris, a relatively new member of the team, since it was his turn in the rotation. Harris shot photographs, while Baty took video with a handheld camcorder, the best technology they had at the time.

When Assistant District Attorney Paul Miovas first informed us that the crime scene tape had been found, I was excited, but also worried, for two reasons. First, on a personal note, though I'd seen the autopsy report and the photos, seeing the video would be something very different. Second, and more important, Miovas told us that since the video had emerged after the start of the proceedings, it would be easy for the defense to request a mistrial. Judge Smith had called a five-day recess, and during every minute of those five days I had expected Miovas or Gruenstein to call with the news that the defense had submitted the motion for mistrial. They never did. I assumed Andrew Lambert was cocky enough to think he could win even with the video.

Now, sitting in my familiar spot once again in Nesbett Courthouse, investigator Tim Hunyor slides a cassette into a VCR at the front of the courtroom, the lights are dimmed, and Jenna Gruenstein presses Play. I can feel my insides going numb as she tells the jury that they are about to see what investigators did the day of Bonnie's murder. So am I—I have not seen this tape until now either.

Captain Baty, looking uncomfortable, avoids eye contact with me and the other members of my family. Whatever the jury is going to see, I need to see, too. I'm worried about what the jury will learn from this video. We are told we will see the video in its entirety. I've known frustration beyond words at what I've always felt was a combination of indifference and incompetence on the part of the Alaska State Troopers. Is that what the jury will see? Will the video justify the troopers' initial decision that Bonnie's death was an accident? I pray it won't come across that way. Regardless of how difficult it may be to watch, I will need to know why they decide whatever they will decide. Before a single frame comes into view, I realize I am already crying.

The camera moves slowly, showing my daughter floating in the shallow waters of McHugh Creek, facedown, clothed, lifeless. I want to recoil, rip my eyes from the screen, but I don't. Some strange thing inside makes me continue to stare. I watch every second of the worst thing I can ever imagine seeing. No matter what happens to us in life, there is nothing worse than wondering about the blanks of an already terrible picture. I don't want to imagine the blanks anymore. I just want to know.

The camera pans from Bonnie's limp body floating in the water up to the cliffside. Throughout the frames, I can see detectives investigating—turning over debris, wading through the water, getting down on their knees and digging through the dirt and soil. I am watching the troopers conduct a careful, thorough investigation of the crime scene, and as Gruenstein pauses the video occasionally to ask Trooper Baty questions, I begin to feel something remarkable: gratitude. Alongside the gratitude is also guilt and relief. Guilt for so long assuming that they had screwed up the investigation and missed critical evidence at the scene. Relief at realizing that they hadn't.

I had for years harbored intense anger at the idea that the troopers hadn't given Bonnie a fair shot, that they'd dismissed her and messed up everything from the start. Now, as I watch them quietly move throughout the frame of the video, their distant voices mixing with the sound of light splashes of water or the rustle of leaves and twigs being pushed aside, I see that they were doing everything that should, and can, be done.

I am astonished to find that watching the tape of the investigation of my daughter's death produces in me the unmistakable feeling of a weight being lifted. Of, incredibly, healing. The part of me that wants Kenneth Dion to be served justice stands separate from the part of me that wants to know my baby was given a fair chance at respect and dignity, even in death. People watching me sob would logically assume that my tears spring from a primitive reaction to the fresh pain of seeing my daughter's dead body. They can't realize that within my tears is something that, although it can't be described as happiness, somehow carries goodness.

I watch tape of the troopers placing Bonnie's lifeless form into a black body bag and zipping it up. They perform the act gently and with care. They have a diver in the water, looking for a possible weapon. He goes to where they anticipate her body would have landed and floats to see where the flow of the water may have carried her. An investigator is crawling around on his knees, looking for evidence. They are not dismissive or careless. They are professional and methodical.

The video ends, and through the subsequent questioning, I learn that the troopers did a lot in the days after the murder. They talked to Bonnie's friends, people she went to school with, people she worked with, anybody who had any connection at all to her. Like me, they walked the same route Bonnie walked that day. They spoke to the papergirl, people jogging on the street, riding the bus. For a week straight, in fact, they talked to people on the bus, to see if anyone had seen or heard anything. No one had. They drove down the Seward Highway, stopped at all the rest areas, looked through the trash. They did everything they were supposed to do and more.

On cross-examination, Andrew Lambert again focuses on what Baty did not discover.

"From Bonnie's house, the two miles to the bus stop at Lake Otis and Abbott, you never, ever contacted a person who said I saw a redheaded guy along that route at any time on September 28, 1994, in the early-morning hours when Bonnie was walking along there?"

"No."

"And you never contacted a single witness that said 'on September 28, 1994, I saw a 1991 black Ford Tempo' anywhere along the route from Bonnie's house down to the bus stop of Lake Otis and Abbott?"

"No, sir."

"And you never contacted a person, let's just go from Bonnie's house to the bus stop at Independence, not a single person that ever said 'I saw a redhead on September 28, 1994'?"

"No, sir."

"Even after September 28, 1994, you never contacted anybody who said they saw a 1991 black Ford Tempo anywhere along the house from Bonnie's route down to the Sentry and Independence area?"

"No, sir."

"Any evidence you have that ever placed Kenneth Dion anywhere near Bonnie's house or along that route on September 28, 1994?"

"I never received any evidence like that."

"And there's no evidence that, or witnesses that you discovered that places Kenneth Dion's car along the routes we talked about on September 28, 1994?"

"No, sir."

Lambert refers again and again to the leaf with the single drop of blood, and to the lack of blood anywhere else. He wants the jury to focus on that leaf because he knows that, outside of Kenneth Dion's sperm, which proves sex but doesn't prove murder, it is the only hard evidence we have on our side. He talks again about impact splatter and castoff, the blood that results from swinging a weapon backward. He keeps Captain Baty on the stand for nearly an hour, asking what amounts to the same questions he asked Dr. Thompson: Wouldn't you expect to see more blood here? How could there not be more blood in such circumstances? How do you explain the lack of drops and drippings and splatterings? His only goal is to get Trooper Baty to make the same types of statements as Dr. Thompson was compelled to make—no, the drop of blood doesn't prove she was murdered. No, there is no incontrovertible evidence that she was raped, only evidence that sex occurred between Bonnie Craig and Kenneth Dion. No, we don't know exactly how or when she fell, or how many times she did or didn't hit her head on the way down. No, they didn't find any duct tape or wire or rope. No, they didn't find anything, or anybody, to tie Kenneth Dion to the murder of Bonnie Craig.

Captain Baty is excused. As he leaves the stand and walks out of the courtroom, my son Adam reaches for my arm in an attempt to calm me. But I'm already up and rushing out of the courtroom.

In the hallway outside, I catch up to Captain Robert Baty. With tears in my eyes, I give him a hug. I saw his pain as he watched the video and testified. I knew he cared.

"Thank you," I say. "Thank you for the respect and diligence you showed. All of you. I'm sorry."

Kristin Denning has been a forensic scientist with the Alaska Scientific Crime Detection Laboratory for seventeen years, about the same amount of time that has passed since Bonnie's murder. Kristin tells Paul Miovas that she was a new addition to the team that did the initial DNA testing on the samples taken from the crime scene and Bonnie's body, and then, as the technology improved over the subsequent years, when retesting was done. She was the one who had initially tested the bloody leaf and declared the blood a possible match to Bonnie's. The Crime Detection Lab is always careful to make conclusive statements, she says—a possible match is the furthest she's willing to go.

By 2003, the technology had improved, and Kristin reexamined Bonnie's jeans and panties as well as the sperm samples found in her. Miovas asks Kristin Denning a series of questions regarding sperm—how long it lives, the typical quantities one expects to see, and the factors that can affect it, like cold water in a stream. It makes me ill to listen to the details. Kristin Denning talks about seepage and drainage, disgusting terms that are nonetheless necessary to discuss. I need to remind myself constantly that if it weren't for Dion doing that, he might never have been found. The sex act could have taken place hours before the discovery of Bonnie's body, she says, or a few days before. Analysis of the other samples, like a fingernail and some debris, lead to the same conclusion.

Miovas passes the witness to Andrew Lambert, who says, "I just have a few questions that I wanted to ask you. And it's specifically related to the clothing here. When you have sperm that you find on clothing, clothing only, that doesn't give you a time frame on when sex occurred?"

"No, it does not."

"All that tells us is that we have some sperm on some clothing that was deposited at some time?"

"That is correct."

"Okay. And sperm's kind of pesky. It can hang around for a while, right?"

"It can."

"And the last thing is, just because we have the presence of sperm doesn't mean that Kenneth Dion murdered Bonnie Craig, does it?"

"I can't answer to that."

"Just because there's the presence of sperm doesn't mean that he sexually assaulted her, does it?"

"I can't answer to that, either, so yes, you're correct."

"That's all the questions I have."

Paul Miovas calls Barry Wilson, another Alaska State Trooper, to the stand. He is currently captain of C detachment, Alaska's west coast. Like Robert Baty, Wilson was part of the Criminal Investigations Bureau, Sexual Assault Unit, in September 1994. He was one of the troopers called to the crime scene at McHugh Creek. In the video, there had been a trooper walking around with a dive mask and dry suit. That was Wilson.

Miovas asks him about how the bottom of the creek looked, and questions why he'd done a "float test," as seen on the tape.

"To kind of get a feeling of why the body ended up where it was at," Wilson replies. "We wanted to know if the marks on the top of the cliff face up on top where the blood was found, if somebody come off there and ended up in the water, where would they end up, and so that was kind of the thought process behind that floating."

When the floating turned up nothing, Trooper Wilson and his colleagues walked Bonnie's route from home to her bus stop. They got on the bus and talked to people on the route, none of whom were able to tell them anything significant. They rode the bus to UAA, talking to people waiting at the stops along the way. They talked to workers at a construction site along the way. They went to the university bookstore and got a list of the textbooks that would have been in her missing backpack. They searched for Bonnie's missing calculator, her student ID, and her key ring. Nothing was found. A week later, they went back to McHugh Creek and did the float test again. Still nothing turned up. On October 5, 1994, they went to the funeral home to take additional pictures because they'd been told that the embalming process might bring out things that couldn't be seen before, but nothing came of it. They got waivers from both UAA and Berkeley to obtain copies of the e-mails between Bonnie and her boyfriend, Cameron, but the exchanges yielded nothing.

On cross, the defense's approach is familiar.

"Trooper Wilson," says Lambert, "as you came down the trail, you didn't see any blood?"

"No, I didn't."

"It didn't look like a trail that there had been a fight on the trail and things were disrupted and torn up and things like that?"

"No, I didn't see any evidence of that."

I feel the tears coming. I keep them at bay.

"Let me just lump it together just quickly. You found no evidence at McHugh Creek that connects Kenneth Dion to being there on September 28, 1994, right?"

"I didn't, no."

"You didn't find any witnesses that connect Kenneth Dion to Bonnie Craig?"

"I did not, no."

"Right. And then, when you got on the bus and you rode the bus, nobody mentioned anything about, hey, I saw a redhead on the bus on September 28, 1994?"

"No. Nobody said that."

"And then, when you went back and you did the subsequent search of McHugh Creek three days later on October 1, 1994, again, you didn't find any physical evidence that connected Kenneth Dion to being there on September 28, 1994?"

"No, sir."

"You didn't come across any witnesses that said Kenneth Dion was there?"

"I did not."

"You didn't come across anybody that said they saw his 1991 Ford Tempo there?"

"I did not."

"And when you walked the trails and the highway, you didn't find anything connecting Kenneth Dion to Bonnie Craig?"

"I did not."

"You never found anything that was potentially a murder weapon?"

"No, I did not."

"Thanks. That was all the questions I have."

After serving as a state trooper for nearly three decades, Curt Harris has now been retired for four years. Prior to joining the Homicide Unit of the Criminal Investigations Bureau in the summer of 1994, Harris had been on uniformed patrol in Matanuska Valley and other parts of Anchorage, and before that assigned to a bush post in Bristol Bay.

It was around three o'clock, recalls Harris, when he received the call to head out to McHugh Creek. Mike Marrs, his sergeant, was out of town, so it fell to him, the new man in the homicide unit, to take charge. The unit was understaffed, just six of them spread across the biggest state in the country. Harris responded to the scene with Barry Wilson and a few other troopers. Despite his junior status, and despite his having never led the investigation of a homicide case or crime scene before, Corporal Baty assigned Harris to be lead investigator. Paul Miovas asks what "lead investigator" means in practice.

"My impression looking back on that time was that, initially, that meant that I was responsible for gathering all the paperwork, making sure that everybody that was involved in it was turning in supplements and reports and so on and so forth," says Curt Harris. "The concept, at least our concept, in the unit at that time was to plan what we would do on kind of a collective basis, if you will."

"Somebody needs to videotape, somebody needs to photograph, that kind of thing?"

"That's correct."

"And, as the lead investigator, you said that it's your job to—it sounds more like coordinating with all the other investigators. You're the person who's making sure all that coordination gets done, ultimately?"

"Well, right from the get-go on this case and others I was involved in, there were always—everyone in the office was involved in major cases initially. The first forty-eight hours or so are critical. And an office briefing was held, assignments were made, people were dispatched to do different things, and so on and so forth."

Harris explains that the investigators would begin at the perimeter looking for evidence, then slowly work their way toward the middle. Miovas wants to show that Harris knew what he was doing even if he was new to the unit. It will be Lambert's job to show that he did not. The prosecution wishes to show that the troopers investigated properly and produced relevant evidence. The defense wishes to show that the investigation was bungled from the start, rendering the evidence meaningless.

Miovas wants to show the jury that Curt Harris was solid in his command of the scene, thorough in his delegation, and meticulous in his procedure. He asks Curt Harris to comment on each of the forty or so pictures taken that day, as though it's a high school presentation. Through the slide show, Harris takes us from the parking lot to the cliffside to the creek, where my daughter lies in eight inches of water, facedown.

"Okay. So you've described that you guys set the body bag up on the opposite side of the creek or that pond, and you were able to remove her and take her out of the area from that directly, is that correct?" Miovas asks.

"Yes."

They describe Bonnie being placed in a body bag. There are questions about blood and debris. As I have done from the first day of the trial, I force myself to listen to every word. It kills me—but this isn't about me.

A few minutes later, Miovas passes the witness, and Andrew Lambert begins his cross.

"Morning, Detective Harris."

"Morning."

"Are you enjoying retirement?"

"I am."

"I think we're all envious. Now, you said that there were a lot of people that you've interviewed in this case, right?"

"That's true, yes."

"All right. And of all the people that you've interviewed, none of them said that Kenneth Dion was at McHugh Creek on September 28, 1994?"

"That is correct."

"None of them has said that his 1991 black Ford Tempo was at McHugh Creek on September 28, 1994, right?"

"That's true."

"None of them said that they heard any yelling, screaming, or fighting or anything that ever went on at McHugh Creek on September 28, 1994?"

"That's true."

"And there were about two hundred–plus tips that came in, right?

"There were hundreds of them, I think, if not more."

"Right. And even as you got interviews there were tips in the interviews, right?"

"That's correct."

"All right. And of the interviews and tips that you did, none of them related to Kenneth Dion?"

"Not that I know of."

"And you found no murder weapon in this case, right?"

"I did not, no."

"And you have no evidence that Kenneth Dion abducted Bonnie Craig on September 28, 1994, from a bus stop?"

"Not that I know of."

"Or anywhere else at all?"

"Not that I know of."

"There's no evidence that Bonnie Craig was forced against her will to go anywhere, right?"

"Not that I know of."

"And there was no evidence that she was forced—there's no evidence that she—that you saw at McHugh Creek that she was ever—you're familiar with ligature marks and binding?"

"That's true."

"You never found anything of that nature that showed that she was subdued in some fashion?"

"No, I did not."

"And as far as the crime scene goes you're familiar with luminal, right?"

"Yes, I am."

"And you didn't use any luminal in the crime scene on September 28, 1994?"

"I didn't, no."

"Okay. Are you aware that they came back at some later date and used luminal there and found no blood?"

"Yes."

"Okay. And are you aware that, in fact, when they did, that

crime scene personnel came to McHugh Creek at a later date and were looking around there and didn't find any blood?"

"That seems right."

"In fact, there's no evidence at all of anything that you found that connects Kenneth Dion to McHugh Creek on September 28, 1994?"

"None that I know of."

"Okay. And there's no vehicle that you're aware of that's connected to this as an alternate murder scene?"

"None that I know of."

"Or an alternate rape site?"

"Not that I know of."

"There's no other residence or location at all, whether it be in a trailer, a motor home, a mobile home, you know, anything like that, that's an alternate crime scene that you're aware of at all?"

"Not that I'm aware of."

"Nothing that connects Ken on September 28, 1994?"

"Not that I'm aware of."

I am watching a handful of people prepare to decide the fate of the man who I'm certain took my daughter's life. I can't tell what they're thinking. I'm getting sick of Lambert's repeated line of questioning, the endless repeating of what wasn't seen or found. I want to scream, "Enough! Stop asking questions about things nobody saw! *Stop!*"

There is nothing I can do but watch, and hope. Samantha asks me if I'm okay. I tell her I am, but the truth is I am nervous. I know very well that Curt Harris may be the weak link in our case, and Lambert is doing his best to expose him as exactly that.

"I think you said you had only been in this unit about two or three months, right?" says Lambert to Curt Harris.

"As I recall."

"How long had you been a police officer at that point?"

"I began my career in 1980."

"Okay. So you'd been an officer fourteen years?"

"Correct."

"Pretty experienced person?"

"Yes."

"And you know as a police officer that I'm assuming as a uniformed patrol officer you've taken photos over the years?"

"Yes."

"Carry a camera in the car?"

"Yes."

"Bring a camera to the scene?"

"There were cameras at the scene, yes."

"Okay. Well, you were taking photos at the scene, right?"

"Yes."

"And the importance of photos are to document evidence that you see, right?"

"That's correct."

"So later on if you're in a situation like this they can be shown to the jury and they can see exactly what you're saying and understand what you're saying, right?"

"That's true.

"All right. And there's a difference between taking just a regular photo and a forensic photo, isn't there?"

"Yes."

"All right. A forensic photo is a photo that's, you know, basically it's two-scale, it's done at different angles, it shows the evidence in different forms?"

"Yes."

"As opposed to just going snap and there's your picture?"

"Correct."

"Okay. You didn't take a single picture of the blood leaf, a forensic photo, did you?"

"No, I did not."

"You didn't do any measuring from the blood on the leaf to just where the edge of the cliff is, not where the slide marks are, but just to the edge of the cliff to tell us how far back the leaf was from the edge of the cliff?"

"No, I didn't do that."

I don't like where this is headed. Lambert has his hooks into Curt Harris, and he isn't letting go.

"And there was a tape measure there, you've told us, because you measured the length of the cliff, right?"

"Yes."

"And you didn't do any measuring from the leaf to the slide marks?"

"No, I did not."

"And you didn't take any forensic photos of the slide marks?"

"I did not, no."

"And while there's a video of it, sometimes forensic photos that are closer up and at different angles can give you different perspectives than just a video that pans in on it, right?"

"That's true."

"Okay. And then you talked about there was some moss at the top of the cliff that you thought was torn off, right?"

"Yes."

"You didn't take any pictures of where the moss was torn off?"

"I don't know if those are depicted in the pictures or not."

"Well, the pictures that we saw are kind of panned away from the cliff, aren't they?"

"Yes."

"I mean, you have no close-up that says, snap, here's the moss and a forensic, you know, ruler in there, you know, to do that, to show this, right?"

"No, I did not take a photograph like that."

I'm hoping Judge Smith will stop Lambert's badgering of Curt Harris, or that Miovas or Gruenstein will come up with a clever objection. Harris's voice sounds more anxious with each question Lambert asks and each answer he is forced to give.

"All right. And then you said that there was, at the bottom on the first ledge, the ledge that's fifteen feet down, that you saw moss and debris on that ledge?"

"Uh-huh."

"I'm sorry, for the record we have to say yes or no."

"Okay."

"It's been a long time, I know it has been for you."

"That's right."

"You certainly didn't take any pictures when you're standing on that ledge, did you?"

"No, I did not. I didn't have a camera with me at that point."

"Sure. But you could have said, hey, somebody—and you could have taken a camera with you, right?"

"True."

"You could have said, hey, can someone hand me a camera?"

"Could have."

I observe the jury members. They are swept up in it. They cannot feel sympathy for Curt Harris because they've been instructed not to. They've been instructed only to listen to the facts and make the best conclusions they can.

"There's a trail that goes right to there, you can walk right up to it, isn't there?"

"You can't walk right up to it, but that's—that's true."

"There's a trail right there and then you have to kind of step around the corner and then down onto the ledge, right?"

"That's correct, yeah."

"But you easily could have got a camera, right?"

"Yes."

"And then we would have been able to see the size of the moss, right?"

"True."

"And we would have been able to see what the actual ledge looks like up close?"

"True."

"And then you talk about there are plants on the ledge, and that those plants are bent in a downward direction with fresh scrape marks on them?"

"Yes."

"You didn't take a single photo of these fresh scrape marks, did you?"

"That's true."

Andrew Lambert goes on for several more minutes about all the things that Trooper Harris and his team did not take pictures of. He goes on to talk about, of course, all the blood absent from the scene.

"Now, when you went out to Bonnie's parents that particular night and you went out there around ten o'clock, right?"

"That sounds right."

"And when you went out there, you told her stepfather that it appeared as if Bonnie had been out hiking at McHugh Creek?"

"That's true."

"And that it appeared that she had accidentally fallen off a cliff and hit her head and died?"

"That's true."

"All right. So that evening the information you provided to the family was it was an accidental death?"

"That was one of the options that I presented, yes."

"Understood there may be other options and I'm sure Mr. Miovas on redirect will discuss them. One of the other options is maybe she was murdered, you know, like we're discussing here today, right?"

"That's true."

"But clearly there was other ways of dealing with it other than telling them that it was accidental?"

"I said some things I shouldn't have said."

I think back to the weeks and months after the murder. Their telling me at first that it was a hiking accident. Sticking to the story despite my arguments.

"And you indicated to them that it appeared she tumbled down about thirty feet of rock, striking her head and dying?"

"I think that's fair."

"Sound about right?"

"Yeah."

I remember going to the funeral home and seeing the bruises on Bonnie's arms, the obvious defensive wounds on her hands. Hounding the troopers relentlessly, only to be met with silence or dismissal, again and again.

"Okay. And I think you indicated also at that point it didn't appear like there was any foul play that we could tell, but we were going to continue to investigate."

"That's fair."

"Okay. And you told them this numerous times that night? It was about an hour-long conversation?"

"More than likely, yes."

"Okay. I mean, you weren't, I mean the idea of it was not to be a ruse and lie to them, right?"

"I was discussing with them one of the options. And like I said, I said things that I probably shouldn't have said. In retrospect it's very clear it was a stupid thing to say, but at that time, as you have already mentioned, you don't want to disclose a lot."

"Sure."

"I was sensitive to the family's feelings."

"But when you went there that night . . ."

"In looking back, you know, at that time, yeah, I said the wrong thing is what I did. And I chose to take a route that would seem to make this something that wasn't as serious as it turned out to be."

I think of Sergeant Marrs telling me that even when they started to suspect it might be homicide, they still didn't want to reveal it publicly because it might scare off somebody from coming forward. I never bought the explanation. To me, they were always just trying to save face. They knew that they'd screwed up, and they didn't want to admit it.

"Okay. So I'm a little confused there. Instead of just simply—I mean you're a fourteen-year experienced officer, all right, right?"

"Yes, that's true."

I remember finally seeing the autopsy report and reading the word *homicide* in association with the case for the first time, at least on paper. Though I'd never seen anything before that had officially designated Bonnie's death an accident, that's what I'd been told in the first few months following September 28, 1994. At some point, the troopers had changed their story. They just hadn't bothered to tell me. I remember the feeling of being always on the outside looking in.

"And instead of just simply saying, hey, your daughter died, we're investigating, you just flat out told them it was an accidental death, from everything you could tell at this point, right?"

"That was one of the options, one of the possibilities, yes."

In redirect, Paul Miovas does his best to soften the damage done by Lambert, who has crafted a strong picture of Curt Harris's incompetency, therefore implying that the entire investigation was botched and that no conclusions from it can be believed. Miovas speaks to Harris like a boss forgiving an employee who has messed up.

"Okay. One more time, why are you telling them accident but not discussing the other theories with them?"

"The other line of thinking on this, the other theories, to begin discussing it would disclose information that only someone who was involved in what happened might know."

"Okay."

"And I did not want that to become public knowledge."

"How many prior homicides had you been lead investigator on before Bonnie's case?"

"None."

"How many prior crime scene, homicide crime scenes had you been the lead investigator on before Bonnie's case?"

"I don't really remember."

"Okay. Any that you can think of off the top of your head?"

"None."

"Okay. I wonder, Investigator Harris, if thinking back on it, as Mr. Lambert pointed out, you could have just said 'I'm not disclosing any information'; is that what you should have done in this situation?"

"That's what I should have done and that would have been the best thing to do."

"Okay. I appreciate that. Thank you, Investigator Harris."

The message from both sides is equally clear. From the defense: *The guy made a mess of the whole thing. The evidence means nothing.* From the prosecution: *The guy made a few rookie mistakes. It doesn't change what happened.* The jury will decide which statement matters more.

———————————

Prosecutor Jenna Gruenstein calls Joe Barr to the stand. Joe, thirtysomething, big, tall, and clean-shaven, grew up in Anchorage but now lives in Texas. He worked at Sam's Club with Bonnie and struck up a friendship with her. They had spoken on the phone a couple of times during the week before she died. The defense has taken great pains to try to paint Bonnie as someone she wasn't—a girl who made the rounds. Gruenstein is trying to restore the proper picture of my daughter—someone who had lots of friends.

She asks Joe, "Were there any particular reasons why Bonnie would call you?"

"Just friends."

"Did she want . . ."

"Just coworkers. She wanted to I believe play pool."

"Was she asking you out on dates? Did she want to go with just the two of you?"

"No, no."

"Was she asking you to go out on a date with just you and she?"

"No, she was not."

"Did you ever end up going out and doing anything with Bonnie . . ."

"Never."

". . . either alone or with a group?"

"I never saw her outside work."

"Okay."

"So my answer is no."

"Were you interested in dating her when . . ."

"No."

". . . you were talking to her on the phone?"

"No, I was not."

"Did she ever talk to you about a relationship that she was in?"

"Yes, she did."

"What would she discuss about that?"

"She always talked very good of her boyfriend and I believe he lived in California or went to school in California."

"Did she ever discuss with you her feelings toward her boyfriend, what she envisioned in the future?"

"I don't believe so. All I know is I remember it was a positive whenever she talked about her boyfriend."

Gruenstein passes the witness, and Andrew Lambert says a kind good morning to Joe Barr. But, as appears often to be the case with Lambert, that kindness quickly gives way to a mix of aggression and hostility. It's clear from Lambert's first few questions that the defense had tried and failed to subpoena Joe Barr themselves.

"You didn't want to come up here for us, did you?" says Lambert. "But you came up here voluntarily for the state, right? When they called you and asked you to show up here, you came up, didn't you?"

"Yes, I did."

"Okay. Now, you still have the transcript there?"

"Yes."

"The testimony in this case is that she babysat for Wendy Goodrich one time and it was on a Saturday night. So she called you at least twice. You never called her at all, did you?"

"No, I did not."

"She called you?"

"Yes, she did."

"And in fact, you told the troopers numerous times in this interview that she had been calling you all week long?"

"I don't recall that."

"You've read the transcript, right?"

"Yes. From what it says in here, I guess I did."

There's more back-and-forth about what exactly the transcript says; then Lambert asks, "Now, even though she said she had a boyfriend, you told the troopers that you felt that she had a crush on you?"

"That's what I said in the transcript, but I don't feel that way today."

"Understood, but in your original testimony to troopers, in 1995, you said, 'I think she—I don't know, I felt like she had a crush on me or something.' Right?"

"Yes, I did, in the transcript."

"And you also told them that, you know, 'I know she had a boyfriend, but I sort of got the impression, you know, he's four thousand miles away'?"

"Yes."

"Right? And that you thought she had a crush on you and wanted to go out with you. Right?"

"Correct."

Lambert searched the transcript for Joe's exact quote, then said, "You indicated that she'd come find you in the building and flirt with you and stuff, right?"

"Yes, that's what I said on here. But again, that's not what I feel. I feel it was just she was really an outgoing person."

"I understand that as we're talking about it in 2011, but I'm talking about when the police came to you on December 12th, 1995. That was your feeling at the time, wasn't it?"

"Yes."

"And that was closer in time than it is today, isn't it?"

"Correct."

"And if you didn't think that back then, you clearly could have told the troopers 'that's not what I thought,' right?"

"Yeah. Yes."

"Let me make sure I got everything. I don't know if I asked this, so it's my last question. Bonnie was calling you throughout the week; that's what you told the troopers, right?"

"Not that I recall, but it says it in the transcript."

"Okay. Thank you."

With Lambert's questions done, Gruenstein stands back up immediately. "In December of 1995, you're about twenty-two years old?"

"Yes."

"And reading through the transcript, I think maybe it comes off a little bit, you're kind of selfish or, maybe a nice way of putting it is, you mention that you had numerous girlfriends, I think?"

"Yeah, I was a typical boy, I guess, that I hung out with. Maybe cocky, overzealous."

"Is it possible that your twenty-two-year-old self might have categorized things somewhat differently than you might today?"

"Yes."

"Going back again to 1995, you're more than a year out past Bonnie's death."

"Yes."

"How clear was your recollection of the exact timeline of when that phone call was made?"

"It would have been a lot better if it would have been right after, but I'm sure I've lost some key points."

"And to be fair, in your transcript you do tell the troopers that you're not really sure?"

"Yes."

"I have nothing further, Your Honor."

The last witness called by the prosecution is Jessica Hogan, a forensic DNA analyst for the Alaska Scientific Crime Detection Laboratory in Anchorage, newly promoted to Crime Scene Response Supervisor. In 1994, she says, they were using a system called DQ-alpha, which essentially gave information about one genetic location in a given DNA sample. Today, the advanced system, called STR typing, reveals information about fifteen locations. Paul Miovas shows some slides that look like microscope exercises from biology class, and asks Hogan to comment on them. They are comparative analyses of the two samples, she says—Kenneth Dion's DNA in one column, the sample taken from Bonnie in the other.

Like Kristin Denning, the forensic scientist at the Alaska Scientific Crime Detection Laboratory who had been part of the team that did the initial DNA testing on the samples, Jessica Hogan is unwilling to state whether a sample matches or doesn't match; she only discusses probabilities. She speaks in deeply technical language, referring to alleles and amelogenin and substrate fractions. But the point she makes is clear enough. In one slide, the two samples match in eight out of ten locations; in the other, in all of the locations. The two nonmatches on the first slide, she points out, are locations where not enough material was available to do significant testing.

Miovas keeps Hogan on the stand for half an hour asking dizzying statistical questions. Finally, he says, "So the conclusion is that Kenneth Dion cannot be excluded as a source detected in the major component of the sample. Once again, you don't say match. You don't say it is him. You say cannot be excluded."

"That's correct," says Hogan. "I mean, then it comes back to the fundamental question that we're trying to answer, and that is can I exclude an individual as a source of DNA. All those numbers that were provided and compared in the reference sample for Mr. Dion as well as the vaginal sample from Ms. Bonnie Craig, they were consistent. And therefore I cannot exclude Mr. Dion as a source of DNA in that sample."

"We have no DNA inconsistent with Kenneth Dion. So what is the implication of this additional phrase?"

"That all of the information that was actually detected can be accounted for by the reference sample for Mr. Dion."

On cross, Andrew Lambert parries. "Now, the fact that there is Mr. Dion's DNA present in and on Bonnie Craig doesn't mean he murdered her," he says. "And that doesn't mean he sexually assaulted her."

"That's correct," Jennifer Hogan says.

When Dr. Arndt von Hippel had contacted me years earlier, during the earliest stages of the investigation, telling me he'd seen Bonnie alive at McHugh Creek the morning of her murder and offering to help solve the case in any way he could, he'd also said he would be happy to testify to that fact. At the time, neither he nor I knew whether his potential testimony would benefit the prosecution or the defense. Now, here he is again, being sworn in, a witness for the state, nearly eighty years old but still trim.

"Well," Dr. von Hippel says now when asked the standard swearing-in questions, "I don't know the whole truth, but I'll give as much as I know of it." He takes the stand and asks the judge if he might get some coffee, seemingly unaware that it's an odd request. The moment of levity is somehow welcome.

Dr. von Hippel has been retired for twenty years from his job as a thoracic and cardiovascular surgeon—or, as he describes it to Paul Miovas, "in the context of Alaska in those days, it was basically anyone who was bleeding bad."

He repeats for Miovas what he said to troopers over the course of multiple conversations in the fall of 1994, and which he has reported in multiple depositions in the years since: that he saw Bonnie with three other young people—two young men and another girl—at McHugh Creek on the morning of September 28, 1994. He says he recognized the picture of Bonnie in the paper because of her epicanthic folds—skin folds on the upper eyelid, which both she and I have—and her denim Levi's jacket. Seeing a picture of me in the paper, he said, he'd recognized those same folds. He called me and asked to get involved, went on TV with me, contributed some money to the cause.

"Bonnie Craig came bounding down what used to be a set of concrete steps over there in a very athletic fashion, and light on her feet," says Dr. von Hippel. "She was looking cheerful, and I commented to her as she passed, 'You make it look easy,' and she sort of gave me a little smile."

Kenneth Dion is sitting in court, as he's been all trial, in a white shirt and black tie, staring straight ahead. After the papers ran a front-page photo of Dion four years before, in 2007, Dr. von

Hippel told troopers that Dion was the man who had been immediately behind Bonnie on the morning he saw her at McHugh Creek. Dion's face was turned to the left in the newspaper photo, and that was the same side Dr. von Hippel said he'd passed him on. When Miovas asks if Kenneth Dion is the same man sitting in the courtroom, however, Dr. von Hippel says he can't be sure.

"Your Honor," says Dr. von Hippel, "if I should run out of coffee, which I appear to have done, would I be able to get some?" I can't tell if Dr. von Hippel is attempting to get off the stand, trying to appear as an unreliable witness for both sides, or plain scrambling. I wonder if he's worried about his original testimony, or how that testimony might contradict things that have been presented so far in the case.

When Miovas passes Dr. von Hippel to Andrew Lambert, Lambert immediately quells the lightness. "Before we start, Dr. von Hippel, I know there's been some laughter in here and there's been some quips that have come out of you, but you understand that we're here for a first-degree murder and sexual assault trial, right?"

"I presume that's what . . ."

"Right, this man is on trial for murder and rape, so you know that this is very important, isn't it; it's not funny, is it?"

"I've never considered it to be. I've spent the last seventeen years looking to see if I could do anything to help."

Lambert asks Dr. von Hippel to stay focused on the questions and give direct answers. "Now, you had indicated that you didn't see any redheads out at McHugh Creek. That is correct. Right? And Mr. Dion has red hair."

"Not in my book."

Lambert looks flustered. I'm enjoying it. "Okay."

"I mean, you have gray hair in some people's book, but on the other hand, some people might say it's dark and some gray in it, and I don't see him as being what I would call a redhead."

"Okay. All right."

"I grew up on the East Coast and there was a lot of really red-headed people, complete with freckles."

"Understood, Doctor. My question is you've stated previously you didn't see a redhead there, right?"

"That is correct."

"All right."

"I don't see a redhead here or there."

"Okay. And I think you described Mr. Dion as he looked straight on as just a boring slug."

"Yeah, something like that. Nothing personal, just that's the description."

"I'm sure he's not taking anything personally."

"That's good."

"And in the picture in the paper, all Mr. Dion's doing is just looking a little to the side with his mouth closed, right?"

"I don't know what he's doing, but it was descriptive."

"Okay."

"It was diagnostic, as we say."

"Sure. Okay. Well, let's go through a couple things and then I think I'm pretty close to done."

"Me, too."

By the time Dr. von Hippel leaves the stand, he has been no help to the defense. I don't know how much help he's given the prosecution either—the jury may have appreciated him mostly for entertainment value—but when I find him outside the courtroom, I give him a big hug, thanking him for the support he has shown us over the years. He has done his best. On a given day, it's all any of us can do.

I have read and heard the name Tammy Aaronson numerous times. When Trooper Tim Hunyor first told me about Kenneth Dion, he'd also mentioned Dion's wife, Tammy, and the baby they'd had not long before Bonnie's murder. It's strange to now see Tammy Aaronson sitting on the stand. I don't know what I expected. Perhaps someone rough around the edges, since I associate her with Kenneth Dion, a criminal. It's quite the opposite. She is so meek, Paul Miovas has to ask her to speak up to be heard, even with the microphone. I guess it makes sense. It isn't strong women whom men like Kenneth Dion target.

Tammy Aaronson, formerly Tammy Gregory, tells the jury about the young wife and new mother she'd been in 1994. She and Kenneth Dion had married in Valdez in April of that year, and their daughter, Amber, had arrived on the scene in September. Apparently, things between Tammy and Kenneth went bad quickly.

"At that point, what I'm going to refer to as late August through the next month or two," says Miovas, "were you living with Kenneth at that time?"

"We were living together, but he wasn't home often."

"Okay. Were there periods of time where he would disappear and you didn't know where he was?"

"Yes."

"Are we talking about sometimes days, sometimes weeks?"

"Most of the time weeks."

"Okay. And one of the things that's very specific that you have recalled is that your daughter's born on the third and the days leading up to your daughter being born and you going into labor he's not around. Is that correct?"

"Uh-huh, that's correct."

"But he shows up, takes you to the hospital, and you have the baby. He's there when you have the baby, correct?"

"Yes."

"Okay. And then after that, my understanding is he disappears for a couple more weeks after you have the baby."

"Yes, he left the day after she was born and I didn't see him for about another week."

"Okay. And once again, does this pattern continue where he will disappear for periods of time?"

"Yes."

"When he would disappear, would he either tell you where he was going or explain where he had been when he gets back?"

"No."

All else aside, it's hard for me not to feel sympathy for this woman, and for her daughter, Amber, now just a year younger than Bonnie was when her life ended.

"All right. Now, you came into town last night, you and I met for the first time ever, correct?"

"Yes."

"And I asked you the same question and you told me that—in passing in coming up here, that you recall that you had been to McHugh Creek before. Is that accurate?"

"Yes."

"Can you tell us the time frame of when it was that you recall going to McHugh Creek?"

"Just . . ."

"Let me just ask you the circumstances. Did you go there with Ken?"

"Yes, I went there with Ken and two other people. I—I mean, all of the . . . the meeting yesterday that we had just really jogged my memory. Passing McHugh Creek on my way up here, it's just, you know, the emotions of this trial, I—things are coming into my brain."

"Okay."

"I don't recall an exact time, but it was definitely after Amber was born."

Miovas has achieved his purpose: letting the jury know that Kenneth Dion was familiar with McHugh Creek. That he had taken his wife there—at least during one of the periods when he was around. Andrew Lambert declines the opportunity for cross. Tammy Aaronson is excused.

I walk out of the courtroom and call her name. Tammy turns around, surprised to see that it is me.

"I'm sorry," I say, and give her a hug. I had hoped Kenneth Dion would accept the plea deal not just so that my family would be spared the nightmare of a trial, but also so that this woman and her daughter would be spared the same. It isn't her fault that she chose a man who she didn't know was evil. There is deep pain in her eyes. Worse, her daughter will now have to live with the public fact that her father is on trial for the rape and murder of an eighteen-year-old college freshman.

"What he's putting you through—I'm sorry."

"Thank you," says the ex-wife of Kenneth Dion, before turning and walking away.

14

Trooper Tim Hunyor is waiting to sell his house and get out of
Alaska. He's been posted throughout the state in various roles
for twenty-five years. Retirement is looking good.

Trooper Hunyor, with his kind, round face, looks like an uncle
you know you can trust. It's nearly impossible for me to look at
him or hear his voice without mentally returning to Club Paradise,
on that remote island in the Philippines, when I received the unexpected e-mail with the subject line *Bonnie*, and everything suddenly changed. Prosecutor Paul Miovas briefly reviews that period
for the jurors—the Alaska State Troopers receiving word from
New Hampshire that a match had been discovered for the DNA
profile in their database, Trooper Hunyor and a fellow trooper going down to New Hampshire, the broad strokes of their hour-long
interview with the suspect named Kenneth Dion.

Miovas asks Jenna Gruenstein to turn off the lights. She does,
and then she presses Play. A black-and-white video comes onscreen,
showing, from an overhead angle, an ordinary-looking man sitting
in a plastic chair, legs apart. Though I know about the interview

the troopers conducted with Dion, this will be the first time I actually see it.

Tim Hunyor appears onscreen, greets the man in the chair, and shakes his hand. We hear Hunyor and Dion speak for a long time, one in a friendly Midwest cadence, the other with a New England inflection.

It's a masterful display of interrogation by Trooper Hunyor. He establishes rapport with Dion via his folksy, conversational manner, then proceeds to subtly disarm him. When he slides Bonnie's picture in front of Dion, the one that ran in the *Anchorage Daily News* after her murder, you can see the man's body language change immediately—he starts to shift in his seat and make nervous jokes, like how his wife would have killed him for hanging around with an eighteen-year-old girl. Trooper Hunyor and his colleague laugh along with Dion, maintaining trust and affinity; then Hunyor keeps at Dion, asking more questions in his nonthreatening, friendly way.

He gets Dion to talk about his stormy relationship with his wife, Tammy, and his regret at screwing up the marriage. Dion tells Hunyor about his cocaine habit, his bad temper, his appetite for bar fights. He talks to Hunyor like a friend at a pub, not realizing how much he is revealing. Dion brags about his martial arts prowess and tells him how, for a period of time, he kept different martial arts weapons in the trunk of his car, among them something called a sai, as well as nunchucks.

The video ends, and the courtroom is silent. The members of the jury regard Kenneth Dion, who stares straight ahead. Trooper Hunyor is excused from the stand. Judge Smith tells the prosecution it may call its next witness. The state rests, says Miovas. It's almost over.

In a murder trial, the defense team is not technically required to present a case and therefore does not need to call any witnesses. The onus is on the prosecution to prove that the accused is guilty beyond a reasonable doubt; the onus is on the defense not to prove innocence but to introduce said reasonable doubt.

Andrew Lambert chooses to call two witnesses before the case is handed over to the jury for a verdict. The first, on Friday, is a woman named Carol Klamser, a sexual-assault-response advanced nurse practitioner educated at Cal State and the University of Tennessee. She seems a strange choice to testify for the defense; many of my nurse friends are cynical about her motivations. Lambert asks her to comment on the injuries to Bonnie's vagina. Klamser testifies that the injuries are not necessarily from rape; under cross, however, she admits it's difficult to ascertain whether sexual assault occurred simply by looking at vaginal injuries.

The second witness called by the defense, on Monday, June 13, 2011, is Dr. Harry Bonnell, a big, round-faced forensic pathologist from California. Dr. Bonnell's double chin presses down onto the collar of his shirt as he takes the stand. He has small bulging eyes, a multifurrowed brow, and a high salt-and-pepper hairline.

Dr. Bonnell was Chief Deputy Medical Examiner for San Diego County for a decade before—as comes out at trial—he was fired, and later, he turned to consulting for attorneys on both sides of civil and criminal cases. He sits on the board of trustees for a group called the Parents of Murdered Children. He is on the Los Angeles Superior Court expert panel. He is part of San Diego's police review standards board. He has performed more than seven thousand autopsies. His credentials are glittering, and Lambert makes sure to highlight them extensively.

Dr. Bonnell has been interviewed extensively by both Andrew Lambert and Paul Miovas. He has been supplied with the autopsy report, the toxicology report, the photos, and Dr. Thompson's testimony. He has watched video of the crime scene.

"As to the cause of death do you agree with Dr. Thompson that the cause of death is blunt force trauma?"

"Yes."

"Is it the manner of death as to what you disagree with Dr. Thompson?"

"It is the manner of death and to a little bit on a cause of death I believe he has contributing factors, hypothermia and possible drowning, and I think that particularly the drowning may have played a greater role in the mechanism of the death. She wouldn't have drowned if it wasn't for the head trauma, but it doesn't appear that the head trauma immediately killed her."

"Now, did you have an opportunity to review the scene video in more detail?"

"Yes."

"Okay. And after reviewing the scene video in more detail, tell us what your opinion is as far as whether it's undetermined, accidental, of that nature."

"At this point in time I think it's greater than 50 percent that it's accidental. I think all of the injuries are accountable for a fall off a cliff, and I've got no knowledge that that fall was at the hands of another."

"So do you think that the injuries are more consistent with a fall from the cliff than a weapon or a combination of a fall from a cliff and a weapon?"

"I think the serious injuries are all consistent with a fall and not consistent with a single weapon."

Dr. Bonnell is on the stand for the better part of the day. He tells the court that in his opinion, Bonnie's lacerations are probably from two rocks, as opposed to one weapon.

"Now, Doctor," says Lambert, "if you fall, can a person have multiple impacts to their head that causes multiple injuries?"

"They can. That's more typical in somebody, for example, tumbling down stairs where there's repeated impacts. Most of it depends upon what surfaces they come in contact with and whether they're flat or irregular."

"Okay. So if somebody, let's say, tumbles down a rock face, it wouldn't be unusual that they hit their head a number of times, and we don't know the exact number, but that could cause multiple impacts in one strike?"

"Correct."

"You could also have single impacts from that also, right?"

"Right. It depends upon the orientation of the head and whatever it's striking. Again, when I was out there and again looking at the old videotape, the creek bed in that area is not flat. It's got elevated rocks and depressed rocks and little . . ."

I feel like Andrew Lambert is trying to pull a fast one at the eleventh hour. I peer at the jurors, trying, as I have tried to do for a month, to read their minds. I cannot.

"In Dr. Thompson's testimony, he indicated that he thought all the injuries to her head looked similar in size, depth, and shape. Do you agree with that?"

"No."

"Why not?

"Well, there, just alone in this photo we have some of them that are less than a half-inch long and others that appear to be close to two and a half to three inches long, penetrate very deeply; others have very little abrasions and go all the way down to the surface of the skull. And if there is access to the direction of the wound, there are several variations in that access."

"Would you say that with those differences in the appearances of all these injuries, including the main laceration, that it's more consistent with a single type of weapon causing it all, or is it more consistent with falling down, striking rocks?"

"It's much more consistent with impacting different shaped surfaces."

"Such as rocks?"

"Such as rocks."

Once again, I reflect on how the defense need not prove a thing, only raise doubt. I don't know if Lambert has succeeded in doing so. I worry.

Judge Smith calls a recess and excuses the jury. Before they are allowed back in at the end of the break, he says, "All right. Mr. Dion, I've previously advised you that you have the right to choose whether to testify or remain silent at this trial. Your attorney has indicated that you've decided not to testify. I need to make sure that's your voluntary decision. Okay? Is that your voluntary decision?"

Dr. Bonnell is the final witness, unless Dion himself is going to take the stand. If that's the case, he needs to be scheduled in.

But Dion sticks to his decision, saying, "Yes, Your Honor."

"Have you discussed this decision with your attorney?" Judge Smith asks.

"Yes, Your Honor."

"Have anyone promised you anything or threatened you in any way to convince you to make this decision?"

"No, Your Honor."

"Are you currently sick or under the influence of any alcohol or drugs or any medication?"

"No, sir."

"Do you think you've had enough time to think about this?"

"Yes, sir."

"All right."

———————

The jury is called back in; Lambert continues. Dr. Bonnell says that the vaginal injury could result from consensual sex. He says it's impossible to tell how old the injury is without a microscopic cross-section, and that the effect of water can make the injury look fresher than it actually is. Therefore, he says, it's impossible to tell whether the vaginal injury is contemporaneous with the head wounds.

On cross, Paul Miovas jumps all over Dr. Bonnell, dissecting his testimony. He refers to an interview he did with Dr. Bonnell a few weeks earlier, on May 22. Miovas specifically notes that Dr. Bonnell had never mentioned rocks being among the potential objects that could have caused Bonnie's injuries. "Do you remember describing those objects to me?" he says.

"I believe I said some of the injuries could be caused by rounded objects, like a tire iron, baseball bat, pipe . . ."

"Something cylindrical."

"Yes."

"At the end of the interview, Mr. Lambert asked you, could it be a rock, and you said, yes, it could be a rock as well?"

"Right."

"But you didn't opine that in the middle of our conversation, did you?"

"Not that I remember."

Miovas keeps at Dr. Bonnell relentlessly, which pleases me. Dr. Bonnell starts to shift in his seat, blinking frequently.

"And you said there's a second object, a sharper-edged object that caused some of the other injuries. Tell me a little bit about the characteristics of this object."

"This object would have a sharper surface impacting the scalp, not a rounded surface. It could be a sharp stone. It could be the blunted side of a two-knife, that kind of thing."

"Two-by-four I think is one of the things you said, the edge of a two-by-four?"

"The corner edge, the sharp edge of a two-by-four could cause the sharper-impact injuries."

"Okay. And on this one you actually said a sharp edge of a rock could cause those injuries, correct?"

"I may have."

Miovas shows photos of Bonnie's injuries on which Dr. Bonnell has drawn circles and squares—circles to indicate injuries made by sharper objects, squares to indicate those made by the other type of object, something rounder and flatter.

"Dr. Bonnell, you said the circles you drew on the photos indicate injuries made by sharper objects. And I'm looking now at this injury right here toward the six o'clock position, and then there's one that has the circle down here, correct?"

"Yes."

"All right. Would it surprise you that you said at the time that the circles were not things that were caused with the sharp object, the circles were ones that are insufficient to cause unconsciousness?"

"Yes."

"It would surprise you that that's what you said?"

"No, it wouldn't surprise me at all, because they're insignificant injuries."

"Okay. When you did the circles, I said tell me if you can circle the ones that are not sufficient to cause unconsciousness."

"Uh-huh."

"And that's what the circles are, not the sharp objects?"

"Well, they're basically one and the same, but yes."

"You say they're one and the same, but now I'm a little bit perplexed because squares are the ones you said are the round, blunt, flat object, correct?"

"Correct."

"But you have this one, it's got a circle and a square?"

"That's correct."

"You circled it because you said it wasn't sufficient to cause unconsciousness; then you put the square on it to show what kind of object it was, not the sharp one, but the round one, the flat one?"

"Correct."

"So you misspoke in your direct testimony about what the circles represent?"

"Apparently so."

Miovas pauses briefly, then continues. "You said 50 percent or better chance, greater than 50 percent chance that it's accidental or consistent with a fall?"

"Based on what I know now, yes."

"Based upon what you know now?"

"Yes."

"And you said all of the serious injuries could be accounted for by a fall?"

"Yes."

"And is that based on your opinion as a pathologist?"

"That's based upon my opinion as a pathologist and experience with these kinds of injuries, yes."

Miovas takes a few steps back over to the prosecutor's table. Gruenstein hands him a few sheets of paper. He scans them for a moment and then looks back up at Dr. Bonnell, who looks like he'd now rather be anywhere but on the stand answering these questions.

"Let's talk about experience with these kind of injuries. Is this something that when it comes to falls, this is actually a specific field in pathology, is it not, falls from height? This is a specific art, if you will?"

"Nothing I'm aware of," says Dr. Bonnell. "It's general knowledge for any forensic pathologist."

"You're not aware of studies that deal with this type of thing studying accidental falls, pushes, people who jumped, you're not aware of any of these kind of studies in your field?"

"Oh. Sure. But they're part of the field; they're not a specialty."

"Right. We have two types of falls that pathologists generally use, right, it's falls from height and falls from ground level, correct?"

"That's very much an oversimplification. With falls from heights, there are so many different variations from one story to . . ."

"I understand that. But what I want to know is this; in your field as a pathologist, do the words 'falls from height' mean something specific in pathology, in forensic pathology?"

"No."

"They don't?"

"No. Because *heights* is too general a word."

"That's interesting. I want to first show you an article, called 'The Retrospective Analysis of Fatal Falls,' published in 2010. Are you familiar with it?"

"No."

"Have you read any articles dealing with falls and accidental falls and patterns of injuries with falls?"

"Over thirty years, yes."

"Can you name one for me?"

"It was probably one of the first ones I did, which was coauthored, 'Falls off the Aurora Avenue Bridge in Seattle.' "

"When was that?"

"That would have been somewhere around 1981 to 1984."

"How about in the last ten years?"

"No."

"The article I gave you is the most recent I was able to find, May 2010, an article about falls, fatal falls, and the analysis of fatal falls. You're not familiar with that?"

"No, I'm not."

"Do you know *Forensic Science International*? Is that a journal you've heard of?"

"I have heard of it."

"When you were asked in this case to offer an opinion about whether or not this was an accidental fall, when was that?"

"I believe it was about a year ago."

"So you've had a year between that point and sitting here talking to the jury about your opinions?"

"I think I basically gave my opinion in December, and then was not contacted and not made aware of it going to trial I think until April or May, and I've not gone back and done a literature search."

"So you rendered your opinion in December. I would assume that means that you had the material to review prior to December?"

"Yes, except for the scene video and the testimony from trial."

It's obvious when a prosecutor smells blood but is still trying to control the tempo of his examination. The witness knows it, too, as does the rest of the courtroom. Dr. Bonnell is squirming badly now. Miovas has no intention of letting him off the hook.

"The way pathologists normally work is you do the autopsy, you look at the object of evidence, and you make a determination as to manner and cause of death, correct?"

"After you reanalyze the circumstances surrounding the death."

"But it is, if you will, scientific method, you start with the observations and then you figure out what the observations show and you come to the conclusion, correct?"

"Yes."

"That's not how it works when you're consulting for a defense attorney, is it?"

"It's pretty much the same except as a defense consultant you normally have the advantage of additional investigation that has not been done at the time you sign a death certificate."

"When you're consulted by Mr. Lambert for a case like this, he doesn't say, look at it and tell me what you think. He says, tell me if you think we can say it's an accident. Is that accurate?"

"What I say is, send me the material and I'll tell you what I think. If it helps you, good. If it doesn't help you, maybe next time."

"Are you telling me that prior to reviewing the material you were never asked whether or not to consider whether it was an accident?"

"I don't remember exactly what I was asked. He could have asked me if it was consistent with a fall versus a homicidal assault."

"Well, let's talk about what you don't recall. You don't recall because you don't write a report, do you, Dr. Bonnell?"

"I don't write a report unless I'm asked to write a report."

"I didn't ask you that question. I asked you did you write a report?"

"Not in this case. I only did an affidavit or statement."

"And that first affidavit was dealing with the vaginal injury, correct?"

"I believe that was one of the things it dealt with, yes."

"The one that fleshed out the idea of the accidental fall would have been the notice I got mid-April of 2011, correct?"

"I'm not sure what you got in mid-April."

"Oh, you haven't been shown the notice of expert?"

"I don't remember seeing it. I might have, but I don't remember that."

"Well, that's interesting because that's kind of what the law asks for. Now, when you were first consulted, you were asked to consider whether or not this was a fall, correct?"

"I'm sure that was one of the options open to me, yes."

"I see you've been flipping through this *Forensic Science International*. This one actually has in the title, 'Pathologic Features of Fatal Falls from Heights.' That's a 2004 article. I'm assuming that you haven't read that article in preparation for trial, either?"

"I haven't read any specific article in preparation for trial."

"Since December, when you offered your opinion, you haven't at any point gone back and read any of the literature about accidental falls, pathologic signs of what are consistent with accidental falls, any of the studies of accidental falls for the past ten years, have you?"

"I did not do any literature research for this case."

"Everything you're testifying about today is just based on your limited understanding and experience, not with any specific studies or specific knowledge about accidental falls or injuries consistent with accidental falls. Is that accurate?"

"No. It's been involved with my education, my training, my common reading of journals, and experience."

"You retired and then starting consulting in 2001?"

"Uh-huh."

"Since 2001, is it your testimony that you haven't read a single article that you can think of about accidental falls?"

"An exact article, no. The odds are I read this one."

Judge Smith calls for an hour break so that the jury can eat lunch and Dr. Bonnell can read the articles.

When we come back in, Miovas latches right back on.

"That was about a one-hour break, Dr. Bonnell. Did you have time to read the articles?"

"Yes."

"I want to go back and ask you one question. You said that you personally authored an article."

"I coauthored it. 'Falls off the Aurora Bridge.' "

"When was that?"

"I haven't the slightest idea. Probably some time back in the '80s."

"All right. I've got your CV. You put your publications on there, correct?"

"Only the publications I was lead author."

"Only the publications that you were lead author. Okay. That one's not on your CV?"

"I was not lead author."

"Were you listed as a coauthor?"

"I don't remember."

"You don't remember?"

"No. I know I was collecting the data. I don't know if I was listed as an author."

"Are you tired, Dr. Bonnell?"

"Yep."

"Dr. Bonnell, during that hour break, how long did it take you to review that article?"

"I would estimate twenty minutes, maybe twenty-five."

"Twenty minutes, maybe twenty-five."

"Uh-huh."

"I came back in the courtroom after about fifteen minutes. Does that sound right?"

"I have no idea when you came back in. I wasn't paying attention."

"You weren't. What were you doing?"

"Probably nodding off."

"Yeah. You've been sleeping for the last forty-five minutes, right?"

Paul Miovas has just expertly decimated Dr. Bonnell's credibility. I'm proud of the prosecutor in an almost maternal way. He has exposed Dr. Bonnell for what he is. I just hope the jury can see it, too.

It is June 14, 2011. We have been coming to this room for just over a month listening to the debate over what happened to my daughter and who was responsible. Or who wasn't.

From TV and movies, most people think of closing arguments as short, polished speeches full of rhetoric and flair. They are in fact methodical, usually long, summaries of everything that has been presented to the jury by both sides, tailored to a specific perspective. Sometimes the style is subtle, sometimes more direct. What closing arguments are not are the perfectly eloquent and gripping two-minute orations we know from the big and small screens.

In speeches that last more than two hours all told, the prosecution and the defense each take their last turn trying to sway the jurors. Paul Miovas goes first.

"I want you to understand what this process is about, ladies and gentlemen," he says. "As I told you before, it's about getting to the truth. I'm not going to make some big, grandiose speech. I think you all understand exactly what's going on in this trial. But I do want to make one point very clear before I start talking about the evidence, ladies and gentlemen. Kenneth Dion is entitled to a fair trial. He got a fair trial, ladies and gentlemen. You don't have to for a second buy anything that they're trying to suggest to you in this case. You get to decide this. He's got a fair trial. You don't have to buy what they're selling."

As he's done throughout the trial, Miovas focuses on Bonnie's character, telling the jury that she was exactly the girl they think she was—diligent, loyal, and good. He shows a number of e-mails exchanged between Bonnie and Cameron after he'd gone to Berkeley.

"The really sad one," Miovas says, "is the one Cameron sent the day Bonnie died. She was supposed to take two tests, turn in a paper, and meet him online at the computer lab. She never made it to the computer lab."

As Miovas reads from the e-mail—*"It's me again. Hope I'm not bothering you. Anyways, just want to tell you that I'll be here at 5:15. I have class. Well, I better go head off to class. Have a good day. I love you. Cameron."*—I turn and see Samantha break. For years, she has been a rock, and now, finally, it is coming out. I hold her close as she sobs great heavy tears, mourning her big sister. Miovas reads from another e-mail, this one sent by Cameron the following morning—*"What happened? Weren't we supposed to talk at Wednesday at 5:15? I thought we were, but I guess we weren't. Either that or something went wrong with your computer."*—and Samantha's tears come harder. Hopefully, this will all be over soon.

Miovas takes the jurors through the timeline again, step by step—Samantha hearing Bonnie leave in the morning, papergirl

Mandesa Byrd seeing Bonnie heading for her bus around 5:20 A.M.,
commuter Eric Behr seeing someone who was probably Bonnie soon
after. "This is a young lady who gets up, she has a class schedule, I
don't know about any of you that have set your college schedules,
but I don't think there are a lot of people that enjoy taking 7:00
o'clock classes. This is a girl that not only takes a 7:00 o'clock
class, ladies and gentlemen, but she gets up at 5:00 o'clock to walk
two and a half miles to catch a bus to go to school. Not your aver-
age young lady."

Miovas cautions the jurors not to get distracted by the red her-
rings planted by the defense, like the troopers' initial interpretation
of the cause of Bonnie's death. "The troopers show up at Gary
Campbell's house and give him what is obviously the most devas-
tating news a parent can ever have. Bonnie has been found dead.
Curt Harris said some things he shouldn't have said. He tried to
calm Gary in a very emotional situation and say, well, it could be
an accident, nothing to indicate foul play. This was his way, inex-
perience in dealing with homicide investigations and trying to calm
a very distraught parent. Don't give Kenneth Dion a break because
an inexperienced homicide detective said something to a family
that he shouldn't have said."

Miovas talks briefly about Dr. von Hippel and his odd, frequently contradictory testimony between November 1994, when
he first contacted the troopers, and the trial, when he seemed to go
back on everything he'd previously said. The bottom line here,
Miovas says, is credibility, and Dr. von Hippel has none. "He didn't
feel comfortable, ladies and gentlemen. Quite frankly sounds like
he regretted that he even went down that rabbit hole in the first
place."

He walks the jury through the forensics of the case a final time,
concentrating again on the eleven lacerations to Bonnie's skull,

which could hardly have resulted from an accidental fall down the cliff. He shows some of the pictures the jury has already seen, like the injuries to Bonnie's hands that demonstrate she was trying to protect herself, to reinforce the point. He asks them to consider the behavior of one of the defense's primary witnesses, Dr. Bonnell. "This was a man that seemed annoyed. He's clearly tired. He was clearly disengaged. He wouldn't even look at me when I was asking him questions. He wouldn't even pick his transcript up when I wanted to talk to him about it. There are articles in the field that deal with this specific subset of forensic pathology, falls from height. He didn't read a single article in the field in the past ten years. I'm not going to say that the man's not intelligent, ladies and gentlemen. Doesn't seem to be at all interested in taking this process serious, but I don't dispute that the man's probably smart. This man's a paid consultant. Seemed he's testified in nineteen states. He's not a practicing physician. This man is a paid consultant. He testifies for a living."

Miovas talks about Trooper Tim Hunyor's interrogation of Kenneth Dion in New Hampshire in 2006, and Dion's claim that he didn't recognize Bonnie, despite the fact that he'd had sex with her, and that the Anchorage community had been saturated with her image for months while he was still living there. "He wants you to believe that he had sex with Bonnie Craig the week she died and doesn't realize who she is when they show a picture. He lived here until 1996, ladies and gentlemen. When shown the picture, he says, 'her, eighteen years old, hell no, my wife would have killed me.' He's not with Tammy anymore, ladies and gentlemen. They broke up a long time ago. There's absolutely no reason he has to lie to the police right now. Men that have gotten away with murder for twelve years don't all of a sudden say to an Investigator Hunyor when he walks in the door, 'oh, yeah, that girl, yeah, I know her, I had sex with her and, yeah, I know she died.' No. He's had twelve years, twelve years since Bonnie's murder to think about what he's going to say if this ever catches up with him. Murderers don't just admit that they murdered somebody. Of course he's going to deny it. We haven't been able to catch him yet; why would he admit it at this point?"

Miovas asks the jury to consider certain questions for which the defense hasn't provided sufficient answers, like what happened to her backpack and key chain, why she didn't go to school that day, and how she got out to McHugh Creek in the first place, more than ten miles away from her bus route.

"Finally," he says, "I want you to think about this. Hundreds of witnesses interviewed, so many investigators have put eyes on this case, so many people have been talked to, so many tips have been looked into, sixteen years have passed, if their explanation that it's an accident is correct, Bonnie must have been out there with somebody because she didn't get out to McHugh Creek on a bus. How did she get out there? What happened to the people that she was with? How come nobody's come forward and said, 'I was with her and this is what happened'? You know why, ladies and gentlemen? Because this man abducted her that morning, raped her and then killed her, and left her body to be discovered. This is murder. This is sexual assault. The evidence mandates that verdict, ladies and gentlemen. I'll have a chance to talk to you after Mr. Lambert. Thank you."

After a twenty-minute break called by Judge Smith, Andrew Lambert stands and faces the jury members. "For seventeen years, you've heard that Bonnie Craig was murdered and raped. I told you at the beginning of this case that it wasn't going to be as clear." That's all the defense needs the jury members to think about:

whether things are less than 100 percent clear. If yes, Kenneth Dion
gets to walk. That's how the system works.

"This is not a case where we're here for Ken Dion or against
Ken Dion or for Bonnie Craig or against Bonnie Craig at all. You
can't convict somebody in this case just to give back to the community or just to give something back to the family that's been sitting
here for the last month watching this case. Voting not guilty does
not mean that you're for or against anyone. All it means is the state
just hasn't proven the case beyond a reasonable doubt. So when
you go back and you vote not guilty and you're going to go home
and you're going to talk to your friends, and you're going to talk
to your family, and they're going to say, 'oh, my God, for seventeen
years we heard that Bonnie was raped and murdered, how could
you possibly vote not guilty?' And you're going to have to look
them square in the eye and you're going to have to tell them, 'this
is what the law required me to do. This is what the evidence showed
in the case and we followed the law and we followed the evidence
and we have no regrets about doing that whatsoever.' If there is any
reasonable doubt in this case, you have to vote not guilty."

Lambert talks about the movie *12 Angry Men*, about a young
Puerto Rican on trial for murdering his father. The jury votes
eleven to one to convict, but one of the jurors reminds the others
that the burden of proof is on the prosecution and that the prosecution hasn't proven its case. Lambert knows that the evidence is
not on the defense's side, so he is taking a different tack. He is,
again, showboating. "The instructions tell you that the presumption of innocence alone is enough to find Ken not guilty. This is
something that's been valuable to us for 200 years. The burden
falls on the state, and the state has to prove it beyond a reasonable
doubt. Really, the question you should be asking yourself is not is

Ken guilty here of anything, the question is not did he kill and sexually assault Bonnie Craig, the question really is, is there reasonable doubt about the claims that are made by the state."

He is talking in circles already, scrambling. This should reassure me of the strength of our case versus theirs, but it doesn't. Lambert continues to deflect and distract. "I want to talk to you more about the facts of the case. You know, Mr. Miovas asked some questions and said, when Mr. Lambert's up there, I want him to answer these questions. Well, these are questions that are not required to be answered in this trial. It's the state's duty to answer those questions if they can. It's not our responsibility to answer the questions at all. Don't let them shift the burden. That's not how it works. It's their job. Make them answer the questions."

For the next hour, Lambert reviews the parade of witnesses that have come forth and dismisses each of them, stressing again that none of them can say they ever saw Kenneth Dion or his car. He notes again that, from the time Bonnie left her house to the time her body was discovered, there is no evidence whatsoever connecting Kenneth Dion with Bonnie on that day, during that period.

He calls Bonnie's character and loyalty into question, just as he has done many times throughout the past month. He scoffs at the argument that she was too busy, and too in love with Cameron, to sleep around. "Through the history of mankind people get together and have sex. And we may want to think that doesn't happen and we want to kid ourselves about that and think everybody should have a relationship and we tell everybody to be in a relationship before you have sex and you shouldn't have one-night stands. I tell you what, if you watch the reality shows on TV, those reality shows are the reality of how life has been for a long time. If you look at those shows, people are hooking up all the time with people they don't know or they don't know well, and they're doing it for a short period of time, and they never see them again, and maybe one night it's one and then the next night it's another. And I'm not trying to imply by any means that Bonnie is a bad girl and that Bonnie would do anything, you know, one night after another with another boy at that time. But we don't know." *What a bastard*, I think. He even cites Arnold Schwarzenegger, the former action movie star turned governor, whose longtime affair and resulting child with his housekeeper has recently been exposed. No one suspected that, says Lambert—and Schwarzenegger's a person in the public eye.

Finally—we know he's headed here—Lambert talks about blood. It is this point to which he gives the most emphasis and on which he spends the most amount of time. "There should be a ton of blood at the scene," he says. "There should be pooling, dripping, spatter all over McHugh Creek. We talked about the scalp wounds, they bleed instantly, they bleed rapidly, they bleed profusely. They bleed all over the place. There should be blood all over the ground up there. It's inconsistent with one drop of blood." He talks a final time about spatter, castoff, dripping, transfer stains. He talks about the lack of blood in Bonnie's hair, on her coat, on the plants around the cliffside.

"In the end," says Andrew Lambert, "it really comes down to are you truly being fair, are you actually presuming that there's reasonable doubt and the presumption of innocence here. Ask yourself the question, does reasonable doubt exist here? Reasonable doubt does exist. After seventeen years," says Lambert, "please let the police and media know they got it wrong. Go back there and check four 'not guilty' boxes."

Judge Smith calls for another twenty-minute break. When it's his turn to rebut, Paul Miovas stands again, buttons his suit jacket, and looks at the jurors.

"Once you concede that she's injured at the top of that cliff, the only thing that you need to resolve is who killed her. Now, I want you to understand this. One of the things I think people have a natural inclination, especially as we sit here in 2011, one of the things we think about in the context of the kind of things we see on TV, the shows, the films we see nowadays, we think nobody in their right mind would ever have sex with a girl, ejaculate in her, and then kill her and just leave her there. Nobody would do that. We all know that's leaving evidence behind. You need to take this into consideration when you think about when this happened: 1994, ladies and gentlemen. We had very primitive—and this was testified to by Jessica Hogan—primitive DNA technology in 1994. Kenneth Dion would not have known that his sperm would link him years later to Bonnie Craig's death. You have to realize that we weren't dealing with the same technology in 1994 that we're dealing with today."

Miovas refers again to the testimony offered by Dr. Bonnell, and goes through the points of impact on Bonnie's body, explaining again why they could not have resulted from an accidental fall, especially the eleven skull lacerations.

"I agree 100 percent with one of the things that Mr. Lambert's been telling you all along: there is no evidence that anybody saw Kenneth Dion with Bonnie Craig at any point, let alone September 28th. You know why? She did not know this man. This man was a complete stranger to her when she left for that bus stop on Wednesday morning at five o'clock from her house. The reason he killed Bonnie Craig is so that she couldn't tell her story. How did the assault occur? We'll never know exactly. A dead victim cannot tell her story, ladies and gentlemen."

Miovas knows he has something more specific to address. Lambert has spent the month talking about blood, and the lack of it at McHugh Creek on that day. So, at this last juncture, he brings something new to the table.

"Mr. Lambert is absolutely correct; there is not a lot of blood out at the scene. All we have is the one drop. When they pulled her out of the water, you didn't see the blood. The blood didn't come until the next day, when they opened the body bag. When they pulled her out of that water, she has those injuries but you don't see the blood then, either. I want you to understand what this is really evidence of. Think about how easy it was for the detectives to get down into that creek where Bonnie was. This is not a deep hole, ladies and gentlemen. This is not a deep body of water. It's very accessible. When Bonnie goes off that cliff, we know she's injured because she drops blood at the top. We already know she's going to get murdered. The reason there's no blood, ladies and gentlemen, is because this man goes down to the creek and finishes the job so that he doesn't leave a witness behind. The man killed her in the water. She'd already been injured. He went down and finished the job."

Inside I am jubilant, thinking Miovas has just torpedoed Andrew Lambert's defense in one fell swoop. He's played it perfectly, keeping this bombshell in his pocket before delivering it and letting it hang in the minds of the jury members. I look over at Andrew Lambert. He is trying to keep his expression neutral, but I think I can see in his eyes that he recognizes the damage that has just been done. I look at the members of the jury. Their faces, too, seem to register the surprise we had hoped for. Still, all it takes is for one person to have doubt. That's all it takes to set Kenneth Dion free. Just one person.

Miovas turns and points to Kenneth Dion. "That man stole

Bonnie's life and took her away from her family. He murdered her, ladies and gentlemen. Do not be fooled. You find him guilty of first-degree murder and sexual assault in the first degree because the evidence mandates it, and so does justice."

———————————

Following court protocol, three jurors from the original fifteen are randomly selected out, leaving three women and nine men to reach a verdict on Dion's fate.

"Thank you, Mr. Miovas. Thank you, Mr. Lambert," says Judge Smith. "Ladies and gentlemen of the jury, we have now heard from both the prosecution and the defense, and they have called all of their witnesses. It is now up to you to render a verdict in this case. In a moment I will adjourn this courtroom, and it will be your duty to begin your deliberations. When those deliberations have reached a conclusion, I will ask you to inform the bailiff. Thank you."

Judge Smith's gavel comes down, leaving the jury to their discussion and us to do nothing but go home and wait.

I go through the motions of getting ready for bed, though I know I will not find sleep tonight. I will merely wait for the sun to rise again, carrying in my heart the hope that the dozen strangers deciding Kenneth Dion's fate will see clearly.

———————————

We are scheduled to do a family interview for Channel 11, the local TV station, late the next morning. I am arriving at the station when I see reporter Grace Jang, who has covered the entire trial, and a photographer zipping out of the parking lot. They see me, looking at them with confusion. We both roll down our windows.

"They're back!" Grace shouts. The jurors have already

returned a verdict; whatever their decision, it hasn't taken them long to reach.

I swing the car around and head to the courthouse while trying to notify as many people as I can, asking them to spread the word.

The courtroom is packed with onlookers. Murmurs run through the crowd. Many pairs of eyes follow me and my family as we file toward the benches and sit. We are all there; everyone has rushed over to the courthouse to be present for what we hope will be the verdict we have dreamed of hearing. The courtroom is so full that the doors are being held open for those straining to see in from the hallway.

Judge Smith calls the jury in, and they sit. He asks the jury foreman, one of the older gentlemen among the group, to confirm that they have reached a verdict. They have, says the foreman.

I am not sure whether I'm breathing. I feel Adam's arm around me and Trina's hand trembling in mine.

Kenneth Dion sits at the defense table in a black shirt, expressionless.

"Please read the verdict out loud," says Judge Smith.

The foreman lifts his chin slightly, taking a small breath. "On the first count, Murder in the First Degree, we find the defendant, Kenneth Dion, guilty. On the second count, Murder in the Second Degree, we find the defendant, Kenneth Dion, guilty. On the third count, Murder in the Second Degree, we find the defendant, Kenneth Dion, guilty. On the fourth count, Sexual Assault in the First Degree, we find the defendant, Kenneth Dion, guilty."

I remember little after that. I am conscious of Adam wrapping his arm tight around me as the blood seems to rush out of my body and I collapse against his chest. I feel him kiss the top of my head.

I'm half aware of other things going on around me—several people in the gallery bursting into tears, a squealing sound from a woman near the courtroom doors. Voices, shouts, the shuffling of bodies. Judge Smith's voice saying something about sentencing. I hope I am not dreaming.

15

That evening, I am in my living room with my dad, Samantha, and Adam, watching one of the jurors being interviewed by Grace on Channel 11. She remarks that she wasn't even ten years old when Bonnie was killed.

"One day," says the juror, "we'd go in and I'd say, 'Oh yeah, he's guilty.' The next day, the defense would present something and we'd go, 'Well, maybe it was an accident.' I think throughout the trial there were doubts."

In the end, says the juror, watching Trooper Tim Hunyor's interview of Kenneth Dion in New Hampshire helped seal the final decision. "Looking at the interview of him being interrogated raised some red flags," she says. "He didn't pick up the picture; he didn't look at it. He automatically said, 'No, I don't remember anything.' But he had said that he remembers faces. The media coverage of this case in '94 was pretty publicized, and you don't remember her face?"

The juror describes her impressions of our family prior to the verdict being read. "The family, holding on to each other," she says. "One of them looking up, like saying a silent prayer. The prosecution was just sitting there waiting. Defense was sitting there waiting. Ken was just sitting there, blank stare, looking forward."

She says her hands were shaking when she and her fellow jurors entered the courtroom. "I was so nervous. When they read the first count, Ken shook his head, then the other three counts, and before they sat down, he looked at us." It was chilling, she says. But she is proud to have performed her civic duty, and she would be proud to do it all over again.

———————————

Halloween 2011. Three and a half months have passed since we heard Kenneth Dion pronounced guilty of raping and killing my daughter Bonnie; Jason, Samantha, and Adam's sister; my father's granddaughter. Today, we'll learn his sentence.

We drive to the courthouse in silence. I prayed for justice for years, and now, finally on the cusp of it, it feels strange. It is a practical and emotional liberation to know that the man who killed will not have the chance to kill again, but at the same time, my feeling of relief is accompanied by the knowledge that nothing will bring back the daughter I lost.

Before the lawyers on both sides are allowed to offer their sentencing recommendations to the judge, and before the criminal is sentenced, those victimized by the act are given the opportunity to address him. It may seem a strange addition to the process, but it is done so that the judge, after having listened to the lawyers arguing and examining witnesses, may obtain a different perspective of the ramifications of the crime through the eyes of those it has impacted most.

It is the only time the family is invited to address the court, and the criminal, directly.

Present are the judge, the convicted, the lawyers, the victim's family, and, sometimes, as in this case, a crowd of supporters and spectators. The trial jurors are not required to be present to hear the victim impact statements. They have fulfilled their civic role. It's possible that some of them may be present in the gallery today, but if so, I don't notice.

Months ago, when we were first told we could have the opportunity to address Kenneth Dion, I asked my children what they wanted to do. I told them there was no pressure and no expectation, and that if they wanted to, they should do it for themselves, not for me. Both Jason and Adam immediately said yes. I looked at Samantha.

"I've wanted to since hearing the verdict," she said.

Now, Samantha rises from her seat, clears her throat, adjusts the sheets of paper in her hand, and looks directly into the eyes of the man who took away her big sister, her hero, forever.

"Kenneth Dion. You will never begin to understand the totality of your actions, and I will never be able to come even remotely close to helping you understand, but this is my attempt. This is my attempt to have you search within yourself for what little regard you have for any other human being. I hope you hear every word I am about to say, every word my family says, every word that was spoken during the trial on behalf of my sister, and every word my sister said to you in the hours when you kidnapped, raped, and murdered her. I hope these words haunt you for the rest of your life. I hope there is never a day that passes where you don't think about them."

Kenneth Dion stares straight ahead.

"Bonnie was beautiful, intelligent, fun, loving, and tenacious. She touched the heart and soul of every person she ever encountered, which is how I now know you have neither a heart nor a soul. I'll never forget the public outcry from not only my family, our friends and Bonnie's friends, but also the public in general. Such a heinous act hurts the very core, shakes the trust and integrity and leaves an unanswered emptiness for our community.

"What you will never be able to take away are my beautiful memories. I will tell you what you did take. You took away my childhood, my sense of self and esteem, my chance at a normal life with a normal family, and, last, my trust. I will never forget the fear and sorrow I felt as a twelve-year-old, being held by my thirteen-year-old brother, when I heard my father collapse to his knees screaming at the news of Bonnie's death. That fear and sorrow is an ache that is within my being every time I want, need, and miss my sister, which is all the time. She was my role model, my support, my stability, and my best friend. At twelve years old, I lost my childhood. I lost my parents and my friends. My parents were too consumed in their own grief and their need to know what happened to realize I was still there needing them. No one knew what to say or how to act around me, and I no longer fit in any crowd.

"I lost trust. I remember learning most victims of rape and murder are done by people close to the victim. I didn't trust my own father as he was being ruled out as a suspect. I have little trust for men in general and carry many stereotypes I wish I could overcome.

"The first time I saw you, scared, pathetic, and unable to make eye contact, I didn't know what to think of you. You didn't exist in my life until then, and I still wasn't sure I could completely hate you. The years after losing Bonnie, I always maintained that I never wished death on you for one simple reason: I'd never want anyone who could have possibly loved you to feel even the slightest bit of loss which I felt. Throughout the trial, you acted cocky and arrogant. I learned and saw details about Bonnie's rape and murder I had been sheltered from. I saw you shake your head and skirt the decisions you made, not take responsibility for your actions. On top of that, you tried to taint the reputation of my sister to cover your own ass. You are a heartless, soulless coward. I will never forgive you.

"I hope you spend the rest of your life in prison. I hope you find the courage to be a man and tell the truth and apologize for the pain you have caused. My hope is that you show the ones you love and care about that you still have some decency and regard for others hidden deep within you.

"Last, I want to thank you. Thank you for being careless and getting caught so you can never hurt another innocent person again. I thank you for making me realize just how real and precious life is and that within moments, one's entire world can change. Finally, I thank you for showing me what evil is so I can cherish the good.

"Your Honor, I ask that you put this man away for the rest of his life and protect our community. This man has no remorse and no regard. He does not deserve to be free. I ask that you show Kenneth Dion, Bonnie, my family, and everyone this has touched that the justice system does indeed seek justice. I ask that you show the jury they are correct and did their civic duty well. Finally, I ask that you show the world that the worth of a human life is irreplaceable."

With an expression combining rage and catharsis, Samantha takes her seat. Jason and Adam are next. But as I look at both of my sons, I see in their faces an overwhelming mix of tension, anger, and sorrow. They both motion for me to go instead.

My knees feel weak. My stomach is knotted, and I can feel my throat going dry. But I am going to address this monster. I force myself to stand. I take a moment to get steady. I inhale.

This is what I say to the man who killed my daughter:

"Since September 28, 1994, days turned into weeks, weeks into months, months into years, and years into decades. It's been seventeen long years for this incredible tragedy to come to the final chapter. No one can count the number of tears our family and Bonnie's friends have shed. No one can count the sleepless nights, the bursts of fury, nor imagine the depths of depression we have suffered.

"We can't describe the pain we have suffered. As a mother, I felt it was like having your guts ripped out of you. The pain goes on and on. You continue to exist with a huge hole in your heart."

I can feel the pain threatening to overwhelm me. But I make myself continue.

"The pain of losing your child is unbearable. It's magnified when it is to a violent act of rape and murder. It is also magnified as you watch and feel the pain your surviving children are going through. And it was magnified yet again when I realized, as a parent, that I wasn't there for my surviving children. I was so focused and intent on catching Bonnie's killer that my children lost me as their mother."

My surviving children look up at me. I know they have forgiven me for my neglect. But I haven't forgiven myself.

"For twelve years, I feared that Bonnie's death could have been the result of mistaken identity, and that I was the intended victim because of my work as an undercover reserve police officer for APD. We had always called Bonnie my Xerox copy. The guilt is so tough for a parent to live with—the thought that your innocent child could have been murdered because of your job.

"Bonnie was always described as bubbly. She was so kind to everyone. She only made it to her fifth week of college. She wanted to be a psychologist. She was sweet and gentle. She never would have hurt anyone intentionally. She was a member of a peer counseling group at Service High School called 'Natural Helpers.' That describes her perfectly; Bonnie was a natural helper. She started SADD, Students Against Drunk Drivers, at Service High School, after losing a dear friend in a drunk-driving accident. She cared so much about all those around her. She never dabbled in drugs. Refused to even try alcohol. She didn't live a risky lifestyle. She was the first girl to make the Service High School wrestling team. She carried pepper spray on her key chain. But how could she ever be protected from an animal like you?

"How can you call yourself a man? How can you call yourself a fifth-degree black belt? You are neither. You are a disgrace and a coward. You did get one thing right when you got the tattoo on your knuckles. You truly are a 'lost soul.'

"You, Kenneth Dion, had so many choices and opportunities to end this madness once you were identified. But you always thought only of yourself. You didn't care what you put our family through. We have been dragged through a private hell because of your continued selfishness. Your own daughter and her mother have suffered a private hell because of your insistence that you could get away with a brutal rape and murder. You chose not to spare our family or yours in hopes that somehow there would be some technicality that would let you get away with murder.

"Over the past five years we had more than thirty-five pretrial hearings, and at each one you chose to continue your facade, claiming your innocence. You then went to an even lower level and decided to try to tarnish my beautiful daughter's reputation. You could care less what your lies about having a secret tryst would do to Bonnie's boyfriend or our family. You disgust me. You are a lying coward. A weasel."

I look at Kenneth Dion. Still there isn't a hint of emotion in his eyes.

"For years I prayed for you, in hopes that you would become man enough to apologize for your actions, take responsibility, and admit to your crimes. I prayed that my children would be spared a trial and all the pain that would come with it. Bonnie's sister and brothers were twelve, thirteen, and twenty at the time of the murder. She had two stepbrothers and a stepsister. All were too young to comprehend such a senseless act, not that such an act could ever be understood no matter what age you are.

"How could you sit there in that chair, seeing the pictures of Bonnie, watching her lifeless, battered body being recovered and put into a body bag? How could you not want to stop the ridiculous charade? Can you imagine what it would be like if something like this was happening to one of your family members?

"As a Christian, I know I must forgive you, but I will never forget. For as long as I live, I will make sure you never walk out of those prison doors. Kenneth Dion, you got only one thing right. You are a lost soul. And unless you make some major changes in the life that you have chalked out for yourself, you will rot in hell."

I sit down, shaking.

Jason and Adam never find the strength to stand and address Kenneth Dion. I hold them close, telling them it's okay.

Paul Miovas stands, doing up the middle button of his suit jacket. It is his turn to recommend sentencing parameters to the judge first.

"Alaska has the highest incident of rape among the country—among the states in the country—but we have a two-and-a-third times higher rate than even the closest state behind us, Judge. We have an epidemic in our state, for sex assault and for violence against women. But what's really alarming is this, and this goes to the general deterrence, Judge—what's really alarming is that only 39 percent of women who are forcibly raped ever report that they've been forcibly raped. Thirty-nine percent. That means that there is 61 percent of the women out there that are being forcibly raped in the communities that do not come forward and do not report this. This is a problem. This is a serious, serious problem in the state of Alaska. It has reached epidemic proportions."

Rapes and murders of women go unsolved all the time, in Alaska and elsewhere. I think about the failings of the state, and the system, to bring justice and respect to the young women lost at the hands of monsters like Kenneth Dion.

"But you are now in the place, Judge, where you can actually send the message that the system needs to; that we protect our women, and that if we—if you violate the women, if you hurt the women, if you rape and murder the women in our community, you will get the most harsh treatment under the law. The women in our community need to know that, and the men who violate them also need to understand that we will not tolerate this in the state of Alaska. I think that there's never been a case better situated for the Court and for the system to address the general deterrence of this epidemic we're facing. This is the best case, Judge. One of the things that you have to look at as well is reaffirming society's norms, and the—acknowledging the community condemnation. Judge, I think throughout the trial, throughout this process, throughout your involvement, you understand how important it is that the community see justice done in this case. The community has been behind the state, has been behind the family, has been behind this prosecution since day one—since the very first portions of the investigation, there was strong community outcry."

There is only one appropriate sentence, Miovas suggests, and that would be the maximum on both the first and fourth counts, equating to ninety-nine and twenty-five years. If the jury were to find Dion guilty on the first count, first-degree murder, which is murder with intent, then the lesser second and third counts—second-degree murder, intent to cause serious injury that accidentally results in death, or second-degree murder with extreme indifference, death accidentally caused during the commission of another crime or while the victim is trying to escape an assault—would by default carry a guilty verdict as well. The fourth count, sexual assault in the first degree, is separate. It is the rape.

The even bigger thing, he says, the thing that is more important in terms of sending a message up through the system, is to restrict Kenneth Dion's ability for parole. It is one thing to identify and convict the man; it is another to keep him where he belongs.

"The thing that the courts have focused on, as you probably well know, are whether or not the defendant has any potential for rehabilitation or has a lack thereof, and whether or not it is necessary to isolate him from society to protect society for the rest of his life. I think both of those are very clearly established in this case. What I've provided you with, Judge, is essentially a very easy-to-follow breakdown in chronology of Mr. Kenneth Dion and his criminal activity."

Miovas points to Dion's long criminal record—eighteen convictions, ten misdemeanors, eight felonies—and notes how, with the exception of three years, from 1999 to 2002, Dion never went more than a year from the time he turned eighteen without having committed "offense after offense after offense. One of the things you look at, Judge, is whether or not he has the ability to be rehabilitated. Well, I would submit to you that it's very easy in this case. Two states have already demonstrated that he is incapable of rehabilitation. Two states have tried. We have tried. New Hampshire has tried. Neither one of us has been successful. Neither one of us has been able to rehabilitate him. We both put him through treatment programs. We both incarcerated him. We both essentially escalated the punishment to see if there was a point at which he would start to conform to society's acceptable standards. Never did he do it. Not once, Judge."

Miovas argues that Dion's prior convictions for violent robberies make him a threat to the community at large. "Make no mistake about it, Judge, robberies are violent assaults. In most of those cases, he actually walked in with a handgun and robbed the person point-blank right there in the actual store. Now, there can be nothing more violent than walking in at gunpoint and robbing a place under those circumstances. But it doesn't stop there, Judge. As you heard in some of the pretrial litigation, there are a lot of women in the wake of Kenneth Dion's life who have suffered at his hands, who have been assaulted, have been verbally assaulted, have been threatened and beaten when they have refused to have sex with him. It is not an isolated situation, Judge. He has convictions for this. There are assault convictions. There are assault convictions against his wife in January of 1994. His wife said that she refused to have sex with him. She was pregnant. He threw her down the stairs and beat her."

"That's a lie, man!" Kenneth Dion says. Throughout the trial, he has swung between stoic and dismissive. This is his first outburst. I wonder if he spent nearly the last two decades thinking he was going to get away with murder, and now the temper he referred to when speaking with Trooper Hunyor is rearing its head. Andrew Lambert places a hand on Dion's arm and quiets him down. But Dion's manner has changed. He is now a man coming to grips with the idea of life behind bars. No matter how many martial arts weapons you carry, the prospect of this will shake you to your core.

"He was convicted of assaulting Tammy Gregory for the

January 28 incident in 1994. He was convicted for an incident of assault when he struck a woman in the Hellfire Bar a month earlier than that. He was convicted for an assault when he was nineteen years old, in 1989. The man has an assaultive past, Judge. That's my point. My point is that he has an assaultive past, and it's been documented that women suffer at the hands of Kenneth Dion."

"Wrong!" Dion cries, still agitated. This time Judge Smith begins to tell Kenneth Dion he will have a chance to speak later if he so chooses, but Dion cuts him off, exclaiming, "I don't like listening to these lies and bullshit, Your Honor!"

Miovas doesn't skip a beat. "That is what makes this such an egregious thing," he says, ignoring Dion. Judge Smith ignores Dion, too, and allows Miovas to continue. "The fact that a man was willing to take a young, vulnerable girl off the streets while she was walking to school demonstrates how dangerous this man is. Whenever there's a police officer that's been shot, the court basically upholds those without hesitation. They say a person who is willing to shoot an armed police officer in the course of their duty has demonstrated that they have violent tendencies that society needs to be protected from. Well, what I would say, Judge, is that I agree with that, but I also agree that a man that would snatch up an eighteen-year-old girl from the streets, rape her, and murder her also has demonstrated that society needs to be protected from him."

Miovas clears his throat. "I'm going to end on one last factor, Judge, and maybe Mr. Dion will prove me wrong, but I doubt it. This speaks to whether or not there's a possibility of rehabilitation in this. There can be no reform, no rehabilitation, without acceptance of what you've done, accepting responsibility for what you've done and admitting it. . . . A person who is unwilling to admit what they've done cannot be rehabilitated, Judge. It cannot be done. Mr. Dion, as the family has pointed out, has never taken responsibility for what he's done."

"And I never will!" Kenneth Dion shouts, "'cause I didn't do it!" He has finally snapped. He is no longer a man coming to grips with the idea of life behind bars. He is a man desperately railing against that vision.

"And that answers your question, Judge," says Miovas. "Nothing further."

Andrew Lambert stands and speaks briefly—only a minute or two, in contrast to the half-hour or so that Paul Miovas has used. Lambert spends most of his time trying to persuade Judge Smith to keep parole on the table for Kenneth Dion, arguing that it has been restricted in only a handful of cases, usually involving "police officers and tortures." Regarding the amount of time Kenneth Dion faces in prison, Lambert speaks even more briefly. And he does so with something I haven't heard from him throughout the trial: resignation. It secretly delights me.

"As far as what sentence to impose, Judge, I think, you know, the reality of this comes down to there's not a whole lot that I can say or do that I think is going to change the Court's view of the facts of this case, Mr. Dion's history, or the outcome of this case. I don't think there's anything I can say that could be terribly influential to you in this at all. So Mr. Dion and I have discussed that, and that there was likely not a whole lot that I could say that would sway you in what you would do, but I am concerned about the parole restriction, and I don't think it's appropriate for reasons I've already said, and reasons that are in my brief without being duplicative about that. So we would just ask Your Honor to be fair and let's move on with sentencing and get it done."

"All right," says Judge Smith. "Thank you. Mr. Dion, this is your opportunity to say anything you want to the Court prior to my imposing sentence. You're not required to say anything. It's not held against you if you choose not to say anything, but if you wish to say something, now is when you would do it."

"I have nothing to say, Your Honor, at all," says Kenneth Dion. In seconds, his ire has mushroomed, and then collapsed. He slumps in his seat, beaten, a man mystified by what he must now mentally accept. I relate to this experience. I went through it on a boat in Florida sixteen and a half years ago.

Judge Smith calls for a twenty-five-minute break. When we return, he summarizes the facts of the case and the arguments offered by the prosecution and the defense. Finally, he says:

"Count One, Murder in the First Degree. The defendant had to grab the victim off the streets of Anchorage as she went to UAA. She was a stranger to him. He had to subdue her. He sexually assaulted her, and at some point, he transported her to McHugh Creek and got her to the top of the cliff to throw or push her down into the creek. The number and locations of the multiple blows to her head reflect a calculated, methodical beating, whether to overpower her or to control her, or both, is unknown. The purpose of leaving Bonnie Craig in the creek would appear to be to attempt to either hide or destroy the evidence of both the sexual assault and the murder. The Court finds a ninety-nine-year sentence is warranted given the facts and circumstances of the case."

Thank you, I say privately. Kenneth Dion will never see the light of day.

"The court also agrees with the pre-sentence report and the state that a flat sentence is warranted. Defendant has shown no ability to conform his conduct to the law or to be rehabilitated, so there will be no suspended time."

I feel another wave of relief. Of course there shouldn't be any suspended time. Kenneth Dion deserves to live out his existence in a tiny cell being reminded of the hell he has created in so many lives.

"As to Count Four, Sexual Assault in the First Degree, the minimum sentence given the three felony prior convictions at the time of the offense is twenty-five years, and the state has argued for twenty-five years consecutive to the ninety-nine years in Count One. The Court concurs that twenty-five years consecutive to Count One is appropriate for all the reasons previously discussed, and that there are different societal interests in prosecuting and sentencing of a sexual assault than a murder."

Judge Smith grants Kenneth Dion one concession: the chance for parole. Since Dion's felony history is clustered around two specific time periods, and not spread out over the course of his life, this is appropriate, says Judge Smith. At first I'm upset, until I think about the timeline. Judge Smith says aloud the calculation I'm trying to make in my head.

"Count One is ninety-nine years flat, Count Four is twenty-five years flat. That's one hundred and twenty-four years. If defendant earns good time, he could be released after serving approximately eighty-two years; however, defendant will be considered for discretionary parole after serving thirty-three years on the murder conviction and six and a quarter years on the sexual assault, or approximately thirty-nine and a quarter years. Now, when the Court considered whether to limit discretionary parole, I took a look at that and said thirty-nine years from now, he's going to do about half his life in prison on these charges even before the parole board takes a look at him. If there's any chance at all he can turn his life around, he's got thirty-nine and a quarter years to figure out how to do that. Does that mean the parole board is going to let him out in thirty-nine and a quarter years? No. It means they'll have a hearing at that time, take a look at what he's done while he's in prison, and make a decision as to whether, in fact, that activity would warrant his release into society. Obviously the family, if they wish, can appear at those parole hearings and have input at that time."

Kenneth Dion will be eighty-two years old when he appears before the parole board. I'll be ninety-five. If I'm still alive, I will be there.

––––––––––

Outside the courthouse, Channel 11's Grace Jang asks to interview us as a family. It is raining lightly, but none of us minds the feeling of the light mist against our skin.

Jason, Samantha, Adam and Trina, their daughter Jayleigh, and I stand together as Grace asks us questions, and we answer with a strange mix of relief and elation, underpinned by the sadness that will never disappear. She asks me what was going through my mind when the verdict was read. I compliment Paul Miovas and tell her we were hopeful for the conviction but frightened for the alternative. Jason says he was doubtful they'd ever catch someone but thankful that they'd collected DNA. Grace addresses Adam as the baby of the family and then apologies for getting it wrong when he corrects her. Adam says he was just praying for a victory. "I couldn't think anything bad about him," my son says, "so I was just praying for justice." Just like Adam. Good to the core.

Grace asks Samantha to show the viewers the item she is carrying with her. "A little plaque that Bonnie had made a long time ago when we shared a room together," Samantha says, holding out the clay plaque that had graced the room she'd shared with Bonnie before the murder. *Samantha and Bonnie's Room*, it reads. "From when I was twelve. Right before she died."

Grace asks Samantha what she misses most about her sister.

"Everything, oh my gosh. Her constant smile, her upbeat attitude, her loving nature. She was incredible. She was everything I always wanted to grow up to be."

She asks Trina, Adam's wife, whether she ever met Bonnie. No, Trina says, she only knew Samantha at the time, but she feels that she has come to know her and her goodness through Adam's spirit and that of the rest of the family.

Grace turns to me last. "What is Bonnie's legacy?"

"That she did die but it was not in vain," I say. "We've had so many changes in the law because of Bonnie, not just here in Alaska but in the rest of the United States. So many states have heard the story and have changed their laws to start collecting DNA on arrest. That's a huge victory for Bonnie, and I think she's right there pushing for this."

Grace asks us as a group what we'd say to Bonnie if she were listening right now.

"We love you!" we chorus as a group, followed by a collective sound we haven't heard from each other in years: laughter.

EPILOGUE

When a child is stolen from you, you learn that the pain has two layers. There is the raw pain of your own loss, and there is the sympathetic pain for anyone else who might experience the same. That's why it's so common to see parents of slain children in front of microphones shedding tears for their own loss but telling the world that they want to do everything possible to prevent it from happening to others. They mean it. *We* mean it.

Kenneth Dion will be placed where he belongs. But there are other Kenneth Dions, and there are other innocent victims. For them and their families, who do not yet know how broken our system is, changes need to be made.

I remember a moment when Bonnie and I were in the car together, on our way to the mall to do some shopping, when she noticed a bumper sticker on the car in front of us that read, *God puts us all on Earth for a reason, but I'm so far behind I will never die.* Bonnie never got the chance to discover her reason. Or maybe her reason was intertwined with mine. Maybe her death, and the pain our family endured, were signposts pointing to something bigger. After Bonnie's murder, I felt something speaking to me, telling me that God's mission for me now was to do everything in my power to help protect other children from a fate like Bonnie's, and other families from the hell our family was going through. There was only one way to do that: change the law. Until it happened, really happened, people like Kenneth Dion would continue to get away with murder, rape, and other heinous acts. With the collection of DNA on all felony arrests, they wouldn't.

If Alaska had been collecting DNA on arrest at the time Bonnie was murdered, Kenneth Dion would have been identified within weeks, and we'd have been spared a dozen years of hell. My quest now is to convince those in power that collection of DNA on all felony arrests and immediate entry into CODIS will save time, money, pain, and, foremost, lives. It will help catch criminals earlier and reduce the number of repeat offenders. It will help solve more cold cases, keep innocent citizens from going to jail, and exonerate those who have been wrongly accused. It will decrease plea bargains, increase the likelihood of guilty pleas for serial offenders, and provide stronger evidence to secure convictions. It will reduce the revictimizations of those already victimized. It will help bring answers to those who have suffered profound loss.

Alaska was the seventh state to start collecting DNA on felony arrest. We got that law changed in twelve days because of Bonnie's murder. People need to speak up—and they need to get the right people to hear them. There is only one effective approach: to demand that the law protect you and your children in whatever ways it can. To tell your lawmakers that collection of DNA on all felony arrests is not just important but imperative.

Even today, only twenty-eight states have passed laws to collect DNA on felony arrest. It isn't enough. The states not doing this remain safe havens for criminals. Delays in collecting and processing DNA profiles into our national database cost us the lives of innocent children. Backlogs of DNA from rape victims give criminals the time and opportunity to commit further crimes, and tear more families apart.

The United Kingdom collects and processes DNA within days of arrest. In the United States and Canada, we can, and should, do the same. There is no good reason not to, other than lack of effort or desire. A DNA profile costs less than thirty dollars to do in the United States, yet it saves countless hours of investigation. Statistics show that 80 percent of those who commit a burglary have, or at some point will, commit a rape or murder, yet in many jurisdictions DNA isn't even collected at burglary crime scenes. The law needs to stipulate that DNA get collected, and crime labs need to be supported in doing their work as efficiently as they can do it.

Alaskan law requires that DNA be entered into CODIS within sixty days. Today, it is typically submitted in less than thirty. Not doing so—that is, waiting for convictions instead, thereby creating backlogs and delays—is the same as allowing murderers and rapists to wander the streets in your community, and giving them the time and opportunity to commit similar crimes again and again.

Our crime labs are the backbone of the criminal justice system. Make sure your lawmakers are funding them enough to do their jobs. If they can only investigate the worst crimes when those crimes are coming up for trial, then they aren't able to protect our communities properly. If they lack the necessary resources and funding, they will always be a step behind. Only the most atrocious crimes get sent to crime labs today. Even those cases can take years to process.

There is a final point. The hell of losing one's daughter is hard enough to manage. Anyone who has lost a child knows that you spend the rest of your life trying to deal with the fact that it happened. There is nothing I or any other parent in the same situation can do about that—the mental part, the human part. There is no undoing the tragic thing that happened, and it is up to us to deal eternally with the psychological and emotional ramifications.

But what didn't have to happen was the five years of hell we endured between November 2006, when Kenneth Dion was identified, and October 2011, when he was finally convicted. Tragedies occur, and people sometimes do very bad things. When someone is taken forever from his or her family, the family members become different kinds of victims. When cases are allowed to sit in limbo in our court system, there is a very real effect on those victims, and an extension of their sorrow and anguish that isn't necessary. Victims' rights to timely disposition of their cases is the final piece of the puzzle.

Years of hell. That is what we went through—me, our family, our friends, and the larger community. It happens far too often. Elizabeth Smart was abducted, at the age of fourteen, in 2002, and thankfully found less than a year later. But it was eight years before her kidnappers were tried. Alaska passed a law in 2012 attempting to take victims' right to timely disposition of their cases into account. It was a small step but an important one. DNA needs to be collected. Crime labs need to be able to do their jobs. Criminals need to be tried for their crimes in a timely manner.

As a family dealing with a tragedy, we were seen as a source of pain, to be avoided. Both my children and I suffered from the avoidant behaviors of those who couldn't bear to be near us for fear that they would say the wrong thing, adding to our pain. It is sad to report that we were abandoned and ignored by people we had considered good friends. Often, it was a wordless hug from a random person that provided the kind of support that allowed us to move on another day and continue the fight.

If you know people experiencing a tragedy of this magnitude, do not ignore them, or their loss—it only adds to the hole in their hearts and increases their pain. Offer that hug instead. It just may give someone going through incredible suffering the unexpected strength to make it through another day.

When tragedy strikes, we have two options: grow from the trauma and honor the person you love and have lost; or wither away and let the pain win.

Only one of these choices can change tragedy to triumph.

Karen Foster, Bonnie's mother, now lives in Florida. She has been featured numerous times in a range of media outlets, including an hour-long 2011 MSNBC *Dateline* special titled "Justice for Bonnie," as well as the 2013 episode "A Mother's Mission" on the Investigation Discovery TV show *Deadline: Crime with Tamron Hall*. Visit her website at JusticeForBonnie.com.

I.J. Schecter is an internationally acclaimed, award-winning author, collaborator, and ghostwriter, whose work appears in top publications throughout the world. He lives in Toronto.